RENEWALS: 691·

DATE DUE

EVALUATING WITH VALIDITY

EVALUATING WITH VALIDITY

ERNEST R. HOUSE

 SAGE PUBLICATIONS Beverly Hills London

Copyright © 1980 by Sage Publications, Inc.

All rights reserved. No part of this book may be reproduced or utilized in any form or by any means, electronic or mechanical, including photocopying, recording, or by any information storage and retrieval system, without permission in writing from the publisher.

For information address:

SAGE Publications, Inc.
275 South Beverly Drive
Beverly Hills, California 90012

SAGE PUBLICATIONS LTD
28 Banner Street
London EC1Y 8QE

Printed in the United States of America

Library of Congress Cataloging in Publication Data

House, Ernest R
    Evaluating with validity.

    Bibliography: p.
    1. Evaluation research (Social action programs)—
United States.   2. Choice (Psychology)   3. Decision-
making—Moral and religious aspects.   I. Title.
H62.H64   361.6'1'072073   80-14695
ISBN 0-8039-1438-5
ISBN 0-8039-1439-3 (pbk.)

FIRST PRINTING
LIBRARY
The University of Texas
At San Antonio

CONTENTS

The learned but imprudent individual, traveling in a straight line from general truths to particular ones, bulls his way through the tortuous paths of life. But the sage who, through all the obliquities and uncertainties of human action and events, keeps his eye steadily focused on eternal truth, manages to follow a roundabout way whenever he cannot travel in a straight line, and makes decisions, in the field of action, which, in the course of time, prove to be as profitable as the nature of things permits.

Giambattista Vico, *On the Study Methods of Our Time*, 1709, p. 35

ACKNOWLEDGMENTS

This book is the culmination of the last five years of my work. Several people have contributed significantly to it. Gene Glass and Rochelle Mayer have edited it and have substantially influenced the ideas. Steve Lapan, Don Hogben, and Barry MacDonald have pursued many of these thoughts with me, sometimes into incoherence. My colleagues at CIRCE—Gordon Hoke, Tom Hastings, Bob Stake, and Harry Broudy—have provided an unusually stimulating environment in which to work.

Mike Atkin, the Dean of Illinois over these years, was especially encouraging. Tom Sergiovanni, my department chairman, was generous in arranging department assignments. A number of CIRCE students have done their best to keep me straight on various issues, and I have acknowledged their help in specific chapters. Another tough chore has been to labor over my handwriting, a task performed courageously by Jeri Willen and Donna Koenig.

PREFACE

This book is directed at evaluators and at those who wish to achieve a deeper understanding of modern evaluation, of what it is and where it is going. The aim is to arrive at a more reflective evaluation practice. To this end the book presents a comprehensive conceptualization of modern evaluation, ranging from the major approaches, to the standards and principles such a practice must entail, to a critique of those approaches by those standards.

The current evaluation scene is marked by vitality and disorder. The scale, ubiquity, and diversity of evaluation activities make comprehension difficult, even for those operating within the field. More alarmingly, a bad evaluation can deface a social program and injure an entire social class. The social import of evaluation is enormous; its self-understanding relatively minute. It is hoped that this book will contribute to a more complete and translucent conceptual order and to a stronger sense of moral responsibility.

The first part of the book is a characterization of modern evaluation efforts. In the first chapter current practice in evaluation is portrayed, indicating how evaluation in a modern context differs not only in scope of endeavor but also in substance from previous evaluation efforts. In the second chapter, it is asserted that there are relatively few approaches to evaluation, in spite of massive effort, and these approaches are described in detail. A taxonomy of basic evaluation approaches is constructed. In the third chapter the basic evaluation approaches are systematically related to each other by their underlying epistemological, ethical, and political assumptions, and these assumptions are explicated. Throughout the characterization of the dominant modern approaches it is assumed that evaluators are operating rationally, i.e., that they have good reasons to do what they do, even when this leads them to different approaches.

The second part of the book is a reflection on the standards—truth, beauty, and justice—that are necessary for guiding and judging the quality of an evaluation. Truth in evaluation entails more than what we normally mean by truth in science—or so it is argued. Beauty, which is manifested in coherence and imagery in the evaluation, has substantial influence on the credibility of the evaluation for a particular audience. Finally, one's underlying sense of justice has important consequences for the type of evaluation one does and for the results of the evaluation. Conceptions of justice and their implications for evaluation are explored.

The third part of the book is an attempt to derive the political and moral principles on which an evaluation should be based. Evaluation is conceived as part of the larger social decision procedures. It is limited to rational persuasion. What it means for an evaluation to be democratically and morally acceptable is discussed. More practically, certain conditions are asserted as necessary for an evaluation to be considered fair. Finally, it is argued that the underlying basis of evaluation consists of moral values conceived within a pluralist conception of justice.

The fourth part of the book is a critique of federal evaluation policy and the major evaluation approaches. Each approach has its strengths and weaknesses, both theoretically and practically, but no approach serves for all occasions. The book ends with a discussion of the nature of validity in evaluation, contending that a valid evaluation should be true, credible, and normatively correct. The aim of the book is to make practice more self-reflective.

APPROACHES TO EVALUATION

The first step to understanding of men is the bringing to consciousness of the model or models that dominate and penetrate their thought and action. Like all attempts to make men aware of the categories in which they think, it is a difficult and sometimes painful activity, likely to produce deeply disquieting results. The second task is to analyse the model itself, and this commits the analyst to accepting or modifying or rejecting it, and in the last case, to providing a more adequate one in its stead.

Isaiah Berlin,
Philosophy, Politics and Society, 1962, p. vii

1

THE EVALUATOR IN SOCIETY

Sorting out the good from the bad has long been a human activity, and one that is essential to society itself. Although institutions have often been accorded authority for making certain value judgments, only in recent times has the evaluation of public programs become so formalized as to constitute a recognizably separate activity—and even a new discipline.

With the advent of large-scale social welfare programs over the past twenty years, evaluation has emerged as an important activity. In the United States alone, tens of thousands of evaluations of public programs are conducted annually. Thousands of people are employed in these evaluations, and hundreds of universities and corporations compete for evaluation contracts. Most of the evaluations are sponsored by the federal government, others by state and local governments. Evaluation of public programs has become a mandated activity, and hundreds of millions of dollars are spent on it each year.

Both the ubiquity and role of evaluation make it socially significant. Public programs are transformed, legitimated, and discredited by evaluation. The sheer number of these evaluation activities makes surveillance difficult. Evaluations of public programs are not always of high quality. Too often evaluators do merely what sponsors want them to do. Too often evaluators misconceive the nature of their task and do an injustice to the social programs that they evaluate. It is not that evaluators are more incompetent or avaricious than people in other professions, but the possibilities for damage are often more widespread, less obvious, and longer-lasting.

This book is directed toward the goal of self-reflection in evaluation. It seems necessary that evaluation be based on some sense of moral responsibility, that its practice be shaped by reflections on its justice, truth, and even its beauty. There must be moral considerations beyond the prospect of hundreds of organizations and thousands of evaluators currying the attention of a few sponsors. Yet these considerations cannot be arbitrarily derived or imposed. They must be developed from a rational analysis of what evaluation is and what is accepted by evaluators as reasonable if they are to provide a basis for conscientious practice.

Private and Public Evaluation

Modern evaluation is a direct descendant of modernism. Modernization was liberation from tradition, a shift from the unquestioned reality given by tradition to a social context in which everything could be questioned and changed. It was a shift from "givenness" to "choice" (Berger, 1974). In the modern world, more things could be chosen. Presumably, this resulted in better material life and in deeper individual fulfillment. In fact, modernization has proceeded to the point where making choices itself has become a problem. Evaluation has been proposed as an aid in making choices.

Most recently, the conduct of formal evaluation on a massive scale, the sponsorship of evaluation by the government, and the proliferation of agencies doing evaluations have created problems not before encountered. Consider an individual making a choice for herself. She goes to a car dealer to buy a new car. She visits the dealers whose cars she can afford and looks at the cars available. After some haggling with the dealer over price, she chooses the small car which is cheapest. She likes small cars and doesn't want to wait two months for factory delivery. Purchase price, size, and availability are important to her. She doesn't care too much about color and accessories. The individual conducts her own evaluation for her own satisfaction.

Now consider the situation in which there are so many choices that the individual is overwhelmed. There are too many cars available even to know where to begin, and the buyer is not a mechanical expert. A group like Consumers' Union offers their services. They will evaluate the cars for her and tell her which is best. She can purchase their evaluation reports on cars. Now, though, the evaluator is separate from the decision-maker. The situations are different in important respects.

How should the evaluator proceed? He must choose standards for evaluation which are relevant for her if the evaluation is to be useful. Without knowing her, he is not likely to guess her personal preferences. He ignores style; she can make that choice without assistance. Availability is a local matter. The evaluator ignores that, too, except as a limiting factor. Certainly, purchase price is something everyone will be interested in. In addition, the evaluator selects fuel economy and the like as relevant standards for the evaluation. He ignores top speed as a criterion.

The evaluator has other important decisions to make. Which cars shall he evaluate? When the consumer evaluated for herself, she defined the field of cars from which she would choose. This is not a trivial problem for the evaluator because the results will vary dramatically depending on which cars he includes in the comparison. He must choose a set for the evaluation. Using the standards he has adopted, he applies the standards to the set of cars. According to how well they fit the standards, he will either grade the cars as good or bad (implying a comparison with all or the "average" car) or rank the cars from best to worst, depending on how they compare within the set. Finally, he publishes his report.

Now the consumer has another choice: she must decide whether the evaluation is acceptable to her. Certain things are required of it. Are the cars the ones she would choose among? Are the standards relevant for her decision? In making his final judgments did the evaluator balance and weigh the standards as she would have? Even more fundamentally, is the evaluation true? Can she rely on it? Was the evaluator himself reliable? Was he paid by one of the car companies? Is the evaluation credible? The consumer is still free to accept or reject the results and the advice rendered in the evaluation. Although the evaluation has become a social process involving a bond between the evaluator and consumer, she retains final choice.

Consider a third situation. An evaluator is funded by the government to evaluate a social action program. For whom is the evaluation done here? For the government? For the public? For the recipients of the program? For the administrators of the program? The answer is not an easy one, for all these people will be affected by the results. Yet there is no single individual, like the purchaser of a car, to whom the evaluation can be directed. Many people are involved, for a decision about the program based on the evaluation will affect everyone. The evaluation is fundamentally and inextricably part of a *public* situation, a collective decision.

Unlike in a private context, the unhappy consumer cannot simply withdraw after finding the evaluation unacceptable, for it will affect her anyway. The public nature of the situation places certain constraints on the evaluation. All the problems of choosing appropriate standards and selecting proper comparisons are magnified many times over. Still, the evaluator must choose, and evaluators have found a variety of ways of dealing with this problem. The approaches evaluators have taken—for this is the modern predicament of the evaluator—is the beginning topic of this book. The appropriateness of these approaches is the ending. In between I shall try to establish the standards for evaluation that lead to these judgments of appropriateness.

The Process of Evaluation

At its simplest, evaluation leads to a settled opinion that something is the case. It does not necessarily lead to a decision to act in a certain way, though today it is often intended for that purpose. One can evaluate Caesar as a great general without any decision resulting from it. Evaluation leads to a judgment about the worth of something.

This judgment often is arrived at by grading or by ranking something according to how well the object fulfills a set of standards or criteria. Evaluation is essentially comparative, and usually explicitly so. This means there must be a set of standards and a class to which the object is compared. If the object is graded as "good" or "bad," the class of comparison is the entire class of objects or the average object of the class. If the object is ranked as "best" or "worst," it is compared directly to a particular subset of similar objects, e.g., a car compared to four other cars in its price range. The cars are ranked in order, indicating each car's relative ranking on these standards in comparison to the other four cars, but not indicating necessarily how worthwhile the cars are as a group. The selection of a class of comparison itself can make a dramatic difference in the evaluation, even when the same standards are employed (Taylor, 1961).

So, in its essence, evaluation entails adopting a set of standards, defining the standards, specifying the class of comparison, and deducing the degree to which the object meets the standards. Having completed these steps, the evaluator would be able to arrive at a judgment about the worth of the object evaluated (Taylor, 1961). Not all evaluations are so rationalistic, however. Many, such as the case study approaches, reveal the standards, comparisons, and judgments more implicitly and intuitively. Some would strive toward understanding rather than judgment.

The value judgment is often expressed as "good" or "bad," or in other value-laden language, but there is no necessity in this. Within a given context, ordinary descriptive words may be used to express a value judgment. Examples and anecdotes may carry the valuing message. The value judgment resides in how words are used rather than in which words are used.

The value judgments resulting from evaluations are not equivalent to directives. One can reasonably direct someone to do something only if it is within his power to do it. One can make value judgments about things one can do nothing about. However, in the modern practice of evaluation, the evaluator is often asked to aid a decision-maker who is trying to decide among general courses of action. The courses of action become the objects evaluated. The value judgments may result in recommendations, but even here the decision-maker is free to reject the advice of the evaluator.

In the simplest case of evaluation in which the evaluator and decision-maker are the same person, selecting the class of comparison and adopting a set of standards are made easier. Yet the actual evaluative process is more complicated than it would appear. People evaluate not only by applying standards but also by checking their judgments against particular situations in which they feel confident that they know the outcome. Actual evaluative reasoning proceeds more as a dialectical process between abstract principles and concrete examples than as a straightforward deduction from standards (Barry, 1965).

Furthermore, in an actual evaluation, the standards may conflict. One wants a comfortably large car and also a car with high gas mileage. One cannot maximize both simultaneously. In such cases, one is inclined to balance one standard against the other, to ask how much room versus how much gas mileage. Rather than assign absolute precedence to one standard or the other, one is inclined to determine relative precedence of the conflicting standards by intuitive considerations of trade-off ratios between them. How much room is one willing to give up for how much mileage? These relative weightings vary from person to person. Evaluation is a complex process even when it is conceived as residing within one person.

When the evaluator and decision-maker are different persons, another dimension is added. The credibility of the evaluator is at issue, and, in addition, the evaluation must now be communicated to the decision-maker in some fashion. There is greater uncertainty as to what the class of comparison and standards should be, and as to how the standards should be weighted relative to each other. Not only must the decision-maker worry about whether the facts are correct, she must worry about whether the evaluator is presenting them truthfully. In modern liberal societies, this relationship is still conceived as a private act but an interpersonal one.

Finally, in the third situation, the object being evaluated is a public program. The evaluator must be concerned about whether the evaluation meets the norms expected of decision-making procedures in the public interest. Evaluation has become not only an interpersonal but a collective affair. There is a larger community of relevant interests which must be considered. This is the predicament of the modern evaluator, and it places the heaviest burden of all on the evaluator. His evaluation must be not only true and credible; it must be just.

Evaluators have approached the solution to their modern predicament in a number of ways. Their resolutions have evolved from their philosophical, professional, and personal beliefs. Training and familiar practice are significant influences. The major approaches to evaluation are presented in the next chapter, and these approaches related to belief systems in the one following.

2

THE MAJOR APPROACHES

There are dozens of advocated approaches to evaluation. Yet most of these approaches can be subsumed under a few basic types. Some call these basic types "models" to indicate that they are designs or structural types advocated by prominent theorists as approaches worth imitating. They are exemplars. You may prefer to call them simply "approaches."

These basic models all have prominent advocates, explicit rationales, discussion in the literature, a group of practitioners, and, not least, actual evaluations that have been conducted according to the basic design. The models themselves are idealizations of evaluation approaches. An actual evaluation is shaped by many different contingencies; thus it may take many shapes even when it begins conceptually as a particular type. A model is an ideal type, in other words.

It is also worth noting that many prominent evaluation theorists—Cronbach, Campbell, and Glass, for example—are not closely allied with any particular evaluation approach. And others, e.g., Guba, have written works advocating two different approaches. I have conducted evaluations using all of the major approaches. So the models should not be identified as the property of any one person or as typifying a particular person.

Figure 1 is a taxonomy of the major evaluation models. In defining these models, I have made extensive use of earlier classifications, especially that of Stake (1976), and also that of Popham (1975) and Worthen and Sanders (1973). No doubt I have unintentionally excluded some types. I have excluded some potential models because they have not yet been employed enough to constitute a school of practice. The models in Figure 1 are the major approaches now being put into practice.

A brief sketch of each approach is in order. In Chapter 11 I will critique each approach from both a theoretical and practical point of view.

The Systems Analysis Approach

In this approach one defines a few output measures, such as test scores in education, and tries to relate differences in programs or policies to variations in the indicators. The data are quantitative, and the outcome measures are related to the programs via correlational analyses or other statistical techniques. Recently, experimental design has been more heavily employed, and "planned variation" of program has been preferred to "natural" variation (see Cooley and Lohnes, 1976).

One of the main antecedents for this approach was systems analysis as developed in the Department of Defense under Secretary McNamara. It has served as the major evaluation perspective in the Department of Health, Education and Welfare since about 1965. In that year, President Johnson expanded the Planning, Programming, and Budgeting System (PPBS) throughout the federal government. Under HEW Secretary John Gardner, a new office entitled the Assistant Secretary for Program Evaluation (ASPE) was created. To fill this office, a group of economists and accountants headed by William Gorham, who had extensive experience with PPBS in the Department of Defense, was brought in. Gorham's deputies were Robert Grosse and Alice Rivlin, who later became Assistant Secretary and head of the Congressional Budget Office.

FIGURE 1 A Taxonomy of Major Evaluation Approaches

Model	Major Audiences or Reference Groups	Assumes Consensus On	Methodology	Outcome	Typical Questions
Systems analysis	Economists, managers	Goals, known cause and effect, quantified variables	PPBS, linear programming, planned variation, cost-benefit analysis	Efficiency	Are the expected effects achieved? Can the effects be achieved more economically? What are the *most* efficient programs?
Behavioral objectives	Managers, psychologists	Prespecified objectives, quantified outcome variables	Behavioral objectives, achievement tests	Productivity, accountability	Is the program achieving the objectives? Is the program producing?
Decision-making	Decision-makers, especially administrators	General goals, criteria	Surveys, questionnaires, interviews, natural variation	Effectiveness, quality control	Is the program effective? What parts are effective?
Goal-free	Consumers	Consequences, criteria	Bias control, logical analysis, modus operandi	Consumer choice, social utility	What are *all* the effects?
Art criticism	Connoisseurs, consumers	Critics, standards	Critical review	Improved standards, heightened awareness	Would a critic approve this program? Is the audience's appreciation increased?
Professional review	Professionals, public	Criteria, panel, procedures	Review by panel, self study	Professional acceptance	How would professionals rate this program?
Quasi-legal	Jury	Procedures and judges	Quasi-legal procedures	Resolution	What are the arguments for and against the program?
Case study	Client, practitioners	Negotiations, activities	Case studies, interviews, observations	Understanding diversity	What does the program look like to different people?

The managerial model promoted and refined by Robert McNamara at DOD and brought to DHEW by William Gorham was drawn from the world of microeconomic theory. ASPE analysts attempted to apply similar theoretical perspectives to human service areas. Implicit in the TEMPO design (*the early Title I evaluation*) were several assumptions that form an economist's view of how the world works. The basic presupposition is that individuals and organizations behave so as to maximize some identifiable outcome or set of outcomes. An analyst, then, should be able to model organizational choices and deduce desired objectives and the relative effectiveness of different strategies for attaining them. This analytical framework presumes the existence of a stable production function, a regular and quantifiable relationship between the inputs to an activity and the outputs [McLaughlin, 1975: 35].

The history of the evaluation of Title I of ESEA, which provides funds for disadvantaged children, is that of an attempt to employ the systems analysis approach. The Office of Education mandated that such an approach be carried out in all 30,000 Title I projects serving five million children. Two HEW officials explained the approach:

> To carry out this legislative mandate, the U.S. Office of Education contracted with the RMC Research Corporation to develop models for evaluating gains in basic skills achieved by local Title I projects. Each of the three RMC models includes pre- and post-treatment testing, a method of estimating "baseline" gains in the absence of Title I services, and procedures for converting local test results into "normal-curve" equivalents that will permit aggregation across projects [Barnes and Ginsburg, 1979: 7].

Thus, these mandated evaluations use test scores as the only measures of success (although duration of services per week, pupil-teacher ratios, expenditures per child, and total number of participants are also collected) and are concerned with maximizing and aggregating, rather than with distribution. All results must be reported in a specially developed "normal-curve equivalent" and aggregated at the state and national level. Presumably, one score can represent the state or nation.

In *Systematic Thinking for Social Action,* Rivlin (1971) wrote that the basic problem was how the government could make better decisions. She considered the key questions to be these: (1) How do we define social problems, and how are they distributed? (2) Who would be helped by proposed solutions and how much? (3) What would do the most good, and how do benefits from different approaches compare? (4) How can services be produced most effectively? The latter two questions were ones to which evaluation could be addressed. Cost-benefit analysis of comparative programs is the hallmark of this approach. The Follow Through evaluation is the paradigmatic case.

Generally, a consensus on goals is assumed, and the problem is to measure the outcomes of the government programs. In order to establish cause and effect relationships between the programs and outcomes, good experimental design is necessary. The randomized control group is the design of choice but not always possible. After the outcomes have been measured—psychometrically, sociometrically, or econometrically—the programs are compared on costs to determine which outcome can be produced for the least money. Social science methodology is relied on heavily in this process.

A book espousing the systems analysis approach is Rossi, Freeman, and Wright's *Evaluation: A Systematic Approach* (1979). For them, evaluations are undertaken for management, planning, policy development, and fiscal purposes. The key questions are these:

(1) Is the intervention reaching the target population?
(2) Is it being implemented in the ways specified?
(3) Is it effective?
(4) How much does it cost?
(5) What are its costs relative to its effectiveness? [p. 20]

The evaluation must be "as objective as possible; that is, to provide a *firm assessment*—an assessment where the results would be unchanged if done by another group or if replicated by the same evaluators" (p. 21). The commitment is to "orderly policy development and implementation." Systematic evaluations are grounded in social science techniques. Rossi et al. disparage commonsense evaluations because they lead to faulty conclusions, and evaluations based on professional standards because they are not based on scientific evidence. Nor does clinical judgment provide a "firm" guide to decisions.

Systematic evaluations produce valid and reliable evidence which can be duplicated by other observers, which could not have occurred without the interaction, and which include information as to whether the funds are efficiently used. A comprehensive evaluation answers questions about program planning, program monitoring, impact assessment, and economic efficiency. Planning information helps planners pinpoint appropriate interventions. Monitoring information tells whether a program is "in conformity to its design." Impact information tells whether the program produced change in the desired direction. Economic information tells whether the program is efficient. Rossi, Freeman, and Wright caution that evaluation cannot be competently undertaken unless policy-making proceeds clearly and explicitly.

All in all, the systems analysis approach is most heavily oriented to a positivist social science methodology, usually to the exclusion of other methodologies. It has received powerful backing from many officials, particularly economists, in the federal government. In addition, it claims the authority of being a social science.

As noted in the preceding chapter, the predicament of the modern evaluator is that he must evaluate a public program for an external audience. The systems analysis approach resolves this predicament by taking the federal policy-makers' perspective, by assuming that the program being investigated is a functional part of a social and governmental structure. If one assigns the program such a role, then there are certain criteria and functions the program must meet. Hence, there are certain questions the evaluator must answer, assuming that role for the program. It is a functionalist approach. Given the function of programs, any program must meet certain requirements.

The Behavioral Objectives (Or Goal-Based) Approach

The objectives approach resolves the modern evaluator's dilemma in a somewhat different way. It takes the goals of the program as stated and then collects evidence as to whether it has achieved those goals. The goals serve as the exclusive source of standards and criteria. The evaluator assesses what the program developers say they intend achieving. The discrepancy between the stated goals and outcomes is the measure of program success. The stated goals relieve the evaluator of having to presume certain functions for the programs, e.g., efficiency.

In education the goal-based model was advanced by Tyler (1950), who advocated defining educational goals in terms of student behaviors. The evaluation of a program should define its outcomes and its objectives in specific individual behaviors. The task of the evaluator was to determine whether the students were exhibiting these particular behaviors after being in the program. This became known as the "behavioral objective" approach or the Tylerian model of program development and evaluation.

The technology was further refined by Mager (1962), who insisted that not only should objectives be prespecified in behavioral terms but that the objectives themselves contain the criteria and goal attainment levels that the developers aspired to. Quantified outcome variables, especially achievement tests in education, were the means of measuring the student behaviors. Bloom (1956) and others constructed taxonomies of appropriate educational objectives. Bloom et al. (1971) and Popham (1975) applied this approach to evaluating different subject matters.

In recent years, the focus of the technology has shifted away from the proper statement of the objectives to a concern about how the objectives are to be measured. The traditional standardized achievement tests consist of test items not based on prespecified objectives. There has been strong interest in developing "criterion referred" tests. These are invariably objective referenced. That is, the test developers arrive at a set of objectives, then base test items on the objectives.

The National Assessment of Educational Progress, championed by Tyler, is of this type. A more recent development is competency testing. The objectives that serve as the basis for the test are often presumed to be minimal objectives for a particular grade level. In other words, every child should have mastered them. The child must get so many items correct to be declared minimally competent. Almost every state has such a competency testing program. In some states, such as Florida, promotion to the next grade level is dependent on the student's test score. The objectives approach is most popular at the state level.

The behavioral objectives approach has achieved currency in other fields as well. For example, management-by-objectives is essentially an objectives approach applied to business and government organizations. Organizations and individuals are asked to define their objectives and are judged on how well they meet them. This is not surprising since the objectives movement grew out of the task analysis and industrial psychology of the early twentieth century.

Suchman's (1967) early evaluation book on public health evaluation was primarily a goal-based approach. The evaluation process was conceived as one of identifying goal activity, putting goal activity into operation, assessing the effect of the goal operation, value formation, goal setting or objectives, and goal measuring (p. 34). In Suchman's

words, "The most identifying feature of evaluative research is the
presence of some goal or objective whose measure of attainment constitutes the main focus of the research problem" (p. 37). A clear program
objective is equivalent to an hypothesis in a research study.

A contrast may be drawn between this approach and the previously
described systems analysis approach. The Follow Through evaluation,
using the systems analysis approach, relied on only four test batteries to
evaluate thirteen early childhood programs. Presumably, what these
four tests measured was critical. Actually, each early childhood program had dozens of explicit goals and objectives. A behavioral objectives evaluation would have determined whether each objective had
been achieved or else reduced the objectives somehow to a measurable
set.

The Decision-Making Approach

All modern evaluation approaches suggest a connection between
evaluation and decision-making, although who the decision-makers are
and how the decisions shall be made vary. The decision-making
approach suggests that the evaluation be structured by the actual
decisions to be made, and usually this means the decisions of the top
decision-maker, manager, or administrator.

In education the main proponent of this approach has been Stufflebeam (1973). "Evaluation is the process of delineating, obtaining, and
providing useful information for judging decision alternatives" (p. 129).
Stufflebeam went on to define three decision settings (homeostasis,
incrementalism, and neomobilism), four types of decision (planning,
structuring, implementing, and recycling), three steps in the evaluation
process (delineating, obtaining, and providing), and four types of evaluation (context, input, process, product).

Whatever the type of evaluation, the evaluation design is focused by
identifying the level of decision to be served, projecting the decision
situation, defining criteria for each decision situation, and defining
policies for the evaluator. After that, the requisite information is
collected, organized, analyzed, and reported. Each phase is broken
down into subtasks for the evaluator (Stufflebeam, 1969).

Guttentag (1973, 1974) attempted a quantitative analysis of the
decision-maker's preference structure. The idea is to identify the
actions or programs that will maximize the decision-makers' various

values. This is done through a multiattribute utilities scaling method developed by Edwards. "Utilities" are the result of a course of action in terms of the decision-makers' values. The object is to identify the courses of action that maximize the overall utilities.

The approach requires one to define the relevant dimensions of value and to have the decision-maker rate the entities being evaluated on these value scales. All this is based on the decision-makers' subjective judgments. The utilities of the action alternatives are summarized across the various value dimensions to determine which course of action has the greatest utility.

A third view of the decision-making approach to evaluation is that of Patton (1978), who emphasized the personal factor heavily in the utilization of evaluation findings. "The first step in the utilization-focused approach to evaluation is identification and organization of relevant decision makers for and information users of the evaluation" (p. 61). Patton contended that evaluation findings are used when some individual takes direct, personal responsibility for getting the information to the right people. The responsibility for determining what information they need belongs to the decision-makers.

The second step in an evaluation is identifying and focusing the relevant questions. The right question has several characteristics. It is possible to bring data to bear on the question, and there is more than one possible answer to the question. The identified decision-makers both want and feel they need information to help them answer the question. The decision-makers want to answer the questions themselves; they care about the answers. Finally, the decision-makers can specify how they would use the answer to the question.

In short, the decision-making approach to evaluation resolves the evaluator's predicament by taking the decision-maker as the audience to whom the evaluation is directed, by taking his concerns and criteria as the significant ones. How the decision-makers are identified and how their decisions are manifested vary. The presumption is that such an approach will increase utilization of the evaluation findings.

The methodology draws heavily from survey methodology, such as questionnaires or interviews, and the evaluator works more with natural variation in program settings rather than trying to arrange experiments. The questions answered are those of the decision-makers, but these usually involve the effectiveness of the program on some dimension, and, in particular, which parts of the program are working.

The Goal-Free Approach

The goal-free approach is a direct reaction to the ubiquity of goal-determined evaluation. Scriven (1973) maintained that not only should the evaluator not base his evaluation on the program's goals, he should remain deliberately uninformed about what these goals are in order not to be biased by them. Goal-free evaluation should be seen within the context of Scriven's larger concern with reducing the effects of bias in evaluation. Goals bias the evaluator. As Scriven put it, "Unfortunately, I can't both evaluate their [the project staff's] achievements with reasonable objectivity and also go through a lengthy indoctrination session with them" (p. 320).

The goal-free model reduces the bias of searching for only the program developer's prespecified intents by not informing the evaluator of them. Hence, the evaluator must search for all outcomes. Many of these outcomes are unintended side effects, which may be positive or negative. As Scriven wrote,

> The so-called "side effects" whether good or bad often wholly determine the outcome of the evaluation. It is obviously irrelevant to the evaluator whether there are "side" or "main" effects. That language refers to the intentions of the producer, and the evaluator isn't evaluating intentions but achievements. In fact, it's risky to hear even general descriptions of the intentions because it focuses your attention away from the "side effects" and tends to make you overlook or down-weight them [p. 321].

Of all the evaluation approaches described here, goal-free evaluation has been least used, even to the point where some people would question it as a major model. In the social services area, evaluators and developers often find it difficult to envision where the evaluator would find criteria for the evaluation if not from the program developer's goals. They presume that the evaluator merely substitutes his own goals for those of the developers.

However, Consumers' Union regularly evaluates consumer products without asking the producers what their goals are. For example, Consumers' Union evaluates automobiles without using General Motors goals as a basis for the evaluation. Consumers' Union focuses on standards and criteria that they think will benefit the consumer rather than the producer. Similarly, goal-free evaluation takes as its audience or reference group the consumers of social programs rather than the managers. The Consumers' Union approach seems to serve as a model for much of Scriven's thinking.

Of course, social programs are not automobiles, and arriving at a set of standards for evaluation is not as straightforward as with a consumer product. To this end Scriven has attempted to develop the concept of "needs" as a basis for the evaluation. Needs, as opposed to mere wants or desires, are discovered through needs assessments. Establishing the objective validity of such needs would provide the evaluator with an authoritative source of standards. Thus, goal-free evaluation rests upon an analysis of consumer needs rather than producers' goals.

The methodology of goal-free evaluation is not so explicit as some of the other approaches. Generally, Scriven espouses a "bias-free" approach to securing objectivity. The evaluator is seen as an expert eliminating and preventing the biases of himself and others from interfering in the evaluation. Techniques include double-blind experiments in which neither subject nor evaluator knows which is treatment and which placebo. Scriven sees goal-free evaluation as triple-blind in that neither are the intentions known. Other techniques include pre- and post-mixing of elements to be judged, calibration of judges through standard examples, buffering of the individual from the program staff, codes of ethics, concurrent replication, secondary analysis by independent parties, and the like (Scriven, 1976).

Scriven (1975) makes much of the independence of the evaluator from the program staff. His principle of independent feedback says that no unit should rely entirely on a given subunit for evaluative feedback about that subunit. His principle of the instability of independence suggests that evaluators continually become co-opted over time and that care must be taken to renew the vigilance of the evaluation. He makes repeated reference to the evaluator as a hunter or a detective out to discover clues and to track down the quarry. In one case he compared the evaluator's job to that of a coroner who seeks to determine the causal connections under nonexperimental conditions (Scriven, 1976). Through the modus operandi method the investigator tracks down a causal chain between the cause and effect. The evaluator must operate similarly.

In the few goal-free evaluations actually attempted, the techniques have varied widely. In an evaluation of some new curriculum materials, House and Hogben (1974) examined pretest results, read expert reviews of the materials, visited classrooms, interviewed teachers and students, and examined the materials themselves. In another evaluation of curric-

ulum materials, Welch (1978) used a panel of judges to rate the
materials on a lengthy checklist. Harrington and Sanders (1979) have
attempted to develop some guidelines for the conduct of goal-free
evaluation.

The Art Criticism Approach

The roles of the art critic, the literary critic, the theater critic, and
the film critic are familiar ones. They are valued ways of judging the
quality of works in the arts. Eisner (1979) and others have explored the
analogous model of an educational or curriculum critic to judge educational programs. The same approach might be employed in other areas
of social endeavor.

In Eisner's conception, criticism is essentially qualitative, like the
work of artists themselves. "The art critic finds himself or herself with
the difficult task of rendering the essentially ineffable qualities constituting works of art into a language that will help others perceive the
work more deeply" (p. 191). Eisner contends that criticism is an
empirical undertaking. The qualities that the critic describes can be
located in the work itself. Furthermore, anything can be the subject of
criticism. Criticism is not the negative appraisal of something but rather
the illumination of something's qualities so that an appraisal of its value
can be made. The test of criticism is in its instrumental effects on the
perception of the audience.

Eisner distinguishes between connoisseurship and criticism. Connoisseurship is the art of appreciation, whereas criticism is the art of
disclosure (p. 193). Connoisseurship consists of recognizing and appre-
ciating the qualities of the particular but does not require a public
judgment or description. It is the necessary prelude to criticism.

Connoisseurship requires that the perceiver have a great deal of
experience to be able to distinguish what is significant about a wine, a
play, an educational classroom. However, there is a difference between
recognition and perception. Mere recognition and classification based
on experience is not enough. One must be able to perceive subtleties
and understand how they contribute to an overall pattern, as in classroom life.

To develop such connoisseurship one must have the opportunity to
attend to happenings and to compare them. Perceptions must be
refined, integrated, and appraised. One must be sensitive to the emerg-

ing qualities of the classroom or whatever program is being evaluated. This also requires a set of ideas—theories, models, or whatever—that enable one to distinguish the significant from the trivial. Proper training, as well as experience, is relevant to these discriminations.

On the other hand, "Criticism is the art of disclosing the qualities of events or objects that connoisseurship perceives" (p. 197). Critics try to "render" a situation in such a way as to point to significant aspects of the situation, object, or program. Here Eisner draws the distinction between discursive and nondiscursive modes of presentation. The critic tries to capture the essence of the particular. The language of criticism is nondiscursive in that it uses forms to present feelings rather than to represent facts.

Properly executed criticism will increase awareness and appreciation. Appreciation does not mean liking something but having an increased awareness. The function of the critic is to apply criteria so that judgments about such events can be grounded in a view of what counts. Such qualitative inquiry allows the reader to participate vicariously in the qualities described.

As to validity and reliability, Eisener speaks of "structural corroboration" and "referential adequacy." Evidence is corroborated when pieces of evidence fit together. Referential adequacy refers to whether one can find in the work or program criticized the features to which the critic points. The necessity of familiarity with the situation is greatly emphasized. Still, one does not expect unanimity among critics. The goal, according to Eisner, is to expand perception, not to arrive at one definitive criticism. The consequence of criticism is the development of connoisseurship in others. So far the criticism approach to evaluation has been propagated mainly by Eisner and his students (e.g., McCutcheon [1978] and Vallance [1978]) and limited to education.

Certainly, there are different approaches to criticism itself. Kelly (1978) drew an analogy between evaluation and literary criticism rather than art criticism. From literary criticism he draws upon such established concepts as metaphor, voice, plot, and theme and uses them to illuminate evaluation. His analysis shows how evaluators employ similar concepts in looking at programs and in writing their reports. In his analysis, description and evaluation merge. Also, the credibility of the critic is more of a problem to him than to Eisner. As Kelly notes, one attends to critics with whom one agrees. So the nature of criticism can vary from one subject matter to another.

Criticism can also vary within a subject area. Jenkins and O'Toole (1978) noted the differences among literary critics. There are the academic critics in universities who judge everything by the standards of the best works. There are the writer-critics who perceive criticism as a by-product of their own work and who attempt to determine the standards of taste by which they might be evaluated. In particular, the criticism of the latter takes on some of the characteristics of creative writing. Finally, there are the free-lance or journalistic critics who appeal to a broad marketplace audience.

Overall, a critic assumes that he is writing for a group of consumers or for connoisseurs. The audience will find out whether the program is a good one but will also have its sensitivity heightened. This assumes that the audience accepts the critic and usually his implicit standards. There is no standard methodology except critical review, which may be accomplished in a number of ways. Immersion and familiarity with the object or program are usually considered vital. Proper experience and training for the critic are essential. Criticism eventually leads to heightened awareness, improved standards, and better performance. The criticism approach to evaluation resolves the evaluation dilemma by designating as evaluator an experienced, properly trained person, in short, a connoisseur of the subject at issue. With his sensitivities the experienced person renders his judgments in such a way as to inform and educate those less sensitive.

The Professional Review (Accreditation) Approach

For more than fifty years, professional associations have conducted evaluations of professional training. Whether they be doctors, lawyers, social workers, or teachers, professional review of schools, as embodied in the North Central Association for secondary schools, has been a major means of evaluating. Conceived somewhat more broadly, professional review includes surgeons or professors or lawyers judging the work of fellow professionals. Usually participation in the review is limited to the professional's peers.

Many of these are evaluations to accredit training schools as being worthy. For example, beginning in 1885, groups of secondary schools organized to standardize entrance requirements to college. From this emerged the National Study of School Evaluation (1978) which publishes *Evaluative Criteria.* This work contains criteria by which secondary schools are evaluated.

The criteria are organized into specific subject matter areas, such as agriculture, art, business education, and so on. Some criteria refer to school services, such as learning media services, student services, or school facilities. The educational program is divided into eighteen subject areas. In addition, there are nine service areas. Within each subject, there are several checklists to evaluate it.

For example, in the English area there are such checklist items as, "English courses are required of all students" (p. 103), or "Some contemporary and classic works are studied intensively, chosen for appropriateness to student abilities, interests, and maturity" (p. 195), "Attention is given to improving study skills" (p. 111). The evaluator marks each item on a five-point scale from "missing" to "excellent."

This approach is designed to engage the school staff in self-evaluation. Before a visit by an outside committee, the school staff is divided into several subcommittees. These subcommittees mark the checklist items. The results are reported to the full school staff. The outside accrediting agency (e.g., the North Central Association) selects an outside committee to validate the self-evaluation. Schools are given veto power over committee members. The committee may vary in size from ten to thirty people.

The visiting committee is divided into subject subcommittees, and each one checks the self-evaluation ratings, changing the ratings where they disagree. Each subcommittee and the full visiting committee prepare written reports. Before the visiting committee leaves the school, a brief oral report to the staff points out major strengths and weaknesses of the school and makes recommendations. Accreditation is awarded the school depending on the report. After the visit, the school is expected to take steps to correct perceived weaknesses. Criteria and procedures differ somewhat, but similar accreditation visits are made of almost all schools, from the most elementary to the most professional, by various accrediting agencies such as professional associations and state governments.

An interesting variation of the accreditation approach to evaluation is the rapidly increasing evaluation of departments or units within a university, usually sponsored by the university administration. One of the earliest of such evaluations was the Council on Program Evaluation (COPE) at the University of Illinois. From 1972 to 1979, all the academic units on the Urbana campus were evaluated.

To accomplish this, a council consisting of nine professors was established, chaired by a central office administrator. Later two graduate and two undergraduate students were added to the council. The council was given authority to evaluate departments on the basis of six criteria:

(1) quality of the instructional program;
(2) quality of research, creative activity or scholarly work;
(3) quality of service to the university and profession;
(4) contribution or importance of the unit to other campus units;
(5) value of the program to society or its uniqueness in the state; and
(6) potential and future expectations.

At first task groups of five to ten faculty members were appointed by the Council to study a particular department. The task groups conducted extensive interviews with department members and eventually wrote a confidential assessment of the department that was submitted to the Council. The Council reviewed the report, and, based on it, wrote its own abbreviated assessment, usually in the form of a letter, which was sent to the vice-chancellor and to the department. The department could then respond to the letter and recommendations contained within it.

After a few years of this method, this process grew to demand so much time that it was decided not to have a task group for every department. An extensive package of forms was developed to be completed by the department. These forms included questionnaires on most aspects of the department operations. The Council reviewed the completed forms and arrived at an overall judgment and set of recommendations based on the formal criteria. In actual practice, the quality of research was heavily weighted in the final judgments. If the department looked particularly weak or needed some other special attention, a task group was appointed to conduct a more thorough face-to-face evaluation (Petrie, 1979).

Of course, not all professional reviews operate in the same manner. For example, board evaluations in the medical specialities are governed by a panel of professional peers, but the physician is subject to a written examination and an oral examination by specialists. In all these evaluations the source of standards and criteria are the professionals themselves. It is assumed that they are best qualified to judge professional merit. Procedures vary but the evaluation culminates in a holistic assessment of a professional program by other professionals.

The Quasi-Legal (Adversary) Approach

Quasi-legal procedures have long been used for evaluating and policy-making. Recently, attention in evaluation has been focused on mock trials or other adversary proceedings, particularly in view of the aggressive action of the courts in determining issues in social programs. Not all quasi-legal proceedings are adversarial in nature, however. In fact, if one considers "blue ribbon" panels and appointed commissions as legal procedures, most are not. Statutory law (e.g., the Civil Rights Act) sets up administrative review processes that adhere to principles of due process but are not adversarial.

For example, the Warren Commission investigating President Kennedy's assassination was a presidentially appointed group that heard evidence from witnesses, conducted its own investigations, and came to a conclusion about probable events. Similarly, the Kerner Commission on Civil Disorders came to a conclusion about probable causes. Often, this kind of panel is used to address controversial issues and to resolve doubt about them. A recent example is the Wirtz (1977) commission on the national decline in standardized test scores. The panel arrived at probable causes for such a decline.

In England, frequent use has been made of such commissions and councils to give guidance to public policy (Kogan and Packwood, 1974). The Plowden Committee of 1967 on primary education and the more recent Taylor Report on the local governance of schools are examples. Prominent citizens are appointed to head such panels and supplied with government assistance.

All social areas have been guided by such panels, and often the panel is established to resolve issues within a profession itself. For example, a panel examining the educational accountability system in Michigan was funded by the National Education Association (House et al., 1974). A similar investigation was sponsored by the same group in Florida (Tyler et al., 1978). Within the Office of Education the Joint Review Dissemination Panel hears evidence and passes on whether federally developed programs are "validated" enough to be disseminated to the rest of the country.

Although these panels and commissions are not part of the legal system, in fact, part of their authority is derived from quasi-legalistic procedures. Evidence is usually rendered before a tribunal. "Witnesses" testify and submit "evidence." Rules are formulated as to who may give evidence and the conditions of the testimony. The hearings themselves take on a courtroom symbolism and solemnity; the rooms are often arranged in the manner of a court. Great care is usually taken to hear all the evidence. In short, the evaluator's predicament is resolved by using quasi-legal procedures which lend the authority of the law to the evaluation.

More recently, legal adversary proceedings have been employed to evaluate programs. The adversary hearing is based on the supposition that the facts in a case can be best ascertained if each side strives as hard as it can, in a partisan fashion, to bring the most favorable evidence for its side to the attention of the court (Owens, 1973). The partisanship of opposing sides reveals vital evidence.

In 1970 the first such adversary hearing was held in Hawaii to judge whether the curriculum *Man: A Course of Study* should be adopted for the public schools of Hawaii. Three judges, all of whom were educators, presided. Both sides spent weeks preparing the case. Another mock trial was held at Indiana University in the evaluation of a teacher education program (Wolf, 1975). Adversary teams presented arguments for and against the program. Over a two-day period, thirty-two witnesses testified. Legal instructions on direct and cross examination were developed. Thirteen education experts comprised the jury.

The designer of the trial said, "Perhaps the most compelling reason for using legal methodology is that it offers a useful system of evidentiary rules and procedures aimed at producing alternative inferences from data prior to the rendering of a judgment. . . . The judicial approach provides for the structured consideration of alternative arguments and inferences to keep the evaluation both intellectually honest and fair" (Wolf, 1975: 185).

Wolf conceived of the process as involving four stages—issue generation, issue selection, argument presentation, and the hearing. In the first stage a series of interviews was conducted to identify thirty issues. In the second stage a survey to faculty, students, and administrators was used to reduce the issues. In the third stage arguments were prepared. In the fourth stage the prehearing discovery sessions and the hearing itself took place. The whole process took six months.

In the face of criticisms about adversarial methods, Wolf (1979) attempted to deemphasize the adversarial nature of his particular approach. "Perhaps the most significant aspect of the judicial metaphor . . . is that the court's mode of inquiry is educative" (Wolf, 1979: 21). Human testimony is the "cornerstone of evidence." "The ultimate evidence which guides deliberation and judgment includes not only the 'facts,' but a wide variety of perceptions, opinions, biases, and specula-tions, all within a context of values and beliefs" (p. 21).

Stenzel (1979) explored the use of the Congressional investigative hearing as a model for evaluation. A committee was established by the Illinois Office of Education to examine the strengths and weaknesses of a third party evaluation of a special education program. The charge to the committee was to explore the validity of the evaluation, to review the recommendations in the report, and to produce a written response to the original evaluation report. The committee consisted of three members of the professional staff of the Illinois Office of Education. The evaluators appeared before the committee to answer questions. Stenzel (1979) outlined the procedures of a congressional committee, which differ significantly from that of a trial.

There are many quasi-legal procedures that might be applied to evaluation, the "blue ribbon" panel and the trial by jury being only the best known. The aim of legal procedures is to resolve issues one way or the other. Most legal procedures feature some kind of hearing in which arguments for and against an issue are presented. The legitimacy of the approach depends on whether one accepts the particular procedures employed, the hearing officer, and the deciding panel or jury. In the common law itself, court action is usually decided by judges alone.

The Case Study (or Transaction) Approach

This approach concentrates on the program processes themselves and on how people view the program. The major question asked is, "What does the program look like to various people who are familiar with it?" The usual methodology is to conduct interviews with many people, to make observations at the program site, and to present the findings in the form of a case study. The qualitative case study is so prevalent as a methodology that I have used this term, along with "transaction," to refer to the approach. One could also do quantitative case studies, but that would be far removed from this approach. The transaction-case study approach is almost entirely qualitative in methodology and pre-sentation. Case history might be a more accurate designation.

The aim of the approach is to improve the understanding of the reader or audience of the evaluation, primarily by showing them how others perceive the program being evaluated. Anthropological proce-dures, or even journalistic and novelistic devices, are analogs. Ethnomethodology is a related approach, and the methodologies are often referred to as "naturalistic." A leading figure is Stake (1978, 1975). Stake made the argument for case studies in this fashion:

> case studies will often be the preferred method of research because they may be epistemologically in harmony with the reader's experience and thus to that person a natural basis for generalization. . . . If the readers of our reports are the persons who populate our houses, schools, governments, and industries; and if we are to help them understand social problems and social programs, we must perceive and communicate in a way that accommodates their present understandings. Those people have arrived at their understandings mostly through direct and vicarious experience [Stake, 1978: 5].

When the aim of inquiry is understanding rather than explanation and propositional knowledge, the case study is often superior to other modes of inquiry. It is legitimate to discover or validate laws through many scholarly studies, but the aim of the practical arts is to get things done. For Stake, case studies feature descriptions that are complex, holistic, and involve a myriad of interactive variables. The data are gathered by personalistic observation, and the writing is informal, narrative, often employing quotes, illustrations, allusions, and metaphor. Comparisons are implicit rather than explicit.

Stake's approach focuses on perception and knowing as a "transactional" process and hence is sometimes called the transaction model. In Stake's "responsive" evaluation, the evaluator usually negotiates with the client as to what is to be done. He "responds" to what different audiences want to know.

> An educational evaluation is responsive evaluation if it orients more directly to program activities than to program intents; responds to audience requirements for information; and if the different value perspectives present are referred to in reporting the success and failure of the program. To do a responsive evaluation, the evaluator conceives of a plan of observations and negotiations. He arranges for various persons to observe the program, and with their help prepares brief narratives, portrayals, product displays, graphs, etc. He finds out what is of value to his audiences, and gathers expressions of worth from various individuals whose points of view differ. Of course, he checks the quality of his records; he gets program personnel to react to the

accuracy of his portrayals; and audience members to react to the relevance of his findings. He does most of this informally—iterating and keeping a record of action and reaction. He chooses media accessible to his audiences to increase the likelihood and fidelity of communication. He might prepare a final written report, he might not--depending on what he and his clients have agreed on [Stake, 1975: 14].

Using a more traditional anthropological methodology, Smith and Pohland (1974) evaluated a computer-assisted instruction program in the Appalachians, and Wolcott (1977) evaluated the installation of a program-planning and budgeting system in a local school. In both cases, the evaluators relied on participant observation, especially field notes, informal interviews, and document analysis.

In England, MacDonald (1974) also advocated the case study approach in what he has labeled "democratic" evaluation.

Democratic evaluation is an information service to the community about the characteristics of an educational program. It recognises value-pluralism and seeks to represent a range of interests in its issue formulation. The basic value is an informed citizenry, and its evaluator acts as broker in exchanges of information between differing groups. His techniques of data-gathering and presentation must be accessible to nonspecialist audiences. His main activity is the collection of definitions of, and reactions to, the program. He offers confidentiality to informants and gives them control over his use of information. The report is non-recommendatory, and the evaluator has no concept of information misuse. The evaluator engages in periodic negotiation of his relationships with sponsors and program participants. The criterion of success is the range of audiences served [MacDonald, 1948: 226-227].

Also in England, Parlett and Hamilton (1977) advocated an approach they call "illuminative" evaluation. The aim of illuminative evaluation is to study the program: how it operates, how it is influenced by the situations in which it is applied: what those directly concerned regard as its advantages and disadvantages; and how students' intellectual tasks and academic experiences are most affected. "It aims to discover and document what it is like to be participating in the scheme, whether as a teacher or pupil; and, in addition, to discern and discuss the innovation's most significant features, returning concomitants, and critical processes" (Parlett and Hamilton, 1977: 19).

More recently, Guba (1978) endorsed this overall approach and attempted to define the difficulties that face a "naturalistic" evaluation. The major problem, as he saw it, is that of authenticity—the establishment of the basis for trust in the outcomes of the evaluation. Other methodological problems are those of setting limits to the inquiry and of focusing on the categories within which the data can be assimilated and understood. Guba would see naturalistic methodology as descriptive not only of the case study approach but of the criticism and quasi-legal models as well.

A contrast may be drawn between the case study approach and that of the critic, to which it is similar. The critic relies on his own experience and applies standards of his choosing. The case study worker reports on the perceptions of other people, as well as his own, and reports their value judgments of the program. In some cases the case study and criticism may look similar.

The case study or transaction approach to evaluation is becoming more popular. Many case study evaluations, formerly perceived as too subjective, are now being conducted, and there is considerable writing in the area. The case study approach resolves the evaluator's predicament by attempting to represent all significant value positions within the case study, drawing its criteria and standards from those positions, and letting the reader of the study weigh and balance these elements within her own mind.

Other Approaches

I have identified as major models of evaluation certain approaches that are both discussed and put into practice by many practitioners. No doubt I have missed some unintentionally. Others I have excluded because they are closely allied to these major types or are combinations of the major types. The idealized approaches are not necessarily mutually exclusive. A new approach that may be emerging is that represented by Apple (1979), Lundgren (1977), Kallos (1978), Paulston (forthcoming), and several others. Although these authors differ substantially among themselves, their general approach is to assume a deliberate theoretical position regarding society. They see society as organized to produce class inequalities and see education as providing the ideological foundations for such societal reproduction.

So far their work has consisted mainly of critiques of existing evaluation approaches rather than formulating a new approach based on such a theoretical foundation. Few evaluations have been conducted employing such an approach. One study is a long-term investigation of beliefs engendered in students during vocational training in Swedish higher education (Franke-Wikberg, 1979). Presumably, such an approach to evaluation would focus on inequalities in the program being evaluated. If such an approach does develop, its underlying assumptions are likely to be distinctly nonliberal, in contrast to the dominant approaches discussed above.

A final caution about the classification of evaluations into idealized types is that the classification must be taken tentatively. Many evaluators will insist that their particular approach is unique and does not fall within the categories I have outlined here. In a sense they are correct. These approaches are idealized types, constructs that are used to clarify thinking in the field. In a sense every approach has some unique features.

On the other hand, I would argue that these basic types account for the vast majority of evaluations now attempted, and that a strong argument can be made for classifying particular approaches into these general categories. That is not to say that every evaluation will take exactly the form of one of these types. Actual evaluations are shaped by particular circumstances and contingencies. What begins as a goal-based evaluation under one set of circumstances may look very different from a goal-based evaluation under different circumstances. Nonetheless, a goal-based evaluation is likely to look rather different from a case study evaluation under most circumstances. The ultimate test of the classification scheme is both whether it is valid and whether it is useful in understanding evaluation. A similar view of the role of category systems in evaluation has been advanced by Alkin and Ellett (1979) and Alkin (1979).

3

ASSUMPTIONS UNDERLYING
THE APPROACHES

Liberalism

One way of understanding evaluation is to compare the numerous evaluation approaches or models with each other. (I will use the terms "approaches" and "models" interchangeably.) There are many possibilities for comparison but perhaps the most significant comparisons are those among the underlying theoretical assumptions on which the approaches are based. In this way, one might see how logically similar the approaches are to one another and determine what logical possibilities do and do not exist.

The basic theme is that all the evaluation approaches are based on variations in the assumptions of liberalism or, if one prefers, the conceptions of liberal democracy. The models differ from each other as the basic assumptions vary. Assumptions I take here in the commonsense meaning of things taken for granted or things taken to be true.

AUTHOR'S NOTE: A version of this chapter appeared as "Assumptions Underlying Evaluation Models," *Educational Researcher*, Volume 7, No. 3, March 1978, pp. 4-12. Copyright 1978, American Educational Research Association, Washington, DC. Reprinted by permission. Helpful comments were provided by Robert Ennis, David Hamilton, and Bruce Stewart.

In the first column of the taxonomy in Figure 1, Chapter 2, the common names of the approaches are listed. In the top row are the critical dimensions of comparison: the audiences to whom the evaluation is addressed, what the approach assumes consensus on, the methodology of data collection, the ultimate outcome expected, and the typical question that the approach tries to address. At one level of abstraction, these are the assumptions underlying the approaches.

In the taxonomy the models are related to each other in a systematic way. Generally, the more one progresses down the column of major audiences, the more democratic or less elitist the audience becomes. The more one moves down the consensus column, the less consensus is assumed on goals and other elements. The more one moves down the methodology column, the more subjectivist and less objectivist the research methodology becomes. The more one moves down the outcomes column, the less the overall concern becomes social efficiency and the more it becomes personal understanding. These are oversimplifications since the actual ordering is more complex.

The major elements in understanding the approaches are their ethics, their epistemology, and their political ramifications. The current models all derive from the philosophy of liberalism, with deviations from the mainstream being responsible for differences in approaches. The ethics, epistemology, and politics are not entirely separable from each other.

Liberalism itself grew out of an attempt to rationalize and justify a market society (Macpherson, 1966) which was organized on the principle of freedom of choice. Choice remains a key idea in the evaluation approaches although whose choice, what choices, and the grounds upon which choices are made are matters of difference. Consumer's choice is the ultimate ideal but who the consumer is is differently conceived.

A second key idea of liberalism is that of an individualist psychology. Each individual mind is presumed to exist prior to society. The individual is not conceived initially as a part of a greater collectivity, although he may submit to one later as in a social contract situation. Liberalism is profoundly methodologically individualist in its intellectual constructions.

Another key idea is the empiricist orientation. Often liberalism is radically empiricist. For example, John Stuart Mill, the apostle of liberalism, believed that even mathematics was inductively based. All the evaluation models here have such an empiricist flavor.

The evaluation approaches also assume a free marketplace of ideas in which consumers will "buy" the best ideas. They assume that competition of ideas strengthens the truth. Ultimately, they assume that knowledge will make people happy or better in some way. So the evaluation approaches partake of the ideas of a competitive, individualist, market society. But the most fundamental idea is freedom of choice, for without choice, of what use is evaluation? Figure 2 presents the evaluation approaches as they are related to liberalism.

Subjectivist Ethics

All the major evaluation models are subjectivist in ethics, although there is no necessity to this. One type of ethical subjectivism sees the end of ethical conduct as the realization of some type of subjective experience. This describes the top four approaches, which I have labeled "utilitarian." Properly speaking, utilitarianism refers to the idea of maximizing happiness in society. Any activity that maximizes happiness is the "right" thing to do (House, 1976). Usually surrogate measures like gross national product in economics or mean test scores in education are used as the indicators of happiness.

Besides the systems analysis, behavioral objective, and decision-making approaches, Scriven's goal-free model is also included in this classification. All these approaches try to arrive at a single judgment of overall social utility. The simplest approach is the homogenous scaling of the systems analysis approach which tries to reduce all variables into a quantitative model like a regression analysis. Only one or a few outcome variables are employed.

The most complex is that of Scriven's in which many outcome variables are considered, including secondary and tertiary effects. All these various scales must be weighted and combined somehow into an overall summative judgment. The analogy is with a Consumers' Union report in which many different criteria are summed up in an overall ranking of ' better" and "best." As in Consumers' Union, the final scaling will be ordinary rather than interval. It is utilitarian in the sense that there is *one* final scaling of merit, leading to best consumer choice and to social utility eventually.

The other four major evaluation models I have labeled intuitionist/pluralist. The ethical principles are not single in number nor explicitly defined as in utilitarian ethics. There are several principles with no set

FIGURE 2 A Scheme Relating Major Evaluation Approaches to the Philosophy of Liberalism

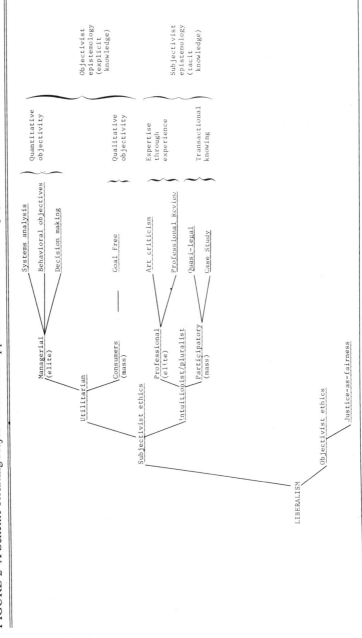

rules for weighing them and the principles are derived from intuition and experience. This captures another meaning of ethical subjectivism— that the ultimate criteria of what is good and right are individual feelings or apprehensions.

In the art criticism model, the critic has arrived at his invariably plural principles by long training and experience. His taste has been refined so that he is an expert judge. Much of his expertise lies in how well he can intuitively balance the principles of judgment. In the professional approach the principles may be spelled out in books like *Evaluative Criteria* (National Study of Secondary School Evaluation, 1978). But their origin and application remain very much a matter of professional intuitive judgment based on long experience.

In the quasi-legal approach, as in a trial, the jury is free to employ multiple criteria in an intuitive fashion. The adversaries are free to introduce anything in evidence that can be construed as relevant. Finally, in the case study approach, plural criteria are introduced by soliciting the judgment of various people involved in the program. The data are weighed intuitively by the evaluator and by the audience of the evaluation. Generally speaking, the utilitarians tend to take explicitly defined techniques as the basis of ethics and knowledge, whereas the intuitionists/pluralists take intuitive tacit knowledge derived from professional experience and participation as the basis.

Although all the major approaches are based on subjectivist ethics, there is no reason why this must be so. It would be possible to have an objectivist ethics within the liberal philosophy. For example, in his *A Theory of Justice*, John Rawls (1971) attempted to base his social ethics on two principles of justice. These principles were not justified on the presumption that they maximized some subjective feeling like happiness, nor on the fact that people intuitively held these principles. Rather, the principles were justified on the basis that rational analysis, namely the theory of minimizing losses, would lead *any* rational person to the same principles. They were objectivist in the sense that they were based on inspectable public logic. Rawls's theory would still fit within the liberal tradition of free choice and methodological individualism.

The utilitarian group is differentiated internally by orientation to different audiences. The systems analysis, behavioral objectives, and decision-making approaches are very much oriented to supplying information to managers. The goal-free approach is aimed more at consumers. This elite/mass differentiation is carried through among the intuitionists/pluralists as well. The art criticism and professional approaches rely on professional experts for judgments about the program being evaluated while the quasi-legal and case study approaches require participation by both the practitioners and the public.

The Liberal Objectivist Epistemology

In their orientation toward management, the managerial approaches look for ways in which management can monitor and improve the programs. Accountability, efficiency, and quality control are major management concerns. Evaluation has something of a watchdog function. The managerial school also tends to be based on a common epistemology, which I will label "objectivist." Evaluation information is considered to be "scientifically objective." This objectivity is achieved by using "objective" instruments like tests or questionnaires. Presumably, results produced with these instruments are reproducible. The data are analyzed by quantitative techniques which are also "objective" in the sense that they can be verified by logical inspection regardless of who uses the techniques.

In its extreme form objectivism in epistemology excludes the non-quantitative entirely. If it exists, it can be measured, the thought goes. Reduction into numbers sometimes becomes equated with objectivity. The origins of much of this extreme empiricism and objectivism can be found in the earlier epistemology of the liberal philosophy.

The origins of liberalism as a philosophy can be traced back in part to the first great British empiricist, Thomas Hobbes. Hobbes was an admirer of Galileo and his thoroughly mechanical view of the universe. Hobbes developed a mechanistic philosophy of mind based on the idea that sensations were produced in the mind by the motions of external bodies. Words have meaning only when associated with these sensations, and truth consists in the right ordering of names with sensations. Clear definitions are critical. Reasoning is equivalent to calculation and will be correct if the signs are attached to consistent images. Cause and effect are a direct reflection of the world. Thus the way to truth is through clear definition and scientific method.

This epistemology was reformulated in turn by Locke, Berkeley, and Hume. Two hundred years later came the last of the great British empiricists, John Stuart Mill, also called the apostle of liberalism. For Mill the mind was a bundle of impressions. Psychological laws of association were the foundation of a science of society. Everything came from and had to be tested by experience to the extent that even deductive logic, e.g., mathematics, had an inductive basis. Mill saw no fundamental difference between logical truths and factual truths. All knowledge, he felt, had to be grounded in and tested by experience. Knowledge was the pooled sum of individual observations.

This extreme methodological individualism ran deep in Mill's philosophy. To Mill, society was a collection of individual persons bound by common interests. His radical empiricism led him to formulate rules for the conduct of inductive inquiry in *A System of Logic.* Since the mind consisted of sensations, feelings and their associations, the categories of the real world seemed to Mill to be easily accessible. But could these categories be relied upon? If they were ephemeral, one could not know anything. To overcome this problem, Mill *assumed* the world consisted of constant uniformities among classes of sensations.

Experimentation was essential for the scientific testing of theories. Valid causal connections could be established only through the meticulous sorting and independent variation of antecedent conditions and consequences. These were often concealed from casual observation. "Unwashed" appearances were deceptive. Only techniques of inductive logic could clean them. It was here that techniques like the method of agreement, method of difference, or method of concomitant variation could be useful. The cannons of induction were to provide a method for sifting evidence of correlations upon which scientific laws were based.

Scientific laws were what one was after. Science should be concerned with causal uniformities which held for all members of a given class. The assumption of the uniformity of nature was the key on which Mill's whole system of logic depended. In Mill's words:

> We must first observe that there is a principle in the very statement of what Induction is; an assumption with regard to the course of nature and the order of the universe; namely that there are such things in nature as parallel cases, that what happens once will, under a sufficient degree of similarity of circumstances, happen again, and not only again, but as often as the same circumstances recur. . . . And if we consult the actual course of nature we find that the assumption is warranted. The universe, so far as known to us, is so constituted that whatever is true in any one case is true in all cases of a certain description; the only difficulty is, to find what description [Mill, 1893].

This extreme empiricism relied on the belief that categories were rather easily obtainable, much like categories in the physical sciences. Using the proper techniques one could define variables and establish relationships among them. Since nature was uniform one could induce laws in social science just as in natural science. Furthermore, this could be done with survey methodology. The extreme emphasis on empiricism to the exclusion of theory has been inherited by evaluation from liberal epistemology: One can find relationships in nature without theoretical constructs.

Hamilton (1977) traces the introduction of some of these ideas into evaluation. A contemporary of Mill, Francis Galton, invented correlational techniques to relate Mill's easily discoverable categories to each other. Galton also provided an important basis for psychometrics in his work on individual differences. Cattell, greatly influenced by Galton, introduced mental testing into the United States.

The use of tests in education for sorting purposes was promoted by E. L. Thorndike. Thorndike also had a strong influence on the "scientific management" movement in education. The scientific management movement introduced efficiency engineering into the schools. Tests, rating scales, and quantitative techniques stimulated by Thorndike's work were used as devices for achieving efficiency in the schools (Callahan, 1962).

In its emphasis on task analysis, prespecification, and many other features, scientific management bears a strong resemblance to the systems analysis and behavioral objectives approaches to evaluation (House, 1978). In fact, one of the leading advocates of scientific management in education was Franklin Bobbitt. Later Bobbitt and Charters adopted a task analysis-job specification approach to curriculum development. One of Charter's graduate students was Ralph Tyler, who later originated the behavioral objectives model of evaluation. The manager orientation to evaluation has long historical roots.

With or without the historical connections the similarity of the managerial evaluation models to Mill's epistemology is strong. Perhaps the leading proponent of the systems analysis approach has been Alice M. Rivlin. She was in the group that introduced cost-benefit analysis to education and other social programs in the Department of Health, Education and Welfare in the 1960s. Most of the large federal evaluation efforts were based on the systems analysis logic (McLaughlin, 1975).

The key ideas in Rivlin's (1971) approach were these (House, 1978):

- Key decisions will be made by higher governmental levels.
- The end of evaluation is efficiency in the production of social services.
- The only true knowledge is a production function specifying stable relationships between educational inputs and outputs.
- The only way to such knowledge is through experimental methods and statistical techniques.
- It is possible to agree on goals and on a few output measures.
- There is a direct parallel between production in social services and in manufacturing. The same techniques of analysis will apply.

Like Mill, Rivlin assumed the physical science paradigm would be appropriate. She saw social services and manufacturing as yielding to the same techniques of inquiry. The result would be generalizations, in this case production functions, that would hold in various circumstances, if one could only find what those circumstances were. Such a mechanistic conception goes back to Hobbes. And the uniformity of nature assumptions were straight out of J. S. Mill. Results would be consistent everywhere. Rivlin also believed, as did Mill, that large samples were necessary to rid oneself of idiosyncracies.

Mill felt that the chief moral problem was enlightenment, and that men were misled by their institutions. Rivlin believed that the major problem was ignorance in not knowing how to produce social services more effectively. Both believed in the use of experts to unravel these problems. Both also believed in using a few measures as surrogates of happiness. These are needed for calculations in order to enable the utilitarian ethics to work.

There is one place where the classic liberal J. S. Mill and a modern liberal depart company, however. To Mill, liberty was necessary for enlightenment to occur. Mill was one of the great defenders of laissez-faire. The government should stay out of men's affairs. For Rivlin, a welfare state liberal, it was the government which would be making the decisions and doing the acting. In order to find out what works, the government would need more control in order to conduct experiments. Mill was not for large-scale social planning, with the exception of special areas like education, where he allowed for planning and even coercion. Rivlin is the epitome of large-scale planning.

The objectivism of the managerial evaluation approaches that tend to equate objectivity with quantification relies on intersubjective agreement as the exclusive indicator of objectivity. Scriven (1972) calls this the quantitative sense of objectivity. One person's perception of something is regarded as being subjective—the disposition of one individual. Being objective is what a number of observers experience. Common experiencing makes the observation public through intersubjective agreement.

Objectivity has come to be equated with externalizing all references so that multiple witnessing can be achieved, since by the doctrine of intersubjectivism what cannot be experienced directly by others cannot be taken seriously. Hence objectivity is often equated with being able to specify and explicate completely all data collection procedures. Complete externalization permits replication, the hall mark of reliability.

In describing systems analysis procedures, the Department of Defense puts it this way:

> Perhaps the most important of these is the scientific method. This means that the data used in the analysis must be capable of verification, either by observation or by deduction from plausible premises, and that the procedures employed in the analysis must conform to accepted rules of logic. Systems analysis is characterized, in the second place, by the use of quantifiable data and mathematical techniques. . . . Explicitness is the final common denominator of systems analysis. The assumptions and criteria employed in an analysis are specified, and incommensurables and areas of uncertainty are carefully delineated [Snyder, 1967: 5].

"Reliable instruments" receive top priority following this reasoning. In fact, the higher the observer agreement (the reliability coefficient), the better the instrument or procedure appears to be. Unfortunately, reliability is no guarantee of validity, and the intersubjective fallacy can lead to the use of "instruments" on which one achieves high observer agreement as opposed to procedures which may have greater validity. Instruments with high reliability are hallmarks of this epistemological objectivism.

There is a sense in which the intersubjective verification principle is carried through in the definition of goals as well as in the measurement of effects. It is assumed in the managerial approach to evaluation that one can reach a consensus on the goals of a particular project. This assumption is critical in the systems analysis and behavioral objectives models, for the consensus defines what the evaluation will look for. In addition, the systems analysis model also assumes agreement on cause and effect relationships. Mill assumed cause and effect to be obvious and discernible in nature.

Hence, in objectivism the notion of objectivity becomes equated with procedures for determining intersubjectivity. This occurs in both the ethics and epistemology. In fact, utilitarianism requires that there be a single standard of social utility against which to compare things.

Although I have placed Scriven's goal-free evaluation in the utilitarian group, it is somewhat more complex. Scrivin employs the *qualitative* notion of objectivity. In this notion objectivity is equated with being free from bias or distortion. Scriven's overriding concern is with the control of bias. He may employ experimental design like the managerial group, but he has evolved an arsenal of organizational and social devices for controlling biases in the broadest sense (Scriven, 1975, 1976).

In Scriven's framework it is possible for a single observer, unaided by any psychometric instrumentation, to be more objective than a battalion of observers loaded with reliable instruments—if the single observer is looking for the right thing and is sufficiently protected from numerous biases. Scriven does not equate objectivity with intersubjective agreement.

Neither does he assume consensus on goals and objectives, as dramatically illustrated by the goal-free approach. Goal-free evaluation probably does assume agreement on the consequences of the program. (Again the choice at issue is consumer's choice rather than that of the manager.) Scriven combines multiple criteria of consequences with ordinal scaling and a relentlessly comparative approach.

The Subjectivist Epistemology

Utilitarian evaluation, then, is based on a subjectivist ethics, such as maximizing a state of mind like satisfaction, but employs an objectivist epistemology in doing so. Once one has determined what is to be maximized, the methodology can then be employed objectivistically to allocate resources to satisfy various desires.

The intuitionist/pluralist evaluation approaches employ a subjectivist ethics of a different sort. Generally speaking their research methodology also tends to be subjectivist. Procedures for how an educational critic or an accreditation team conducts its investigation are general rather than specific. Explicitness of detail and externalization of procedures so that others might observe the same thing are not the common demominators. Reproducibility is not the major criterion.

Likewise, how the jury will come to a decision or how a case study worker chooses certain material over other material is not made totally specific in the quasi-legal and case study approaches. There is a good deal of subjectivity in how the key actors conduct their investigations.

Whereas the objectivists rely on explicitness of detail in defining techniques which others can use, the intuitionists rely on training and experience to ensure that truth is served. At the extreme in these approaches, both validity and utility are defined subjectively. Validity is conceived as being relative to the conditions of the human mind either because of universal limitations on the way people think or because of personal limitations. (In the objectivist framework validity often is conceived as predicting one observable category from another.)

Subjective validity means that truth is relative to human nature and perhaps even to particular humans. What is valid for one person may not be valid for another. Likewise, the subjective utility of something is based on personal judgment and personal desires. Each person is the best judge of events for himself.

Actually, the subjectivist epistemology is not quite as anarchic as it appears. Whereas the objectivist position is based on externalization and total specification of techniques, the subjectivist position is based on the tradition of the "closed case." Through training, experience, and socialization, the evaluator incorporates precedents into his judgments. The law is the most obvious example of a set of cases that guide judgment.

The subjectivists are less interested in arriving at a proposition that is "true" (in the generalizable sense) than in relating the evaluation to the particular experience of the audience. They attempt to obtain valid insights within the frame of reference of the group for whom they are working. It is assumed that there is a gap between language and experience. Tacit rather than explicit knowledge is what the evaluator seeks. The evaluation is intentionally context-bound, and findings are interpreted in context. Since the audience may well have a firmer grasp of the context, based on greater experience, the audience's interpretation of an event may be superior to that of the evaluator. Subjectivist evaluators are more concerned in their work with specific causal statements (internal validity) than with general causal statements (external validity) (Ennis, 1973). Generalizations may be left to the audience.

The subjectivist methodology tends to be naturalistic. It aims at naturalistic generalization (based on the experience of the audience), is directed more at nontechnical audiences like teachers or the general public, uses ordinary language and everyday categories of events, and is based more on informal than formal logic. Informal interviews and observations are the favorite data collection devices. These are often written up as case studies.

The evaluator tries to collect multiple perspectives, although the perspectives may not agree with each other. Historical investigation and the following of events over time are also critical. The historical mode of investigation is more appropriate than the natural science mode. Emphasis is on the qualitative rather than the quantitative.

In the subjectivist methodology, utility is in terms of the observer's interests. Theory and practice are blended together. Improving the understanding of particular individuals is the goal. In the objectivist approach, there is a rigid separation of observer and facts—highly abstract theory separated from application. Prediction is the goal.

The technique of the closed case and use of the precedent give stability to the judgments derived from the subjectivist epistemology. In fact, tradition is so strong in these evaluation approaches that this is a criticism of them. This is because the subjectivist approaches rely heavily on practitioner judgment, which is, in turn, based on the experience of the classroom. The subjectivist models treat education and teaching as a craft rather than as a set of explicit, externalized techniques.

The case study approach to evaluation focuses on events occuring in and around the actual program in context. It is based on perception and knowing as a transactional process. In one version of transactional psychology, human perception is dependent on three features (Ittelson and Cantril, 1954). First, the facts of perception are always presented through concrete individuals dealing with concrete situations. Hence, one can study perceptions only by studying particular transactions in which the perceptions can be observed. Neither perceptions nor the object perceived exists independently of a life situation. The situation is a transaction. All parts of the situation enter into the transaction as "active participants." The parts owe their existence to this active participation and do not appear as separate already-existing entities. Hence, active participation is a key idea.

Second, perceiving is always done by a particular person from his own unique position, experiences, and needs. There are as many points of view as there are participants. Even the scientist-observers enter into the situation as participants. They affect the situation and are, in turn, affected by it. Hence, the scientist-observer's viewpoint is only one of many. He is part of the transaction.

Third, each person creates his own psychological environment by attributing aspects of his experience to the environment. He believes the environment exists independently of his experience. In other words, he externalizes his experience. Consequently, the world as it is experienced is the *product* of perception, not the cause of it.

These presuppositions about perception are strikingly different from those of J. S. Mill and Hobbes. In the mechanistic Hobbesian view, the environment acts on the organism to produce perception. In the transactional view, the organism also works on the environment in an active manner so that perception is a product of the two. Categories are not easily discernible from the environment because they are inextricably entwined with one's own perceptions.

In the Hobbesian-Millean point of view, the world is taken as given. The mechanistic uniformity of nature assures that. Perceptions can be isolated and studied. One can communicate statements to another scientist which are reducible to what the other scientist will experience if he does certain things—the operational viewpoint. In the transactional point of view, reliability is not so easily obtained. What one observes is a function of the unique position and experience of each observer and even of the observer's purposes. Perceptions can only be studied in concrete real-life situations.

Not all the proponents of the case study approaches to evaluation would subscribe to all these presuppositions. But this description captures the transactional viewpoint as a dialectical interaction of people and their environment which results in perceptions. Individual perceptions are a focus of study, and active participation is essential to knowing.

Political Assumptions of the
Models—The Utilitarians

Liberalism is not only an ethical and epistemological theory; it is a profoundly political theory too. As indicated earlier, although Rivlin and the modern liberals accept J. S. Mill's utilitarian ethics and extreme empiricism, they differ dramatically with Mill over the role of government in making decisions and taking action. Rivlin's welfare liberalism holds that the government must make the major decisions, whereas Mill was the champion of laissez-faire, of keeping the government as far removed from decisions as possible. In this regard, the intuitionists are closer to classic liberalism than are the utilitarians.

For Mill, enlightenment was necessary for happiness and liberty. Freedom from government interference was necessary for enlightenment. For Rivlin, enlightenment will occur through government-sponsored research, and on the basis of this knowledge, the government will then take steps to alleviate the problems. In both cases knowledge will make men happy.

For Mill, there were two distinct spheres of activities—the internal and the external. The internal included the individual's own mind, body, and private actions. In the internal sphere the government had absolutely no right to interfere no matter what. The individual could amuse or abuse himself as he saw fit in matters that concerned only himself (Wolff, 1968). The scope of government was limited to only that which concerned others, the external sphere.

Even in the external sphere in Mill's framework, societal interference was justified only on the basis of the principle of utility. That is, governmental interference was justified only when it would promote the greatest happiness of the greatest number of people by maximizing satisfaction.

> Actions are right in proportion as they tend to promote happiness; wrong as they tend to produce the reverse of happiness. By happiness is intended pleasure and the absence of pain; by unhappiness, pain and the privation of pleasure [Mill, 1861].

Mill's arguments were strictly utilitarian, i.e., based on an estimate of future consequences of various alternatives. If the empirical estimates of consequences change, so will the conclusions. The modern welfare state liberals have changed the empirical estimates and hence the conclusions. According to the modern liberals, the principle of utility requires that the government take strong action. The calculation of the utility principle leads to welfare state liberalism eventually (Wolff, 1968).

For Mill, every person was the best judge of his own interest. (It should be noted that Mill was writing at a time when the masses had no vote. His theories applied only to the more "enlightened" citizenry.) For modern liberals like Rivlin (1971), this is not the case. The government is often the best judge. In Mill's framework, complete freedom of speech led to a competition of ideas which strengthened truth. In a free market of ideas, the consumers would buy the best without government interference. For the modern liberal, the government must provide indices of effectiveness on which judgments are based and often make the choice in the public interest. The classic and modern liberals agree on liberal political principles but disagree as to whether government interference will help or hurt.

Mill felt that government interference would result in impeding individual development; in centralization and abuse of power; in inefficiency; in government doing indifferently and poorly what interested private parties could do better; and in suppression of individual initiative, which would lay the groundwork for despotism. However, even Mill felt that if the buyer were not the best judge of a commodity, then the competition of the market did not exist. In cultural and educational affairs Mill did not think that the uncultured were the best judges. Therefore, the state might legitimately interfere—a position close to that of modern liberals.

In the private sphere, which consists of liberty of thought, conscience, opinion, feeling, "tastes and pursuits," and association, Mill felt everybody was indubitably the best judge of his own interest because he was the person most concerned about his own well-being. His knowledge of his own feelings and circumstances was far superior to what anyone else know about him. Therefore, the individual was best left to make his own judgments, even when they appeared wrong or injurious to himself.

But, generally, the calculation of the utility principle leads to strong government interference rather than away from it. It is not surprising, then, that all the utilitarian models of evaluation—systems analysis, behavioral objectives, decision-making, and goal-free—are based on strong government action, usually even government mandates. Most of these models also take as their major audiences the managers and administrators of government programs. The one exception is goal-free evaluation, which takes the consumer as the major audience.

Political Assumptions of the
Intuitionists/Pluralists

How is one to conduct an evaluation if there is no single principle like the principle of utility to use as the criterion? There are two types of answers found among the intuitionist/pluralist approaches. One is professional authority, as in the educational critic and professional approaches, and the other is a combination of scientific authority and participation in the evaluation by those involved in the program. The professional approach began as a voluntary association to ward off government interference and is based on the idea of expertise through experience.

The participatory approaches are attempts to establish more direct participation of the people who are most closely involved in the program. The quasi-legal approach does this by involving people in a decision-making operation like a mock trial. The case study approach involves people through negotiation, interviewing, and responding to drafts of the evaluation, although it is still the evaluator who writes the report. If people are to participate as major audiences, the evaluation must be immediate and comprehensible. The participatory school is aimed at establishing a more direct democracy among program participants rather than in relegating decision-making to the government, as in utilitarian evaluation. Pluralistic principles are derived by the participation of diverse individuals and groups.

There are two distinct approaches to political pluralism. One is derived directly from the classic liberal philosophy of J. S. Mill, without his epistemology or utilitarian ethics. Classic liberalism sees society as an association of self-determining individuals who cooperate with others for self-interested ends. Following from Mill, it is essential that they have a direct hand in governing themselves since they know themselves and their interests best. This version of pluralism accepts individual idiosyncracies and interpersonal conflicts as inevitable (Wolff, 1968).

The sanctity of the individual against the intrusion of society is paramount, and the inner sphere of the private man must be held inviolate. There can be no interference with his thoughts and practices. Individuality and diversity are encouraged rather than suppressed.

Society is conceived as a market place in which each individual pursues his own private goals. Each man is free to pursue his own goals compatible with others pursuing theirs. In the public sphere, society has a right to impose some rules of equity. Otherwise the market will automatically work things out.

The ideal society envisioned is that of a large diverse city like London or New York. Classic liberalism sees man as a rational calculator of pain and pleasure. Rationality is calculating prudence. Each individual views others as instruments in the pursuit of his private ends. Others are means to some end, not ends in themselves. This is sometimes called the "instrumental" theory of pluralism (Wolff, 1968).

Justice is the protection of the inner sphere of the person and a more or less equal opportunity for all to pursue their private goals. In more sophisticated versions, the pleasure maximizing is softened somewhat, and the pursuit of higher goals is emphasized. Nonetheless, society is still viewed as a collection of independent "centers of consciousness" each pursuing its own private goals and confronting others as alien objects (Wolff, 1968).

Associated with this version of pluralism is the "referee" theory of government. The government will establish ground rules for individual and group competition but will not interfere in any other way. Action is to be *direct* action by the individuals and groups concerned and not action by the government. Each person must be free to engage directly in the decision processes, and this role cannot be delegated or usurped by government or anyone else. This version of direct democracy grows out of classic liberalism in which *each individual's* choice is maximized.

The evaluation approach which most closely corresponds to this version of liberal pluralism is MacDonald's (1974) democratic evaluation. MacDonald sees the evaluator as "broker in exchanges of information between groups," representing a range of interests, presenting information accessible to nonspecialists, giving informants confidentiality and control over the data, having no concept of information misuse, negotiating with sponsors and participants, and not making recommendations. The evaluator feeds information to audiences and lets the market work things out. Each person makes use of the information as he sees fit with the evaluator removed from interpretation. The evaluator operates on a set of procedural regulations which controls information flow.

MacDonald has also been most adamant about protecting the sanctity of the "inner sphere," giving informants veto power over what goes into the report. This is captured by his phrase, "People own the facts of their lives." Interference by the evaluator in either the private sphere or public sphere is rejected except to facilitate information flow which will increase knowledge and presumably happiness by allowing individuals to pursue their goals better.

A somewhat different version of pluralism prevails in the United States. Based on the idea that every person achieves his identity from primary groups, it does not see man as a totally detached individual as does classic liberalism. Since ethnic, religious, economic, and cultural groups determine what a person is, his interests must be expressed through the larger groups to which he belongs. This version, called "democratic pluralism" or "conservative liberalism" recognizes tolerance for established, diverse groups but not for idiosyncratic individuals. It is considered good for an individual to conform to some groups, but good for the groups to differ.

In this vision of pluralism as the conflict of permanent interest groups, community is a much stronger value than in classical liberalism. Pluralism is based on group rather than individual diversity. The ideal society is more like a small town than a large city. Tolerance and mutual acceptance are exercised among groups.

Associated with this vision of pluralism is the "vector-sum" or "balance-of-power" theory of government. The purpose is to get the government to act in a certain direction. The individual must work through his groups in order to do this since only they have the influence to guide the ship of state. As in classical liberalism, the individual must have immediacy, effectiveness, involvement, and participation in his group. The government (and evaluator) act as a middlemen, absorbing directions and responding to shifts in pressure. In both types of pluralism the capacity to see competing claims as legitimate is essential to make the system work.

Stake's "responsive" evaluation comes closest to the democratic pluralism version. The evaluator must remain responsive to any legitimate interests and pressures around the program. But he is not obliged to represent any point of view, nor is he obliged to represent points of view in the evaluation unless there is an interest group involved in the program which is actively promoting that point of view. Active involvement is a criterion for representing a group's viewpoint in the evaluation.

Issues are defined by legitimate groups, and only a few issues are to be explored. Methods of investigation are to be chosen to fit the issues.

Problems are best solved directly by local people close at hand (Stake, 1975). This is in contrast to utilitarian evaluation in which the government evaluates, defines the problem, and takes action. The pluralistic evaluations tend to maximize local and individual choice rather than social utility. Both forms of pluralism tend to be identified with the free play of opposing individuals and groups, as the working out of a free market requires.

Although all these evaluation approaches differ in the ways suggested, what they share are some of the basic tenets of the liberal ideology. This includes the principle of freedom of choice. Although who shall make the choice is at issue, choice is maximized. They are based on a strongly individualist psychology, and their intellectual constructions reflect that. They are also thoroughly empiricist in orientation.

All the evaluation approaches also presume a free market of ideas in which, ideally, consumers will select the best. Through a competition of ideas, truth will be strengthened and the social services improved. Finally, the approaches all assume that increased knowledge will make people happy or better or satisfied in some way, an interesting assumption reaching back to the Enlightenment.

STANDARDS FOR EVALUATION—TRUTH, BEAUTY, AND JUSTICE

When it comes to the matter of prudential behavior in life, it is well for us to keep in mind that human events are dominated by Chance and Choice, which are extremely subject to change. . . . As a consequence, those whose only concern is abstract truth experience great difficulty in achieving their means, and greater difficulty in attaining their ends. . . . Since, then, the course of action in life must consider the importance of the single events and their circumstances, it may happen that many of these circumstances are extraneous and trivial, some of them bad, some even contrary to one's goal. It is therefore impossible to assess human affairs by the inflexible standard of abstract right; we must rather gauge them by the pliant . . . rules, which does not conform bodies to itself, but adjusts itself to their contours.

Giambattista Vico, *On the Study Methods of Our Time*, 1709, p. 34

4

THE LOGIC OF EVALUATIVE ARGUMENT

I choose the word "argument" thoughtfully, for scientific demonstrations, even mathematical proofs, are fundamentally acts of persuasion. Scientific statements can never be certain; they can only be more or less credible.

Joseph Weizenbaum, *Computer Power and Human Reason,* 1976

Generalizations decay.
Lee J. Cronbach, *Beyond the Two Disciplines of Scientific Psychology,* 1974

The Coming Great California Earthquake

I sit in Los Angeles but wonder why I stay. A sudden one-foot uplift has appeared along a hundred-mile strip of the San Andreas fault. Based on seismic wave readings, a California scientist has predicted a major earthquake for the Los Angeles area within a year (*Science,* May 1976). Based on different readings, a radio evangelist warns of a major quake. Both scientists and seers agree in their prophecies. Neither provides the kind of information I need.

I talk to the natives about these ominous signs. Their response is shaped by the necessity of living in such circumstances; they shrug their shoulders. The President has been informed, but no one seems to know exactly what to do. Washington officials suggest setting up a new array of scientific instruments along the fault, although what will result from more measurement is not clear.

AUTHOR'S NOTE: This chapter is a shorter version of *The Logic of Evaluative Argument,* Monograph #7, Los Angeles: Center for the Study of Evaluation, UCLA, 1977. I wish to thank Lee Cronbach, Bob Ennis, Gene Glass, and the CSE staff for detailed comments.

Meanwhile the weather is perfect, the setting in the Santa Monica Mountains splendid, the lifestyle sybaritic. Calculations of probabilities of long-term seismic events do me no good; I need to know when the earth will move in relation to myself. The vocabulary of action is complex. Everyone agrees that information somehow informs decisions, but the relationship is not direct, not simple. Often the more important the decision, the more obscure the relationship seems to be. Consider the decision to marry. For most people, it is a long, arduous process, one which takes shape over a period of time. No single piece of information serves as a decision-point. Quite the contrary. The decision proceeds slowly, almost imperceptibly, until it arrives. Reason after reason is advanced and tried out. Finally, a multiplicity of arguments serves as a rationale for the decision, which is often made long before all the arguments are advanced.

The most significant decisions are those that have long-range implications but defy easy extrapolation, that are so entangled with everything else that they resist precise formal analysis. To those we are forced to apply our intuitive logic, our common sense. It is in the nature of these complex problems that knowledge about them is limited, that it is less than determinate. In the face of uncertain knowledge, the task of entangled decision-making becomes less one of absolutely convincing ourselves with proofs than one of persuading ourselves with multiple reasons. The criterion becomes not what is necessary but what is plausible.

Equivocality of Evidence: Certainty vs. Credibility [1]

Why, then, do government officials, the public, and even members of the evaluation community call for definitive proof of the success of educational programs? There is a tradition as old as Descartes which says that the *only* knowledge is that which is certain. Descartes's method of analysis was one of total skepticism: to doubt everything that could be doubted. In his search for certain knowledge, he arrived at the *self-evident* as the ultimate mark of reason. For something to qualify as knowledge it had to start from clear and distinct ideas and be extended by deductive proofs. Propositions so derived were thus necessary and compelling to the intellect; they could not be rationally denied.

This method excluded the merely credible from consideration as knowledge. In the Cartesian ideal, the only true reasoning is analytic. Formal deductive logic, the method of proof used in mathematics, is the method par excellence. Knowledge can be reduced to self-evident propositions. In certain knowledge there can be no disagreement. As Descartes wrote, if there is disagreement over a matter between two men, one of them must surely be wrong. There is a true and a false, and logic works by compelling proofs to determine which is which.

Later, those who pursued this line of reasoning confronted the fact that rational men often seemed to reason differently and arrive at contradictory conclusions. Some of Descartes's own propositions looked suspicious. Pascal introduced the explanation that such disagreement, as well as the reluctance to accept necessary conclusions, was a result of irrationality. Man was seen to possess an irrational side which often led him astray in his search for knowledge. The apparent irrationality of those who do not accept conclusions which others perceive as compelling is a common motiff in contemporary evaluation.

From the Cartesian perspective, certain knowledge can be obtained by deductive processes, and it must lead to absolute conviction. Such reasoning may work in geometry, but it does so by excluding most of the sensate world. As Hume pointed out, our beliefs, even in concepts as basic as causality, are not certain when a thorough skepticism is applied to them. Deductive reasoning succeeds in producing certain knowledge primarily by eliminating most of the every-day world.

The sensate world was epistemologically salvaged for our use by John Stuart Mill. Just as logicians had constructed formal deductive logic by reflecting on the nature of mathematical proofs, Mill reflected on the associationist psychology of his time and formulated an inductive logic that purported to introduce certainty into inductively derived knowledge. To do this Mill made several assumptions that still pervade survey research today. According to Hamilton (1976), the axioms include the following:

- There is a uniformity of nature in time and space. This lends to inductive reasoning the same procedureal certainty as to conclusions drawn from syllogistic logic.

- Concepts can be defined by direct reference to empirical categories and laws of nature can be inductively derived from data because of the above.

- Large samples can suppress idiosyncracies and reveal "general causes."

- The social and natural sciences have the same aim of discovering general laws (which provide a basis for explanation and predictions).

- The social and natural sciences are methodologically identical.

- The social sciences are merely more complex.

Thus, Mill contended that certain knowledge was derivable from inductive reasoning as well as from the deductive. One could define categories and relate them to each other by now familiar techniques. In fact, Mill concluded that the inductive method was the *only* way of discovering new ideas since deductive logic could only reveal what was already there. (Mill was so certain of his method that he contended that ethical principles could also be derived by inductive reasoning and hence had a scientific base.)[2]

Mill's first assumption is the important one. In Mill's own words, "The Universe, so far as known to us, is so constituted, that whatever is true in one case, is true in all cases of a certain description; the only difficulty is, to find what description" (Mill, 1893). How familiar that idea is to anyone who has engaged in survey research, and how fallible the inductive logic on which it is based!

The procedure of reasoning from "some" to "all" is clearly a logical fallacy. Each confirming instance is supposed to make a hypothesis more likely. Yet if the hypothesis is "All men are less than 100 feet tall" and one finds a man 99 feet, this is a confirming instance that weakens the hypothesis considerably rather than strengthens it (Gardner, 1976). Does every day that goes by in Los Angeles without the predicted great quake make it more or less likely? It is also quite possible in statistical studies to confirm a hypothesis by two independent studies and yet disconfirm the hypothesis by using the total results of the two studies taken together (see Simpson's paradox in Martin Gardner, 1976).

Nonetheless, in spite of serious flaws of logic, "science" based on inductive logic seems to work with some degree of success. Certainty of knowing, however, is lacking. Even the best established scientific facts must be held as tentative. As one scientist put it:

> The man in the street surely believes such scientific facts to be as well-established, as well-proven as his own existence. His certitude

is an illusion. Nor is the scientist himself immune to the same illusion. In his praxis, he must, after all, suspend disbelief in order to do or think anything at all. He is rather like a theater-goer, who, in order to participate in and understand what is happening on the stage, must for a time pretend to himself that he is witnessing real events. The scientist must believe his working hypothesis, together with its vast underlying structure of theories and assumptions, even if only for the sake of the argument. Often the "argument" extends over his entire lifetime. Gradually he becomes what he at first merely pretended to be: a true believer. I choose the word "argument" thoughtfully, for scientific demonstrations, even mathematical proofs, are fundamentally acts of persuasion.

Scientific statements can never be certain; they can be only more or less credible. And credibility is a term in individual psychology, i.e., a term that has meaning only with respect to an individual observer. To say that some proposition is credible is, after all, to say that it is believed by an agent who is free not to believe it, that is, by an observer who, after exercising judgment and (possibly) intuition, chooses to accept the proposition as worthy of his believing it [Weizenbaum, 1976].

Evaluation as Persuasion

If demonstrations in the physical sciences are fundamentally acts of persuasion, inquiries in education are more so. Mill's assumption that the social and natural sciences are methodologically identical seems much more dubious today. Cronbach (1974), for one, doubts the advisability of imposing physical science ideals in social science. In the physical science paradigm, events are explained and predicted by "a network of propositions connecting abstract constructs."

After reviewing twenty years of aptitude treatment interaction studies, which were based on such a model, Cronbach concluded that social phenomena are too open to interactions with other variables to support stable generalizations. The positivistic strategy of fixing conditions in which to reach generalizations assumes steady processes that can be separated into independent systems for study, a fragile assumption in social systems.

Cronbach has suggested interpreting data in context rather than trying to arrive at generalizations. An observer in a particular setting can describe and interpret effects within local conditions. Whereas experimental control and systematic correlation ask formal questions in advance, local observation is more open to the unanticipated. Short-term empiricism is sensitive to the context. In being context sensitive, the researcher may give up some predictive power. He gives up constructing generalizations and theory-building and instead develops "concepts that will help people use their heads." So Cronbach contends.

Evaluations themselves, I would contend, can be no more than acts of persuasion. Although sometimes evaluators promise Cartesian proof and use J. S. Mill's methods of induction, evaluations inevitably lack the certainty of proof and conclusiveness that the public expects. The definitive evaluation is rare, if it exists at all. Even a scientific methodologist as sophisticated as James Coleman is faced with continued and trenchant criticism of his work. Subjected to serious scrutiny, evaluations always appear equivocal.

Expecting evaluation to provide compelling and necessary conclusions hopes for more than evaluation can deliver. Especially in a pluralistic society, evaluation cannot produce necessary propositions. But if it cannot produce the necessary, it can provide the credible, the plausible, and the probable. Its results are less than certain but still may be useful.

Proving something implies satisfying beyond doubt the understanding of a universal audience with regard to the truth. To produce proof that a universal audience comprising all rational men would accept requires overcoming local or historical particularities. Certainty requires isolating data from its total context as, for example, in the terms of a syllogism. Logical certainty is achievable only within a closed, totally defined system like a game.

If evaluation is limited to certain knowledge provided by strict deductive and inductive reasoning, it must abandon a great amount of reasoning power that people ordinarily use in the conduct of their lives. Such a limitation results from confusing rationality with logic. They are not identical.

If absolutely convincing all rational men is too heavy a burden for evaluation, persuading particular men is not. In place of the compelling propositions derived from rigorous logic, one may substitute the non-compelling arguments of persuasion. In place of the necessity of self-evidence, one may substitute variable adherence to theses as presented to particular audiences. The thesis may be more or less credible. The audience is free to believe or not believe after inspecting the arguments and exercising its own judgment.

Evaluation aims at persuading a particular audience of the worth of something or that something is the case by an appeal to the audience's reason and understanding.[3] For this purpose, uncertain knowledge is useful although the ideas themselves are always arguable. The appropriate methods are those of argumentation, which is the realm of the "credible, the plausible and the probable" rather than the necessary (Perelman and Olbrechts-Tyteca, 1969).

Argumentation is contrasted to demonstration. Demonstrations rest on formal logic which avoids ambiguity by the internal consistency of its symbol system. In deductive logic the origin of the axioms is extraneous. When one moves from deduction to induction, all manner of issues become arguable, such as the validity of measurement. But the search is still for "certain" knowledge.

In evaluation, the social and psychological contexts become particularly relevant and the knowledge less certain. Under those conditions argumentation aimed at gaining the adherence and at increasing the understanding of particular audiences is more appropriate. Persuasion claims validity only for particular audiences and the intensity with which particular audiences accept the evaluative findings is a measure of this effectiveness. The evaluator does not aim at convincing a universal audience of all rational men with the necessity of his conclusions.

Persuasion is directly related to action. Even though evaluation information is less certain than scientific information addressed to a universal audience, persuasion is effective in promoting action because it focuses on a particular audience and musters information with which this audience is concerned. Personalized knowledge that induces people to stop smoking may be different from scientific generalizations linking smoking to heart disease or cancer. Finding out about the heart attack of a close relative is more likely to induce one to exercise than are charts and tables. Evaluative argument is at once less certain, more particularized, more personalized, and more conducive to action than is research information.

In summary, evaluation persuades rather than convinces, argues rather than demonstrates, is credible rather than certain, is variably accepted rather than compelling. This does not mean that it is mere oratory or entirely arbitrary. The fact that it is not limited to deductive and inductive reasoning does not mean that it is irrational. Rationality is not equivalent to logic. Evaluation employs other modes of reasoning. Once the burden of certainty is lifted, the possibilities for informed action are increased rather than decreased.

The Evaluation Audiences

If persuasion becomes the aim of evaluation, the audiences to whom the evaluation is addressed are important. For years evaluators have been counseled to think of their audiences and the kind of information the audiences will need. What is relevant for one group may not be relevant for another. Argumentation presupposes that a "community of minds" exists, that there is intellectual contact, and that there is agreement on at least a few issues on which deliberation is to begin.

There must be a common language and a desire on the part of the evaluator to persuade the audiences and to take their concerns seriously. Often these conditions are not met. The audiences are misconceived or not taken seriously. It is not uncommon for the evaluator to muster information appropriate to an audience of psychologists but which has little meaning for a teacher or a government official.

The agreement of a universal audience (all men at all times) is likely to be secured by formal logical reasoning based on self-evident concepts. Thus the tighter the experimental design, the more convinced a far-removed universal audience wil be of the cause and effect relationship, regardless of the context. A particular audience closer to the scene may assume cause and effect without such proof. Of course, the universal audience is not "aggregatable" at any given time, but various elite groups in fact serve as a surrogate for it. Perhaps philosophers more than most represent this type of audience. The arguments that move philosophers are not always the same as those that move teachers.

The more an argument is directed toward a universal audience, the less "arguable" it is. There is little to argue about in pure deductive logic. Evaluation techniques are often presented as being nonargumentative, as, for example, being based on valid and reliable instruments, as employing sound statistical procedures, and so on. In fact, all statements made on the basis of an evaluation are subject to challenge and are arguable—if properly challenged. The more technical and quantitative the evaluation, the less a naive audience will be able to challenge it, and the evaluation will appear to be more certain than it is.

In evaluations using statistical metaphors, one can argue that treatment effects differ because there is a probability that two mean test scores belong to different populations and, hence, that the experimental program is better than the control. The extensive use of numbers in the statistical procedures and the test scores gives a semblance of certainty and unequivocality to evidence.

Actually, many assumptions lie concealed behind the numbers (as indeed behind every evaluation). One can almost always challenge the validity of the tests, the appropriateness of the statistical procedures, and the control of the experimental design. The challenge does not invalidate the evaluation. But once the premises are challenged, the nature of the evaluation as argumentation becomes apparent. The evaluator may defend his study either successfully or unsuccessfully. In any case, he must resort to nondeductive and more equivocal reasoning if he is to defend it. Although the evaluation has the appearance of appealing to the definitive rationality of the universal audience, it ends in direct appeals to particular audiences. I believe it is impossible to construct an evaluation otherwise.

Even a broad-based evaluation operation like *Consumers Report,* which uses "objective" procedures and sophisticated experimental designs to evaluate consumer products, is an appeal to particular audiences. Its arguments, directed at the upper-middle class, have little meaning for either the lower classes or the upper classes, and its evaluations are little heeded by them.

Thus the situation the evaluator faces is almost always an appeal to particular audiences which he can define with some precision. If he cannot define his audiences, the evaluation is indeterminate. He must address issues and construct arguments that appeal to particular audiences. Furthermore, the audiences are likely to be a composite of several groups, which complicates his task considerably. Effective appeal to particular audiences changes the limits of applicable rationality. One is not confined to the most restrictive modes of reasoning. If evaluation becomes more equivocal, it also becomes more possible.

One ideal of two-party argumentation is embodied in the Socratic dialogue. The dialogue develops as a rigorous chain of reasoning between a questioner and a responder. The one-person audience is persuaded by getting her to agree on certain principles point by point. The audience's particular concerns are ultimately addressed in the interaction. The Socratic dialogue is also powerful to third parties who might read it.

The actual audience most evaluators face seldom consists of one person, however. It is most often several different groups. Some evaluation theorists have suggested modes of evaluation in which the evaluator engages in frequent exchange with the audience throughout the study. Whatever the mode of evaluation, I would contend that evaluation which succeeds in being persuasive must engage the audience in fundamental discourse, although that discourse may occur in different ways.

Discourse conducted in this fashion is more than a mere debate in which different points of view are presented by partisans. The dialogue must be a discussion in which the parties seriously and honestly search for mutual answers. This restriction severely qualifies the use of adversary methods as persuasive devices since one may adjudicate a conflict without persuading anyone of anything.

Kemmis (1976) has advocated oneself as the audience—"evaluation as self-criticism." He sees the primary audience as being the program staff itself. Believing a dialectic between knowledge and action to be the only way to improve practice, he has suggested that evaluation standards be derived from the program participants themselves and that the data consist of the progress as seen by participants. Evaluation thus becomes therapeutic self-criticism. The ultimate goal is increased understanding and insight of the participants themselves, which can then lead to effective action.

Whoever the audience, in argumentation, the audience must share responsibility. Since the information is not compelling, the audience is free to choose its own degree of commitment. It must actively choose how much it wishes to believe. This requires an active testing of the evaluation by the audience itself rather than a passive acceptance or rejection. The audience must make a personal commitment and share responsibility. This rational decision belongs to the audience, not to the evaluator.

Premises of Agreement

The development of an evaluation argument presupposes agreement on the part of the audiences. The premises of the argument are the beginning of this agreement and the point from which larger agreement is built. Just as common sense admits unquestioned truths that are beyond discussion, some of the major premises of an evaluation are tacit rather than explicit.

According to Perelman and Olbrechts-Tyteca (1969), there are two classes of premises: the "real" and the "preferable." The real includes facts, truths, and presumptions and generally claims validity vis-à-vis the universal audience. On the other hand, the preferable is identified with a particular audience and includes values, composite value hierarchies, and value premises of a very general nature called "loci."

Facts and truths are those data and notions which are seen as agreed upon by the universal audience, i.e., held in common by thinking beings, and hence needing no justification. Whether a datum is a fact depends upon one's conception of the universal audience. If the audience changes, so can facts and truths. However to hold the status of a fact or a truth means that for the purposes of argument the datum is noncontroversial and uncontested. If the datum is questioned, it loses its status as a fact and becomes itself an object of argument rather than an object of agreement.

Where there is agreement on the conditions for verification as in modern science, there can be many facts. Many data are not accorded the status of "facts" by modern science. Polanyi (1958) pointed out how science protects its own system of beliefs from inconsistency by denying that various data which conflict with other beliefs are factual. Thus for many years science did not recognize hypnotic effects as occurring at all. These data were not recognized as factual because they conflicted with the current general scientific belief system. This belief system may change from time to time, but regardless of what it excludes, arguments within the belief system must be based on uncontested facts and truths.

Arguments also proceed from presumptions which do not have the full authority and confidence of a fact or truth. Presumptions cannot be proved but are nonetheless widely accepted as being tentatively true. Many presumptions are connected to the concept of the normal. In evaluations employing statistical models and metaphors, the assumption that attributes within a population are normally distributed is almost universally accepted.

The second class of objects of agreement is that of the preferable. Objects of preference claim the adherence of only particular groups rather than that of the universal audience. Values are the most conspicuous examples. Agreement with regard to a value is an admission that there is a specific influence on action or a disposition toward action that the evaluator can make use of. Although relevant for a particular group, a value is not regarded as binding on everyone.

In science, values enter primarily in the selection of objects of interest for investigation since one cannot investigate the entire world (Polyanyi, 1958) and possibly in the acceptance of scientific conclusions by overall human judgment (Weizenbaum, 1976). But during most of the argument, especially in the exact sciences, values are supposed to be excluded. Ennis's (1973) analysis of cause and effect relationships leads one to question this. In evaluation there is no question that values enter at every stage. Values are used to persuade the audiences and to justify choices to others.

Various combinations of arguments can be compressed into a few general groupings called "loci" (Perelman and Olbrechts-Tyteca, 1969). The most common loci are those of quantity and quality. Arguments grouped around the loci of quantity affirm that one thing is better than another for quantitative reasons—greater number, higher degree, more durability, etc. The effectiveness of means will often be justified by quantitative loci. The idea of the normal and the norm are also based on quantity.

Contrasted with quantity is the idea of quality. Something has high value even though it defies number. Associated with quality is a high rating of the unique. One can be in possession of truth while the multitude is in error. For example, Scriven (1972) contended that the notion of objectivity is not necessarily linked to the number of people holding an idea, nor subjectivity to one person's perception, as is often believed.

Besides general agreements on facts and values, there are special agreements particular to certain special audiences and particular to each evaluation. To the extent that the evaluation is addressed to a technical audience, that audience will share certain agreements and conventions. A group of educational researchers is such a technical audience. Evaluations directed toward a lay audience cannot rely on the same agreements.

Perhaps the most important agreements peculiar to a particular evaluation are those derived from the negotiation that often precedes the evaluation—agreements between sponsors, program personnel, and evaluators. In this exceedingly important negotiation, agreement can be reached on criteria, methods and procedures, access, dissemination of results, and so on. Disagreement on these points can destroy the entire credibility of the evaluation.

In summary, at the beginning of an evaluation, the evaluator must build upon agreements with the audiences. These agreements may be implicit as well as explicit. In fact, it would be impossible to specify all these understandings, although it is dangerous to assume agreement on important points where there is none. The evaluator must start from where his audiences are, even though the beginning premises may not be acceptable to other parties nor to the evaluator himself. Otherwise the evaluation will not be credible and persuasive. There must be at least some common understanding. If the basic values are too discrepant, the evaluator has the option of not doing the study. Of course, those basic understandings are subject to prevailing conceptions of decency and justice in the society as a whole, and the evaluator has the option of drawing upon these larger social understandings.

That is not to say that the evaluator should be in total agreement with his audiences. Presumably, there are areas of disagreement or there would be no need for argument. Presumably, the audiences wish to learn something new or there would be no need for evaluation. But the evaluation proceeds from areas of agreement to those areas where agreement is problematic.

Quantitative Argument

The most popular approach to evaluation is the quantitative. Some see it as the very essence of rationality and scientific method. Many good evaluation studies have resulted from it—and many bad ones. Since this approach is taught in the graduate schools and promoted in the literature, there is little need to further extoll its virtues—they are many. In this section I would like to show that even quantitative methodology is essentially argumentation and is subject to similar considerations. Properly used, it can be a valuable tool of analysis; improperly used, it is dangerous.

Quantitative methodology is a body of mathematical methods and measurement techniques available to the evaluator. The utility of the methodology depends on similarities between the theoretical problems dealt with by the methodology and the substantive problems dealt with by the evaluator in the local setting. For his part, Cronbach (1974) has already determined that the fit on the theoretical and substantive problems is not a good one. The educational context is too complex.

A Rand Corporation mathematician (Strauch, 1976) examined the difficulties of quantitative methodology as it applies to policy studies, i.e., questions arising from the government decision-making process. According to Strauch, insofar as the methodology is mathematical, it is a self-contained system the structure of which is determined by the premises defining the system. Mathematical analysis is the exploration of that structure as it follows logically from the premises. The results are connected to the premises by logical inference. In the sense that their validity can be determined on the basis of that chain of reasoning, the results are "objective"—there is no need to appeal to the competence or judgment of the person who produced them nor to the audience to whom they are directed. The results are necessarily logical. In argumentation, by contrast, the results cannot be totally separated from the person who arrives at them.

The application of quantitative methodology to a substantive problem uses a mathematics model as a simplified representation of the problem. The results depend in part on the mathematical analysis—but equally on the fit between the model and the substantive problem. In the simplest applications, such as in physical science, the substantive problems are rigorously quantifiable. Experimental control enhances the ability of the evaluator to make the substantive problem conform to the mathematical model, i.e., randomness in statistical models. In such cases, the conclusions are "objective" in the sense that they are subject to independent verification on the basis of the logic and fit, without reference to the judgment of the person who produced them. However, the more behavioral or political the substantive problem the more difficult it is to define it unambiguously in mathematical terms. The links between the substance and the model become tenuous.

Strauch identifies the following components of such a quantitative study: *Formulation* involves defining the formal problem from the substantive problem, then finding a mathematical model for the formal problem. This is a process of reduction. *Analysis* involves computation within the mathematical context defined by the model. It results in mathematical statements. *Interpretation* means converting the statements back into the formal problem and finally interpreting these conclusions depends on *both* the logical validity of the analysis and the validity of the linkages. While the logical validity can be determined without reference to the subjective judgment of the analyst, the linkages cannot. They are founded upon the subjective judgments of the analyst. Both formulation and interpretation are subjective processes. Formulation requires reducing the substantive problem to something smaller that can be handled by the analysis and possibly adding some assumptions which make the analysis easier but may be questionable on substantive grounds, e.g., the independence of events.

Interpretation involves restoring the contextual considerations that have been eliminated and possibly adjusting for the simplifying assumptions. Both formulation and interpretation require considerable doses of intuitive judgment. Hence the conclusions are not really "objective" as claimed. (See the discussion of objectivity in a later section.)

The usual way of dealing with the subjective part of the methodology is to ignore it. For one thing it is not such a great problem in the natural sciences where quantitative methods have been so successful. Evidence of "objectivity" there is taken as proof of objectivity in other areas. When these links are challenged, it becomes clear enough that quite arguable premises underlie them.

Good insights are often derived from quantitative studies, but they usually result from the analyst making the right intuitive judgments rather than the right calculations. Those successes are often attributed to the quantitative methodology itself rather than to judgment. Critiques usually focus on the technical quality of the mathematical analysis rather than on the quality of judgments associated with formulation and interpretation. When quality of judgment is challenged, justification must rely on the kind of reasoning common to all argumentation.

One result of underplaying the role of judgment is what might be called "method-oriented analysis," according to Strauch. The analyst ignores the complexities of the context and plunges ahead with his favorite method. With superficial thought the methodology is applied in a straightforward manner as if there were no problems of fit. A few caveats are thrown in at the end suggesting that it is the readers' problem to decide whether the fit is a good one.

In its extreme form there is a school of thought which Strauch calls "quantificationism" which holds that quantification is a positive value in itself. A quantitative answer is always better than a qualitative one. Any problem can be reduced to a quantitative solution, and no problem can be properly understood until it is. Therefore quantitative methods should be applied to all problems. This position may be a straw man in that few people would really subscribe to it.

Such an attitude, which favors "scientific" methodology, is based on a reductionism that treats a phenomenon as an isolated system, develops a quantitative model for that system, and uses that model as a surrogate for the phenomenon. As suggested previously, reductionism may be one element of physical science not transferable to social phenomena.

The image the quantificationist projects is of a purveyor of objective "fact" based on hard data. He takes no personal responsibility for conclusions reached by his methodology since they are not of his making. He has simply uncovered them. He is merely reporting the results of his objective methods. He disdains qualitative data as subjective.

This attitude is close to what Polanyi (1958) described as "objectivism" in science. This is an attempt to define an objective method such that it relieves the observer of any responsibility for his findings. Polanyi contended, on the contrary, that the holding of a belief requires personal commitment and responsibility even in science. Objectivism has sought to represent scientific knowledge as totally impersonal.

Often quantificationism and objectivism also suit the decision-maker in that he may justify his decision by reference to a "scientific" finding. It may help him avoid personal responsibility. Attempts to quantify problems that are not quantifiable and to ignore the judgmental factors eventually distort decision-making.

Strauch suggests that one way to eliminate such distortion is to use quantitative methods as a *perspective* rather than a *surrogate* for the substantive problem. Accepting the mathematical model as a valid representation of the substantive problem means using it as a surrogate. Using the model by incorporating findings into *knowledge one already has* means using it as a perspective.

For most substantive problems, the audiences of the evaluation already have well-developed images of their own. The quantitative analysis may give the audiences an additional but not necessarily better or more valid insight into the problem. The interaction between one's own images and additional insights must take place in the heads of the audiences, the decision-makers or whoever. Using quantitative methodology as only one perspective reduces the problem of the fit between the model and the problem.

On the other hand, both the evaluator and the audiences must take more personal responsibility for the findings since they do not necessarily follow from the analysis. The conclusions cannot be justified entirely on the basis that they follow logically from the assumptions. Evaluation of individual assumptions must be supplemented by holistic evaluation of the total.

Quantitative argument, then, should always be used in conjunction with human judgment, and human judgment should be given the superior position. The implications for quantitative argument in evaluation are strong. Quantitative methodology should be seen to be based on human judgments and on intuitive reasoning and should be justified accordingly.

Qualitative Argument

In his paper on qualitative knowing, Campbell (1974) indicated that scientific knowing is dependent on common sense and that particular facts from either science or common sense are known only within the body of a great many other facts. "The ratio of the doubted to the trusted is always a very small fraction." Indeed, the knowledge of any detail is context-dependent, and, according to Campbell, qualitative knowing of "wholes and patterns" provides the context necessary for interpreting quantitative data. For example, generating alternative hypotheses requires familiarity with the local setting, a qualitative act.

Campbell believes that qualitative knowing has been neglected in favor of quantitative methods. At the same time he would prefer to see qualitative and quantitative methods used together to cross-validate one another. Quantitative methods, he believes, can provide insights that the qualitative do not, in spite of the prior grounding of the latter. Also, since all knowing is essentially comparative, he thinks qualitative techniques like case studies could be improved by experimental design considerations, which he would not see as being a part of quantitative methodology.

In rethinking the necessity and even the priority of qualitative knowing, Campbell (1975) has reconsidered the "anecdotal, single-case, naturalistic observation." Quantitative generalization will contradict such knowledge at some points but only by trusting a much larger body of such observations. In the classic paper on experimental design, Campbell and Stanley (1966), the case study was described as having no basis of comparison and hence providing no justification for drawing causal inferences.

Now Campbell has modified his position considerably, coming to believe that the case worker makes many predictions on the basis of his theory which he can disconfirm. The process is one of "pattern-matching" in which aspects of the pattern are matched against observations of the local setting. Campbell sees the single-shot case study as being a more secure basis of knowledge than he did in the past.

How is it in Campbell's view that we can know anything? He traces the current epistemological difficulties back to a quest for certainty in knowing. The effort to "remove equivocality by founding knowledge on particulate sense data and the spirit of logical atomism point to the same search for certainty in particulars" (Campbell, 1966). Certainty was to be established by defining "incorrigible particulars." This would result in unequivocally specifiable terms and in a "certainty of communication."

Campbell now sees this brand of positivism as not being tenable in either philosophy or psychology. Things out of context are not interpretable. But how can one still "know" something from a group of events which are each in themselves indeterminate? Campbell's answer is that this is achieved through "pattern-matching."

In events of cognition like binocular vision, the eyes recognize common objects by a process of triangulation. The more elaborate the pattern the more statistically unlikely a mistaken recognition becomes. Through memory various patterns can be compared. Pattern-matching itself Campbell sees as a trial and error process. This is essentially analogical thinking and Campbell sees it as being ubiquitous in the knowing process.

In fact, scientific theory is the most distal form of knowing, and the relationship between formal theory and data is one of pattern-matching with the error ascribed to the measurement of the data ("true" scores and "estimated" scores) except when it is agreed that the theory is in need of overhaul. There are two patterns to be matched, that of the theory, and that of the data. Acceptance or rejection of the theory is subject to some criterion of fit between the two. Actually, a theory is never rejected on the basis of its inadequacy of fit except when there is an alternative theory to replace it. It is the absence of plausible rival hypotheses that makes a theory "correct."

Campbell sees these considerations as directly relevant to program evaluation issues. "I believe that the problems of equivocality of evidence for program effectiveness are so akin to the general problems of scientific inference that our extrapolations into recommendations about program evaluation procedures can be, with proper mutual criticism, well-grounded."

If I understand his position correctly, Campbell is arguing that evaluation is a part of scientific inquiry and subject to similar epistemological concerns. However that may be, in this chapter at least, I have reversed the ground-figure relationship somewhat by treating science as an argument aimed at a universal audience and hence concerned with establishing long-term generalizations, and evaluation as an argument aimed at particular audiences dealing with context-bound issues.

In evaluation one may think of pattern-matching occurring not only in the evaluator's mind as he constructs his study and inspects the fit between his description of the program and the actual program itself, but also in the minds of the audiences as they compare the evaluation study to their own experience. The audiences themselves have images, memories, and theories of the program under evaluation. In using the evaluation as a perspective (in this case a verbal model), the audience matches its conception of the program to the evaluation. Where it attributes the error depends on the persuasiveness of the evaluation. The audiences thus serve as independent points of validation for the evaluation and must assume an active role in interpreting the evaluation and personal responsibility for the interpretation.

In Campbell's terms the basic pattern-matching process is analogical rather than logical (although the process must surely involve many forms of reasoning). In fact, one can go further than this. In an epistemology based on removing equivocality and establishing certainty of knowledge by defining "incorrigible particulars," deductive and inductive reasoning are the proper way of relating these particulars. Formal logic depends on unambiguous terms operating in a closed system.

To the extent that the terms are ambiguous and the system open (or not reducible to isolated subsystems), formal logic can be applied only argumentatively. The reasoning must include other varieties of thought or one must accept the fact that one cannot do rational analysis. Rational analysis is possible in evaluation but only rarely will it assume syllogistic form.[4]

Objectivity, Validity, and
Impartiality Reconsidered

What does it mean to say that an evaluation study is "objective" or "valid?" Few concepts have been so confused and have caused so much mischief. Many people are reluctant to accept or believe qualitative evaluations simply because they are based on only one person's observations. Observations by one person are considered in and of themselves to be subjective and hence illegitimate for public purposes.

The crux of the confusion lies in misconceiving "objectivity." Scriven (1972) has written brilliantly about this confusion, tracing the unfortunate history of how objectivity has been defined. The theme of most definitions of objectivity is that there is something outside the mind that is verifiable through public or intersubjective agreement and that one can express or prove such things without influence from personal feelings. An evaluation which can do so is objective. But can one person's view ever be "objective"? The difficulty lies in confusing objectivity with procedures for determining intersubjectivity.

Scriven (1972) contended that there are two different senses in which objectivity is used—the quantitative and the qualitative. In the quantitative sense of the term, one person's opinion about something is regarded as being subjective—the disposition of one individual. Objectivity is achieved through the experiences of a number of subjects or observers. The common experiencing makes the observation public through intersubjective agreement. More formally, one might say that with a number of individuals one is more certain that one has properly represented the population—a sampling problem.

The qualitative sense of objectivity is quite different. It refers to the quality of the observation regardless of the number of people making it. Being objective means that the observation is factual, while being subjective means that the observation is biased in some way. Is it possible for one person's observations to be factual while a number of people's observations are not? Indeed it is. So an observation can be quantitatively subjective (one man's opinion) and also qualitatively objective (actually unbiased and true).

In fact, one might contend that the types of biases that affect the opinion of one person are somewhat different from those biases that plague group opinions. For example, an individual may succumb more easily to idiosyncratic viewpoints since he can hold only one perspective. On the other hand, there are social and cultural biases to which a group is more susceptible than is a particular person, e.g., jingoism. The individual's qualitative objectivity can be assessed by his previous track record on such matters and by his current self-interests. In any case, one who subscribes entirely to the quantitative notion of objectivity is not going to be satisfied with approaches like case studies.

How did the quantitative notion equating the number of people making an observation with its truth gain such ascendancy, even to the point of excluding qualitative objectivity? Scriven traces this distortion to psychology's attempt to root out introspectionism and philosophy's attempt to purge obscure metaphysics. Both tried to do so through the verification principle. Intersubjectivity became operationalized as *the* criterion for objectivity. In its extreme form the equating of objectivity with the quantitative notion of intersubjectivity was manifested in methodological behaviorism and in operationalism. But the fallacy of intersubjectivism pervades all fields.

Scriven cites the example of an evaluation of a television antenna in an electronics magazine in which the evaluator can see and report a better picture resulting from one of the tested antennas. Yet the evaluator apologizes for being "subjective" in his approach *since he did not use an instrument to measure decibel gain.* In fact, as Scriven notes, it is possible to get intersubjective agreement without instruments on the performance of electronic equipment, and it is the case that these pooled judgments of quality do not correlate highly with any instrument readings. Why then is an instrument reading objective while one person's judgment is subjective in the perception of this confused evaluator?

The reason is that the evaluator is only one person making the observation; and even though he knows he could have his observation confirmed by calling in his colleagues, he believes an instrument would be better because he can get even higher agreement among observers on the meter reading itself—even though the meter reading is not highly indicative of quality. In this case the quantitative notion of intersubjectivity has supplanted the quality of the perception.

In operational terms "measuring on a quantitative scale by mechanical means" becomes the indicator of truth because the interjudge reliability is higher, according to Scriven. Simultaneously, one has actually sacrificed validity for reliability because the meter reading, while reliable, is not a good indicator of picture quality. This is one of the common errors of evaluation—the substitution of instruments for direct observation of quality, the substitution of reliability for validity. And it is an error of the first magnitude.

From this idea—that what cannot be directly experienced by others cannot be taken seriously as science (intersubjectivism)—has developed the concept of objectivity as the externalization of all references so that multiple witnessing can be achieved, a gross oversimplification according to Scriven. In educational inquiry this has been manifested in equating objectivity with the ability to specify and explicate most completely all data collection procedures. Complete externalization and objectification permit replication, the hallmark of reliability. In education being objective has come to mean having a "valid" instrument—just as with the electronics evaluator.

What exists, in fact, are highly reliable instruments the validity of which is questionable. They do not always correlate highly with judgments of quality. The distortion of the intersubjectivist verification principle has resulted in equating objectivity with externalized, replicable procedures—even though these procedures may be infected by biases and hence be qualitavely subjective.

The identification of objectivity with a completely specifiable external procedure has another important effect. It relieves the evaluator of responsibility for the results and consequences of the evaluation. After all, if these "objective" instruments and procedures give these results, how can the evaluator be held liable? Science is to blame. Polanyi (1958) calls this position "objectivism." Objectivity in this sense comes to mean that observations are subject to independent verification without reference to the person who produced them.

Now it is not possible to specify all knowledge explicitly nor to verify it completely by independent-external procedures. Scriven contends that even in mathematical proofs in which the steps of the proof are reduced to the self-evident, intuition plays an inevitable and important role. Not only is intersubjective verification not a guarantee of truth, it is not necessary. Truth is an ideal which can only be *approximated* through an interplay of introspection and public verification.

Because of their complexity, many intuitive judgments can never be fully explicated. Yet conclusions may be no less true because of one's inability to explicate them. Agreement among many may be necessary for explaining the truth to someone else but it is not necessary for the truth itself.

How is it possible to establish the validity of a claim if one cannot separate it entirely from the person making the claim? One way is to check the reliability of the observer in previous instances and to check the observer's freedom from bias. These are not guaranteed to produce truth, but there are no guarantees. There are knowledge claims that are hybrids of the internal/external split, e.g., tendency statements, analogies, approximations, that are true yet are not the types of claims one usually associates with scientific statements, according to Scriven. He calls them "weak knowledge" claims and suggests they represent the type of knowledge available in the social sciences.

Such knowledge claims are manifested more as explanations than as predictions. Explanation and understanding are functions of the way information is coded in the mind. Explanation implies a person who is understanding the explanation. It does not exist by itself. The understanding is ultimately reducible to something familiar in the mind of the audience doing the understanding—or else it is not an explanation.

Similarly, unless an evaluation provides an explanation for a particular audience, and enhances the understanding of that audience by the content and form of the arguments it presents, it is not an adequate evaluation for that audience, even though the facts on which it is based are verifiable by other procedures. One indicator of explanatory power is the degree to which the audience is persuaded. Hence an evaluation may be "true" in the conventional sense but not persuasive to a particular audience for whom it does not serve as an explanation. In the fullest sense, then, an evaluation is dependent both on the person who makes the evaluative statement and on the person who receives it.

Prediction is not necessary to demonstrate understanding. Inferring an event from a correlation coefficient plus a few antecedent conditions is not necessary as a test of validity or objectivity. Rather, the basic reasoning pattern is closer to one of pattern-matching, of finding reasonable interpretations and explanations and understandings *within a given context.* The test of an explanation is not accuracy in predicting an event but whether the audience can see new relations and answer "new but relevant" questions.

Finally, about the question of objectivity one must conclude one of two things: either objectivity cannot be exclusively identified with an externalized procedure totally separated from the minds that produced the observations and comprehended them; or else a great deal of truth is subjective in character. In the first case, objectivity means something more than it is commonly taken to mean; in the second case, it means something less.

What about validity? One definition of validity is that it is based on objective procedures. Validity carries with it notions of being properly related to intent, of being correctly derived, and of being sanctioned by authority. In the narrow sense of quantitative objectivity, validity is equated with prediction—with checking the data against a criterion. But that assumes a single intent and assumes intersubjectivism as the verification principle. This is too narrow a procedure. Ultimately, says Cronbach (1971), validity is dependent on how the data are to be used and "utility depends upon values, not upon the statistical connections of scores."

If one cannot arrive at a single score presumably indicating validity, how is validity determined? Perhaps the best answer to the question is to examine the sources of invalidity. An evaluation may be invalid in a number of ways. One way is for the "facts and truths" upon which the evaluation is based to be wrong. Facts and truths are accepted without question by everyone. Other data must be determined by recognized data collection procedures, which are, in turn, sanctioned by a particular discipline and subject to public scrutiny. Often validity refers to using the accepted data collection procedures themselves, as Cronbach's article on test validation suggests.

Another way in which validity is at issue is in relating conclusions and interpretations to the data. As Cronbach asserts, it is not the test or the data collection procedures themselves so much as the interpretations that are valid or invalid. This is the validity of an inference. Is the inference correctly derived from the data and premises?

There is also the question of whether the interpretation can be properly applied to situations other than the one from which it was derived, since all generalizations are context-dependent. These concerns have been dealt with in experimental design somewhat systematically as threats to internal and external validity.

In qualitative studies it is more difficult to provide evidence of validity—which is not a sign that it does not exist. Demonstrating validity in naturalistic studies usually consists of confirming one kind of data with another kind. In proposing case studies of science education, Stake and Easley (1978) saw personal biases and past experience as the main threat to the credibility of the case studies. They proposed extensive tape recording of interviews, extensive use of direct quotations where possible, and reporting disagreements among respondents where they existed. People familiar with the local situation could read the written case to judge the accuracy of portrayal. Field workers would be keyed to "hints of inconsistency" for fruther pursuit. Contexts for observations would be documented and elucidated. Securing the observations of several participants about a particular issue or event was a way of "triangulating" what actually happened.

Most of these threats to validity are seen from the perspective of a universal audience. But there is another way of looking at validity in evaluation—whether the evaluation is valid for particular audiences. After all, validity is always concerned with purpose and utility for someone. If the evaluation is not based on values to which the major audiences subscribe, these audiences may not see it as being "valid," i.e., relevant to them in the sense of being well-grounded, justifiable, or applicable. The evaluation may simply miss the main issues as far as particular audiences are concerned. At the same time the evaluation may be valid in the sense that the facts are correct and the inferences from the data correctly derived. From a particular audience's perspective, the premises may be the wrong ones.

An evaluation can also be invalid in this secondary sense if the argument forms employed are wrong. For example, in this society "means-ends" arguments, particularly cost-effectiveness arguments, are particularly potent. If one were to employ an argument based on maximizing excellence instead of choosing the best available alternative, it might carry little weight although being equally true and valid from the perspective of the universal audience. So validity can apply to evaluation in rather different ways. (The debate between Glass and Scriven in Appendix A is over the form of the argument as much as anything.)

It is also the case that the more "naturalistic" the evaluation, the more it relies upon its audiences to draw its own generalizations (external validity). For example, a case study may be interpreted in different ways by each reader, since each reader has her own universe of cases in her mind for comparison. The reader can see similarities and differences based on her own experience and can draw her own interpretations.

Conceiving the process of generalization in this way alters even the first sense in which validity is used. The evaluator is still responsible for ascertaining and reporting "true" facts and statements, but part of the interpretation is beyond him. Since, as Cronbach says, the ultimate issue is the validity of the interpretation, which only the reader knows for sure, the audiences must assume considerable responsibility for the validity of their own interpretations. The evaluator must ultimately assume rational processes in the thinking of the audiences.

As Ennis (1973) noted, internal validity and external validity refer to rather different phenomena. External validity is concerned with the generalizability of general causal statements. Internal validity bears on specific causal statements that do not entail generalizing to new cases. Generalizing always assumes that one knows the relevant laws involved in extrapolating into new realms. An internally validity study, by contrast, only claims causality in the past within the specific circumstances. It claims no extrapolation and is hence less dependent on outside assumptions.

However, neither specific causal statements nor general causal statements follow perfectly logically from observations, even in the best experimental designs. Some empirical assumptions are needed even in the tightest design. In addition, identifying a particular event as a cause inescapably involves a judgment of responsibility that a particular event is responsible for the effect, according to Ennis. This ascription of responsibility requires much background knowledge and a value judgment. It involves a probable assignment of praise or blame and suggests a place for intervention.

Most evaluators would assume responsibility for specific causal statements that "x caused y" in this study (internal validity), although this in itself necessarily involves a set of assumptions. But some would refer the generalizability of the findings to the audiences' judgments, since generalizability is based on outside information which the audiences but not the evaluator may have. The audiences might make some of the responsibility ascriptions based on their own background knowledge and values. Some evaluators, particularly naturalistic ones, might argue that this would ultimately result in superior generalizations.

There is yet a further related problem with objectivity. Is it really sufficient to say that an evaluator is objective? If objectivity is taken in the commonly used sense of employing an externalized, specifiable procedure which produces replicable results, then it is certainly an insufficient criterion for an evaluation. The administration of standardized achievement tests is a totally externalized, specifiable procedure which produces replicable results. At the same time such tests are thought to be highly biased in many ways, particularly toward minority groups. In this sense, one has an objective but biased instrument. In fact, one can produce an instrument in which the bias is in the other direction. (To further confound matters, if racial discrimination is the intent of such an instrument, one could have an objective, valid instrument for that purpose.)

An evaluation must be free from distortion and bias (qualitatively objective), and being externalized, specifiable, and replicable does not sufficiently address possible biases. Even qualitative objectivity is insufficient for evaluation, for it carries the aura of neutrality. People being evaluated do not want a neutral evaluator, one who is unconcerned about the issues. A person on trial would not choose a judge totally removed from his own social system.

Being disinterested does not give one the right to participate in a decision that determines someone's fate to a considerable degree.

Knowledge of techniques for arriving at objective findings is inadequate. Rather, the evaluator must be seen as a member of or bound to the group being judged, just as a defendent is judged by his peers. The evaluator must be seen as caring, as interested, as responsive to the relevant arguments. He must be impartial rather than simply objective.

The impartiality of the evaluator must be seen as that of an actor in events, one who is responsive to the appropriate arguments but whom the contending forces are balanced rather than nonexistent. The evaluator must be seen as not having previously decided in favor of one position or the other.

The evaluator may resport to objective criteria to resolve the issues; but when his own impartiality is at stake, it is not enough that he give evidence of objectivity. He must give evidence of his impartiality by showing how he has acted contrary to his own interests in the past.

Evaluative Discourse: The Good Life
(Along the San Andreas Fault)

It has been several weeks since I began this chapter. The great Los Angeles earthquake has not yet come. Beautiful day succeeds beautiful day, each one much like the last; so it seems tomorrow must be like today, a pleasant dream extending indefinitely.

Each day that passes makes the quake seem less likely than before. Yet if it is to occur this year, it should become *more* likely. I reason that the time I have remaining here is only a small fraction of the coming year, so the chances of the quake coming now are less than for the entire year of the prediction. I reason that even if the quake should come, the effects will not be disastrous. In addition, the Midwest is racked by tornadoes. Besides, would many of the smartest men in the country, including the seismologists, live here if the danger were so great? I feel reassured. My anxiety lessens.

Meanwhile within the last few days, the *New York Times Magazine* heightens the drama in its Bicentennial edition (July 4, 1976). As symbolic of "America at 200," it features a report on "The Good Life (along the San Andreas Fault)." On the cover is a painting of a fragment of a freeway jutting out into the empty ocean, the remains of Los Angeles after the next earthquake. The article begins with a six-paragraph scenario of the effects of the anticipated quake.

Those who live on top of the nine-mile deep fault have their own reasons for living there. As his backyard crumbles away daily, a postal worker, who has three cars, would like to move but cannot sell his house. A ranch manager, who finds life better in California than anyplace he has ever lived, explains, "I'm not leaving. Is there any place that doesn't have some catastrophe?" For some, precariousness itself makes being here all the more precious. A dropped-out investment counselor living on the fault says, "You're living on a crisis point. Everything you have can be taken away from you at any time."

These are not the reasons I would give but they may be right. Each person is free to weigh his own reasons. Each is free to make his own choices. So it must be when faced with such uncertainty of knowing. Judgments cannot be based on an irrefutable reality. Even when earthquakes are much more predictable, there will remain room for choice in how to respond. In social decision-making certainty seems remote if not impossible.

Faced with such difficulty in arriving at an irrefutable reality, there are those who try to force simplicity atop the complexities of life. They insist on pretending there is agreement where there is none, whether of facts or of values. Often in positions of power, they impose simplified definitions of reality for the sake of action. Yet, no matter how widely accepted the simplification, reality is still there. Whatever twenty-one million Californians believe, the great earthquake will come eventually.

The alternative is not necessarily a descent into irrationality. If opinions cannot be indisputably based, neither must they be regarded as entirely arbitrary, as being merely "value judgments." Such a classification limits knowledge to that which is clear, distinct, and unambiguous. This distinction establishes a schism between objectively true theoretical knowledge on the one hand and action based on irrational motives on the other. It culminates in designating as irrational those who do not agree with one's perspective. Classifying people as irrational justifies ignoring their opinions and perhaps their dignity and interests. It even legitimates using suggestion and force on them.

The alternative is to treat all men as rational. Between the conservative authoritarianism of tradition and the liberal authoritarianism of scientism, between the certainty of fanaticism and the evasion of responsibility of skepticism lies rational deliberation. One must take seriously the opinions of other people and engage them in serious discourse. This is the realm of argumentation and the proper sphere of evaluation.

The starting point is that groups of people adhere to opinions with variable intensity, and that these opinions can be put to the test of serious discourse. Even facts and values may be so considered. Rational discourse consists of giving reasons, although not compelling reasons. In the realm of action, where few things are clear and distinct, motivation can be rational. Practice can be reasonable.

The evaluator must engage his audiences in a dialogue in which they are free to employ their reasoning. This means that the audiences must assume personal responsibility for their interpretation of the evaluation since the reasoning presented to them is neither completely convincing nor entirely arbitrary. This means that the evaluator must also assume personal responsibility for his judgments since he cannot hide behind blind method. Both must exercise their natural reason.

NOTES

1. For this distinction and many other ideas in this paper, I am indebted to Perelman and Olbrechts-Tyteca's excellent modern work on argumentation *The New Rhetoric: A Treatise on Argument*, Scranton, PA: Univ. of Notre Dame Press, 1969.

2. At the end of his masterpiece on inductive logic, Mill considers the logic of a "practice" or "art." "There must be some standard by which to determine the goodness or badness, absolute and comparative, of ends, or objects of desire. And whatever that standard is, there can be but one; for if there were several ultimate principles of conduct, the same conduct might be approved by one of those principles and condemned by another; and there would be needed some general principle, as umpire between them" (John Stuart Mill, *A System of Logic*, New York: Harper, 1893 [8th Edition]).

This leads Mill to impose a single universal standard by which to judge practical affairs, for the only alternative is by "supposing a moral sense or instinct" or "intuitive moral principles." General ethical principles can be known only by induction. Since inductive certainty presupposes a uniformity of nature, the resultant psychology is deterministic. Morality is natural since only a naturalistic assessment will allow scientific methods of proof. Hedonistic utilitarianism is the basis.

In a sense, Mill was preventing disagreement over moral issues since it is always possible to reach opposite conclusions when there is no previous agreement on a criterion. The result of this reasoning is utilitarian calculation which conflates all human desires into a single configuration and satisfies them by the criterion of maximum total satisfactions derived. The judging is done by an "impartial spectator," who in modern times demonstrates his impartiality by employing "objective" techniques of analysis.

3. Kelly (1980) has pointed out the hidden premises in my own arguments here. It is impled that the evaluator acts to persuade the audience of a point of

view because it is "true," and he has some way of establishing this. Truth can be held with varying intensity, however. Kelly also claims, correctly I think, that I am making the Aristotelian distinction between theoretical argument that leads to truth and practical argument that leads to reasoned action.

I am less certain about his claim that evaluation persuades someone to act rather than persuades them that something is the case. Action is the ultimate goal of evaluation, but there are so many other considerations involved in action that it seems unlikely the evaluator would be able to assess, or even identify the major contingencies. It seems to me that evaluation persuades as to the worth of something. Under some circumstances this may be a course of action, but ordinarily the action entails additional considerations.

4. For an extended analysis of an evaluation as argumentation, see Appendix A. For an analysis of "naturalistic evaluation," see Appendix B.

5

COHERENCE AND CREDIBILITY
The Aesthetics

The Drunken Driver

Humankind lingers unregenerately in Plato's cave, still reveling, its age-old habit, in mere images of the truth.

Susan Sontag, *On Photography*, 1977: 1

Consider two different images of the drinking driver. One may imagine the ordinary social drinker who happens to overindulge, and who, missing a stop sign, is detained by the police, thereby getting into trouble. Or imagine the drunken driver, one who is habitually drunk, a reeling, stumbling, insensate hazard to everyone on the road, including himself. The image that one constructs of the driver who drinks has much to do with the recommendations for action that one might embrace as a means of curtailing drinking drivers.

AUTHOR'S NOTE: This chapter was published as "Coherence and Credibility: The Aesthetics of Evaluation," *Educational Evaluation and Policy Analysis,* Vol. 1, No. 5, September-October, 1979, pp. 5-17. Copyright 1979, American Educational Research Association, Washington, DC. Reprinted by permission. Helpful comments were provided by Gene Glass, Jo Friedman, Donald Hogben, Rochelle Mayer, John Nisbet, and Helen Simons.

Until the past decade, the drinking driver has been perceived as the social drinker, a civil problem susceptible to correction by legal actions such as imposed penalties and fines. Over the past ten years or so, however, a series of studies has been influential in changing the dominant image of the drinking driver so that he is now perceived as more of an habitual, pathological drunk. The resulting recommendations for remediation are medical and are directed at a small subset of offenders rather than at all drivers who drink.

The sociologist Gusfield (1976) analyzed the rhetoric of these studies—how data were presented to persuade the reader of the conclusions. What he found is provocative. It has been axiomatic in social science that although a novelist may persuade a reader with emotion, a scientist persuades only with logic. Gusfield referred to this idea of language neutrality as the "windowpane" theory of language: language will reveal reality transparently without embellishment. He demonstrated that in actual practice scientific studies are valued in part for their dramatic use of language.

Gusfield analyzed in detail the most influential of the drinking driver studies, "Identification of Problem-Drinking Among Drunken Drivers" (Waller, 1967). Using Burke's (1945) categories of scene, act, agent, agency and purpose, Gusfield showed how Waller's study works as a persuasive rhetorical device. Since the literary style of science is one of neutrality, the scientific study must appear not to be literary, not to be concocted from a personal point of view. In Waller's drinking driver study, the neutrality of scene is set by the role of the author, a medical researcher, writing in the *Journal of the American Medical Association.* Once the neutral authority of the scene is established, the author as a person does not intrude.

The form of the report is narrative, with a definite dramatic structure. Tension arises over the choice between the two types of drinking drivers, the tension finally being released in a denouement. The dramatic progression is from the problem drinker as social drinker to the problem drinker as drunken driver. In the progression it is important, according to Gusfield, that the change in perspective (which is the actual outcome of the study) be seen as the culmination of external data derived by scientific method. To this end the voice of the report is impersonal: "Recent reports have suggested . . ."; "It is increasingly becoming apparent. . . ." The passive voice places the action in the external agency of the data and method, rather than in the author. It reinforces the idea that the conclusions emerge from the impersonal data world.

The resulting "scientific" style is clinical, detached, impersonal, and lacks imagery. The author presents the external world and allows it to persuade the reader. The style suggests that the observer is governed by method and by the rules of scientific integrity. Attention to detail and meticulous description of procedures, such as carrying numbers to several decimal places, give the impression of accuracy. According to Gusfield, this style reinforces the basic epistemological assumption: by use of the same method, different observers must come to the same conclusions.

Although the discussion of the methodology is conducted with painstaking neutrality, the implications for action are handled quite differently. The facts are converted into imagery. In his study of drinking drivers, Waller repeatedly referred to "drunken drivers," thus conjuring up powerful images, as opposed to describing in more neutral terms like "drivers who get into accidents after drinking." Even the title of the study uses the term "drunken driver." In actuality, the category of drunkenness was defined operationally by alcohol content of the blood, a legal definition carrying quite a different emotional loading than the image of the drunken driver.

According to Gusfield, once Waller identified "drunken drivers" as the problem drinkers through his survey of civil records, he drew the action implications from the imagery of his original classification. Thus the medical scientist made sense of his data by reduction to imagery. The drunken driver imagery extended the meaning of the primary data to meanings already commonly accepted and known by the audience. It was not a simple extrapolation of the data.

In substance, the drunken driver image attributes responsibility to the agent, to the driver himself, and not to the scene within which the driver acts. Drunken driving becomes an attribute of self which requires medical treatment. It implies pathological rather than normal behavior, and correspondingly different courses of remediation. Even a different subgroup of people is implicated. The civil delinquent is transformed into a patient.

Gusfield suggested that this study is typical in rhetorical style, although particularly influential, among the drinking driver studies. More generally, he argued that science works through such reduction. Generalizable knowledge is created through linking specific objects to universal categories. "It is implicit and inherent in the enterprise of defining, describing, and interpreting data through verbal or written communication insofar as conclusions and generalizations imply meanings for action" (p. 31). And later, "To be relevant or significant, data must not only be selected, they have to be typified and interpreted" (ibid.).

Although not all evaluation studies employ such vivid imagery, similar issues arise in evaluation. Imagery, dramatic structure, and mode of presentation are central considerations for the import of an evaluation. These elements, often thought of as merely cosmetic, can affect what people believe and do. How do these elements function and what is their relationship to the content, the "truth value," of an evaluation? Evaluators do employ such elements, although not always consciously and not to the same degree. As Gusfield notes, "What is at stake, however, is the necessity of the interpretation and the close connection between that interpretation and its form of presentation, its artistic element" (p. 32).

Similarly, in his analysis of the role of images in defining problems in social policy, Schon (1979) contended that social problem-setting is mediated by the stories people tell about troublesome situations. The framing of the social problem depends on the metaphors underlying the stories. How the problems are framed is critical to the solutions that emerge. For example, a pervasive story about social services is that they are "fragmented," and the implicit solution is that they be "coordinated." But services seen as "fragmented" could also be seen more benignly as "autonomous." The underlying metaphor gives shape and direction to the problem solution.

Schon contended that we are guided in our thinking about social policy by pervasive, tacit images, which he calls "generative metaphors." They involve a carrying over of one frame of reference to another situation. Usually, these metaphors are induced by immersing oneself in the experience of the phenomenon. These guiding images are necessary to our thinking.

For example, there are two rather different views of urban renewal. One view sees the slum as a once healthy community that has become diseased. A social planner with such an image envisions wholesale redesign and reconstruction as the cure to urban blight. Quite a different view of the slum portrays it as a viable, low-income natural community which offers its residents important social benefits. The second view implies strikingly different prescriptions for improving the community.

The story of the slum as blight was dominant in social planning in the 1950s. In the 1960s the story of the slum as natural community arose as a countermetaphor to vie for public and expert attention. According to Schon, from a reality that is "ambiguous and indeterminate," each story selects features that become the themes of what the story is about. In the first vision, terms like "blight," "health," "renewal," "cycle of decay," and "integrated plan" become important. In the second vision, "home," "patterns of interaction," "informal networks," and "dislocation" are key ideas.

Each story presents a view of social reality by selecting, naming, and relating elements within the chosen framework. According to Schon, "naming" and "framing" are the key processes. By selecting certain elements and coherently organizing them, those processes explain what is wrong in a particular situation and suggest a transformation. Data are converted to recommendations.

Naming and framing proceed by generative metaphor. The researchers *sees* the slum as blight or as natural community. In seeing A as B, the evaluation implicit in B is carried over to A. The first metaphor is that of disease and cure. The second is that of natural community (versus artificial community). The transferred evaluations are based on images deep-seated in our culture. Once we see a complex situation as health/disease or as nature/artifice, we know in which direction to move.

Seeing A as B greatly facilitates our ability to diagnose and prescribe. On the other hand, it may lead us to overlook other important features in the situation that the metaphor does not capture. Since generative metaphors are usually tacit, important features may pass undetected. Schon argued that we should be more aware of our generative metaphors, and that this is best done by analyzing the problem-setting stories that we tell.

The "deep" metaphor accounts for why some elements are included in the story while others are not, why some assumptions are taken to be true in spite of disconfirming evidence, and why some recommendations seem obvious. It is the image of the drunken driver or the metaphor of the slum as diseased that gives shape to the study and direction to one's actions.

The Story

That is to say, the first thing we *do* with images is to envisage a story; just as the first thing we do with words is to

tell something; to make a statement. . . . Pictures and stories
are the mind's stock-in-trade.

Susanne K. Langer, *Philosophy in a New Key,* 1942: 128

Consider an evaluation. First, there is a series of events, the reality as
it were, which will always remain somewhat indeterminate. The evaluator faces an ambiguous world. Through various social and psychological
screens, the evaluator portrays these events in a report. The report itself
is an artifact. As such, the report has coherence and form, some kind of
aesthetic structure, even if the structuring is not entirely conscious.

The report is interpreted by readers, and this interpretation will vary
from reader to reader, depending on her circumstances and her background. If the readers find the report credible, they are more likely to
assume a corresponding valuing position vis-à-vis the object being evaluated. Furthermore, the readers may be led to action, depending on their
disposition and other circumstances. The action may or may not be
recommended by the evaluator.

As an artifact the evaluation report will have aesthetic qualities,
appearances that engage interest, but there is something more basic to
an evaluation report than this. Every evaluation must have a minimum
degree of coherence. The minimum coherence is that the evaluation tell
a story. There must be either an explicit or tacit sequence of events (or
more accurately, an interpretation of events) for the reader to use the
evaluation as a guide to valuing. There also may be recommendations
by the evaluator, but the recommendations are not necessary. The story
is.

In this sense, images by themselves cannot be evaluations. As Sontag
(1977) noted in her analysis of photography:

> Desire has no history—at least, it is experienced in each instance
> as all foreground, immediacy. It is aroused by archetypes and is,
> in that sense, abstract. But moral feelings are embedded in
> history, whose personae are concrete, whose situations are always
> specific. Thus, almost the opposite rules hold true for the use of
> the photograph to awaken desire and to awaken conscience. The
> images that mobilize conscience are always linked to a given
> historical situation. The more general they are, the less likely they
> are to be effective [pp. 16-17].

Photographs may be used to reinforce valuations and even presented
in sequence to tell a story (Templin, 1978). The story itself is neces-

sary, however, to interpret the events. Events must be presented in a specific historical context. The story, even more than the image and the metaphor, is the basic underlying structure of an evaluation.

There are at least two conventional ways of telling the story. One way is to present the evaluator as a neutral, scientific observer. In this case, the story line is implied. It runs something like, "I am a detached, neutral observer who has made measurements according to the canons of science and have found certain things to be so. The program was conducted as I have described it, and I have found the following outcomes. . . ." In establishing this voice, the evaluator meticulously specifies his methodological procedures to enhance his credibility. Readers are expected to believe the results because of the objectivity of the methodology and because of their previous experience and belief in such a methodology. Usually the story line concludes that "the program was implemented, and such and such were the results." Actual description is often sparse. The drunken driver study is an example of this story line. The usual presentation is to describe the project or the goals of the project, the treatment, the results or effects, and the conclusions.

The second major way of telling the story is for the evaluator to stand closer to the program, as reflected in the narrator's "voice," and to tell the story by describing the events in detail. To this end the evaluator may use emotionally charged language and a narrative presentation. The story may look like a newspaper report. The first approach to story telling lends itself to quantitative and the second to qualitative methodology. But in both cases there is an ordering of events that tell a story, even though many of the events are assumed rather than explicit. The more formal the presentation becomes, the more things are assumed.

One ought to distinguish the "story," which is an interpretive ordering of events basic to all evaluations and prerequisite to valuation by the reader, from dramatic form. The dramatic form may vary, and the same story may be presented in a number of different ways. An evaluative story may be made more compelling, interesting, and pleasing by the dramatic form and by other aesthetic elements. However, although the story is more basic, the aesthetic rendering is not merely cosmetic. Both good art and good science lead the reader to experience an event in somewhat the same way as the creator experienced it (Bronowski, 1956). As Gusfield showed in his analysis of the drunken driver studies, the aesthetic rendering can have an important effect on the recommendations and meaning of a policy study, even a scientific one.

It is not too surprising that the "story" of an evaluation is more basic than the aesthetic rendering, since the story line relates events to each other in specific ways, such as in cause and effect relationships. The events of the story may be presented in different dramatic forms, but both the story and the aesthetic elements contribute to overall coherence. All things being equal, greater coherence leads to greater credibility on the part of the audiences. Things fit with more certainty. However, if the report is unrealistically coherent, credibility is lost.

One may think of the difference between the story and the dramatic presentation as the difference between "content" and "form," or in Polanyi's terms (Polanyi and Prosch, 1975), the difference between the "story" and the "frame." The frame may include imagery, meter, or other "artificial" modes of presentation. This is not to say that the "frame" is purely cosmetic. The meaning of a work is the integration of its appearance with its content. The meaning of a poem is not merely the content of the poem written in prose.

The story differs from a chronology of events in that the story consists of inferences and interpretations of events. Events are integrated with each other, and parts are ordered to the whole. The story itself can be more or less tightly integrated, and it provides the necessary coherence for the evaluation as a whole.

A key concept here is that of coherence. Coherence consists of logical connection, congruity, or "consistency in reasoning or relating, so that one part of the discourse does not destroy or contradict the rest; harmonious connection of the several parts so that the whole 'hangs together,'" as in the coherence of an argument or report (Oxford English Dictionary).

Following Polanyi (Polanyi and Prosch, 1975), I wish to expand the scope of "coherence" to include imagery, dramatic structures, and other aesthetic elements. For example, one might consider the logical consistency of the *concept* of the drunken driver as it is used in argumentation. But also, one might consider the *image* of the drunken driver as it is used harmoniously with other elements.

The image itself serves as a condensation of entangled meanings, emotional as well as cognitive, with its own dense coherence. It relates to the every-day, "real" world in a way that the concept does not. The concept can be defined explicitly, the image by a tacit sharing. The multilayered meanings implicit in images and other aesthetic elements make it possible to convey complex, elaborate, and highly refined evaluations of the objects under study. The aesthetic elements convey intensity, unity, and complexity (Beardsley, 1958).

Aesthetic elements, like images and dramatic structures, are distinguished from logical entities in that aesthetic elements are apprehended immediately without recourse to formal arguments. In this sense they are like perceptions. Aesthetic elements inhere in appearance only, and they are apprehended by tacit influence, by an unconscious integration of their parts (Polanyi and Prosch, 1975). So if one reads the drunken driver study, one assimilates somewhat unconsciously the tacit meanings conveyed through the images and dramatic structure. There is a considerable strand of "subliminal perception" in the learning, though one can easily detect the aesthetic elements if they are pointed out.

Furthermore, the reader participates actively in such learning. The reader becomes actively engaged in integrating the parts into tacit meanings and often becomes deeply engaged by the process, though the depth of engagement will vary from reader to reader. Eventually, the tacit inferences and the explicit inferences will be integrated into one's global image, one's "subjective knowledge structure." It is one's world image that ultimately affects one's behavior (Boulding, 1956).

I would like to argue, explicitly not tacitly, that greater coherence makes the evaluation report more credible, more worthy of belief and confidence. An incoherent report is not credible at all, and the more coherent the report (up to a point), the more credible it will appear to be—all other things being equal.

Usually the evaluator also strives to be persuasive—to win the audience to a point of view or even a course of action through reason and understanding. Most of the burden of persuasion falls on explicit argumentation, but here too coherence reinforces the persuasiveness of the argument. Less frequently, the evaluator may even aspire to secure commitment, to bind or obligate the reader to a particular position. These are the most powerful of the evaluations, but they pay the price of reduced scope of audience in exchange for deeper commitment of a few. From credibility to persuasiveness to commitment, one moves closer to action. In most evaluations, coherence plays the humbler role of enhancing credibility.

Form

> Science is nothing else than the search to discover unity in
> the wild variety of nature—or more exactly, in the variety of
> our experience. Poetry, painting, the arts are the same
> search . . . for unity in variety. Each in its own way looks for
> likeness under the variety of human experience.

J. Bronowski, *Science and Human Values,* 1952: 16

If the content differs from the dramatic structure of its presentation, what is it that comprises aesthetic form? In a classic article on "The Problem of Esthetic Form," Parker (1960), following Aristotle, suggested that aesthetic form can be analyzed in terms of six principles: organic unity, theme, thematic variation, balance, hierarchy, and evolution. The master principle is that of organic unity, and, in different ways, the other principles are subservient to it. Organic unity enhances total coherence.

The principle of unity demands that the work contain only necessary elements. In a sense, aesthetic form is in contradiction to life, which contains many unnecessary elements from an aesthetic point of view. The other five principles are manifestations of the unity principle. In an evaluation report, one must have a "theme," and this theme must not only persist but reappear in variations if the total effect is to be achieved. Often in evaluation studies, this effect is achieved by presenting data which build a common theme. Such building and syncopation of data reinforce veracity. They mobilize the reader.

"Balance" entails an equality of opposing elements playing back and forth within the form. It provides dramatic tension. "Hierarchy" is one way the separate parts may be organized. Finally, Parker added the principle of "evolution," suggesting how a total meaning can be created by an accumulation in which earlier parts determine that which happens later. Evolutionary unity can be achieved by a climax at the end, or by the end itself assuming greater importance than the other parts. In an evaluation, the report may evolve into conclusions which have emerged from the data presentation.

These aesthetic principles are perhaps most easily seen in a dramatic narrative. Woodward and Bernstein's *The Final Days* (1976) is not an evaluation, but it is an interesting treatment of presumably factual material. The final days of the Nixon regime are recounted day by day. This daily countdown to the inevitable denouement when Nixon resigns adds to the dramatic intensity of the piece. Woodward and Bernstein do not simply relate one person's account of events and then relate another's, which must have been the way the information was collected. Rather, they blend various perceptions into an overall complex pattern, shifting from the thoughts and actions of one person to those of another. From this interweaving, certain themes emerge.

Forces converge on a defiant and recalcitrant Nixon. One by one, in differing ways, his closest supporters become convinced that he is guilty and must resign. These little personal vignettes within the larger drama are repeated in thematic variations which contribute to the overall theme of Nixon's support continually eroding. Nixon himself is uncertain as to whether to resign or to stay in office. This balance shifts day by day, hour by hour. Growing from the theme of Nixon's increasing isolation emerges a transcendent theme—his personal disintegration. These themes are skillfully woven together until they evolve into the denouement of his disgrace, his resignation from office, and his collapse as a man.

Similar aesthetic principles apply to quantitative material, though their effects are sometimes less easily discerned. The simplicity, economy, and elegance of a particularly appropriate experimental design or multivariate analysis are manifestations of the unity principle. In fact, some scientist-philosophers like Polanyi believe that in the higher reaches of thought, the mathematician is guided primarily by his aesthetic intuition.

Consider, for example, the aesthetic appeal of a multivariate analysis as compared to a long string of bivariate data analyses. Such compression harbors an appeal beyond the fuller truth value a multivariate analysis might entail. It is at least partially in such satisfactions that the pursuit of more elegant designs lies. Or consider the nested appeal of a Guttman scale. The parsimony of such a scale, and of hierarchical theories based on such an ordering, appeals to aesthetic sensibilities. One even looks for problems and data that will fit such designs.

The aesthetic appeal of quantitative studies is reflected in terms such as "coherence," "elegance," "economy," and "power." There is a sense in which "elegant" solutions are compact, simple, swift. They give one a sense of control, utility, and mastery similar to searching for and finding the "right word" in describing something. Elegant solutions dispense with unnecessary steps and procedures. They are compelling.

It is not only in quantitative studies that one finds such coherence. Nor must the structured elements be numbers or symbols. One of the primary reasons for the persuasive nature of Glass's (1972) evaluation of AERA instructional tapes is the way he fits the arguments together into an overall pattern (Appendix A). The arguments are the elements. Glass achieves an integration of the logical parts of the evaluation within a coherent overall rhetorical structure. Elegance in this case means that there are few parts not necessary to the overall logic of the evaluation. There is a clear, if complex, guiding structure with the parts fitted neatly and properly to the whole.

In addition to elegance and coherence, one might say of Glass's work that it is credible because of "voice," the attitude of the narrator toward his subject matter. Glass projects a "persona" such that it appears the narrator will be convinced by the data no matter how the data turn out. The image of the narrator is that of a "rational" man ready to be persuaded by the evidence. To identify this as an effect of style is not to question its authenticity.

"Outward Bound"

> To evoke in oneself a feeling one has once experienced and having evoked it in oneself then by means of movements, lines, colors, sounds, or forms expressed in words, so to transmit that feeling that others experience the same feeling—this is the activity of art.
>
> Tolstoy, "The Communication of Emotion"

Smith, Gabriel, Schott, and Padia's (1976) evaluation of Outward Bound was unusual in that it used both quantitative and qualitative methods. The two parts were handled separately, and both were included in the final report. The opening lines of the study set the problem and dramatic tension:

> What happens to the young person who elects to undergo the physical challenges associated with the rocks, cliffs, snowfields and streams of the Rocky Mountains and the interpersonal challenge of a small group isolated in a foreign environment? Proponents of the Outward Bound program, alumni and staff, maintain that the psychological effects are unique to each participant and cannot be anticipated. In contrast, many others claim that the program causes profound, predictable changes in the participant's feelings about himself and others [p. 401].

The tension introduced in these opening lines provides drama, significance, and interest. The basic question was addressed in two ways—by quantitative measurement and by the qualitative participant observation. Both reflected the overall evaluation story.

In the quantitative part four variables were chosen as outcome criteria: "self-esteem," "self-awareness," "self-assertion," and "acceptance by others." Psychometric instruments were developed to measure all four variables. The "voice" of the quantitative section was that of the neutral, scientific narrator. An opportunity for elegance came in the design of the study.

With groups of participants proceeding through the training at different times during the summer, the evaluators randomly assigned students to groups and administered the questionnaires only once to each group at different times. Thus they were able to employ a complex time-series design in which groups acted as controls on each other. Forty-four means were collected and analyzed for each of the June, July, and August courses.

Unity was achieved by neatly graphing the forty-four means so they could be compared to each other visually as well as mathematically. A four-by-three table succinctly summarized the considerable mass of data. The only aesthetic failing was that the four outcome variables were not related to each other in any way, thus disrupting the unity of the analysis. The same basic question was also addressed by participant observation. Dramatic tension was established by a first-hand account. The style was personal and involved, rather than neutral and detached.

> The six-hour bus ride from Denver to the San Juan Mountains let our fears and expectations incubate. My own fears centered on the difference between myself and my fellow Outward Bounders. I guessed that I was twice as old as the rest and wondered if their strength and endurance would surpass mine. The prospect of failing physically and being a social outcast was cheerless. Like the children around me, I knew something of what Outward Bound was supposed to be and to do to me. I was aware of its military origins and the rumored physcial dangers of the program. There was also the intimation that one would experience the mystical entry into adulthood. Although I had long since entered adulthood, certain aspects of myself raised doubts about the coming 23 days; my fear of heights, my inexperience with competitive situations, my intransigence when pushed. The doubts were repeated mental questions. Would I be left behind? Would I panic

halfway up some steep rock face? Would I fall into an adult role, take too much responsibility, and be rejected? Would I quit? The silence on the bus led me to believe that the others were also ruminating on the experiences ahead. We each had our own private visions and nightmares [pp. 411-412].

Interest in the study was intensified by the personal drama and by the expression of feelings. The headings of the separate sections indicated the dramatic progression: "Expectations," "Competencies," "Expeditions," "Solo," "Social Challenge," "Final Expedition," "Marathon." The climax of the narrative was a dangerous mountain ascent and an exhausting race. The writing was both insightful and colorful.

I decided that Outward Bound was especially designed for people like Chris. She had never worked, never been challenged, never really lived except vicariously through her parents and the media. The course forced her into a series of compacted experiences, causing her maturation to be accelerated. One could almost see her stamina and confidence grow as the course progressed. She tried hard, but never stopped complaining. She could not give up her play of professing weakness and hiding her strengths. The strategem must have worked for her; didn't it get her a free ride across the Rio Grande on my back? [p. 417]

The neutral voice was abandoned for an intense first-person account of events. Outcomes like self-assertion, self-esteem, and self-awareness were registered in personal manifestations. This rendering of events provided a different level of understanding and meaning than the findings that the Outward Bound course had a positive impact on participants' "self-assertion" and "self-esteem" but did not affect measurably participants' "acceptance of others" or "self-awareness," which were the results of the measurement of the four variables in the quantitative part of the evaluation. However, both sections were structured aesthetically. Together, the two components provided a highly qualified but credible and persuasive answer to the question set in the first paragraph of the study.

Together, the two analyses tell only one story about what happened, and the same story could have been presented in different dramatic forms. For example, the overall structure might have been a dramatic narrative throughout, with the quantitative data spliced in for support.

Or the report might have consisted primarily of the quantitative analysis with a bare-bones explanation of the effects included in the "discussion" section. Alternatively, the evaluation report might have been written as a Socratic dialogue or a play. Smith et al. (1976) chose to give equal weight to the quantitative and qualitative.

Whatever the form, the evaluation story would be the same, though it might differ in aesthetic power. The credibility of the evaluation depends partly on the correspondence of the quantitative part to the principles of measurement, the correspondence of the qualitative part to the personal experience of the audience, and the correspondence of the parts to each other—their coherence. If all these elements fit together properly, and the evaluation is aesthetically rendered, then the entire evaluation will be seen as highly credible. In this case, the parts do cohere, and the audience is likely to be convinced of the efficacy of the Outward Bound training. The one failing is that the quantitative and qualitative parts are not explicitly united, so the overall unity is not as intense as it might have been.

Whether an evaluation abounds in metaphors or coefficients, dramatic structure or mathematical economy, every evaluation must do one basic thing: it must tell a story. The story may be explicit, truncated, or implicit, but the story must be there if one is to draw implications. An evaluation must interpret events occurring across time.

In many quantitative evaluations the story is often assumed. For example, in the Outward Bound quantitative evaluation, one assumes that there was a program of some kind, a series of events, and that the evaluation instruments measured the outcomes of these. The purpose of the experimental design was to find out if the assumed events were the causes for the changes in the measures. If so, certain inferences follow. Whether the evaluation was aesthetically pleasing resides in the elegant use of the experimental design, the statistics, and the like.

In the qualitative section of the evaluation, events were portrayed in a personal way, rather than assumed. The aesthetics resided in the images and dramatic structure. Direct observation in every-day categories rather than readings of scientific categories on instruments were the sources of data. The inferred story mobilizes the reader, and the better the presentation of the story is aesthetically, other things being equal, the more the reader is mobilized.

Authenticity

> A work of art is authentic or true not by virtue of its
> content nor by its "pure" form, but by the content having
> become form.
>
>   Herbert Marcuse, *The Aesthetic Dimension,* 1978: 8

Why is it that aesthetic elements like images and dramatic structure
carry such import? There are many explanations, mostly drawn from
theories of aesthetics or art, but no single accepted explanation (Dickie,
1971). It is clear that we see our lives in the form of scenarios and
stories, that images are shaped in the language of our every-day
thoughts. Concrete images are the stuff of which our minds and
memories are composed.

The anthropoligist Turner (1973) contended that affect is "inherently concrete, particular, and associated with the unique relationship
of the self to its objective environment" (p. 354). Abstract principles
are inadequate for acting in the real world. Such an integration into the
environment must be accomplished through particular, affective con-
densations such as only imagery, symbol, rituals, and myths can supply.
These devices convey "affective and motivational power" within the
subjective meaning framework of the person.

Similarly, Sullivan (1977) suggested that it is the role of the imagination to provide integrating images and myths. The individual always
acts within a particular personal and historical context. Highly formal
and abstract theories of action and behavior overlook this deeper level
of contingent motivation.[1]

While such analyses are astute, they may underestimate the mythic
power of science itself. People do sometimes act on the basis of results
they consider to be "scientifically" derived. Science has both its own
myths and its own mythic authority. Nor does the necessity of concrete
imagery entirely explain the effects of the more abstract aesthetic
patterns.

For example, why is dramatic form so effective? According to
Broudy (1972), although dramatic form is not equivalent to moral or
metaphysical meaning, it is the first "intimation" of it. Literal truth is
usually confusing and insignificant. It must be converted into "plausible
fictions." Illusions are necessary for human import. Aesthetic renderings become searches for significance in human events. Furthermore,

people often judge the credibility of reported events on the basis of aesthetic criteria like vividness and inherent unity—on appearances.

An aesthetic experience, then, is *an* experience rather than merely experience. The artist selects events that are cumulative in impact. Tension arising from the dramatic structure commands the audience's attention. For example, in the drinking driver study, the researcher maintains tension between the two competing images of the drinking driver. In Broudy's view, the alternative to imaginative portrayal is insignificance. Aesthetic presentation tries to capture the "essence" of events rather than their literal reality.

Polanyi, too, sees significance as the underlying issue:

> Our lives are formless, submerged within a hundred cross-currents. The arts are imaginative representations, hewn into artificial patterns; and these patterns, when jointly integrated with an important constant, produce a meaning of distinctive quality. These artificial patterns are . . . what isolate works of art from the shapeless flow of personal experience and public life. They make of works of art something detached, in many cases portable and reproducible, and potentially deathless [p. 101].

From a more radical perspective, Marcuse (1978) emphasized the importance of both personal feeling and artistic form in social reform. Subjectivity—the inner, personal history of the individual—can be a liberating force when it is expressed in a work of art. The "given reality," the reality shaped and verified by the dominant social institutions, can be reshaped in the art work. The art work constitutes an alternative reality which is in opposition to the "given" reality. Thus an art work challenges the monopoly of the established institutions in defining reality.

In this process, aesthetic form transforms the content into a new, self-contained whole. This new vision reveals the repressed dimensions of reality in a "fictitious reality" which captures only the essence of events. Through concentration, exaggeration, emphasis on the essential, and a reordering of facts, the audience's consciousness is restructured. Experience is intensified.

The content of the work is subjective feeling, and aesthetic form transforms the content into a self-contained whole, enabling the work to stand against the "given reality." When the content has been properly converted into form, the work has the ring of authenticity. Thus Marcuse can say, "The authentic utopia is grounded in recollection" (p. 73).

The Beauty of the Drunken Driver

Wisdom, the ability to go to the heart of the matter in
concrete situations, is acquired slowly; it is a discipline of
experience, imagaination and story, not of naked intelligence.

M. Novak, *Ascent of the Mountain,*
Flight of the Dove, 1971: 58

The documentary film maker Frederick Wiseman, well known for his
films portraying social institutions, such as the welfare system and the
meat-packing industry, described his television documentaries as "reality fiction," as a "fictional structure with the illusion of truth"
(O'Conner, 1976). From the "formless glop" of fifty hours of film,
Wiseman shapes the documentary in the editing process, where he
introduces the elements of pacing, style, and structure. Although selecting arbitrarily, the film-maker attempts to capture a portion of the
"truth" as he sees it, according to Wiseman.

Yet evaluation is not fiction, or at least it should not be. The dicta
that apply to art, even documentary art, are not necessarily those that
shape evaluation. One expects more veracity from an evaluation report
than from a novel or a film. To return to the original question, how can
one justify artistic presentation of data that affects the very interpretation of the study itself?

Langer (1942) suggested that there are at least two major types of
meaning, the literal and the artistic. Literal meaning deals with explicit
content and is expressed as propositional fact. It can be either true or
false. Artistic meaning deals with tacit form and is expressed as feeling.
It can be either adequate or inadequate. Correspondingly, factual
reference and poetic significance are two rather different relations
between symbols and their meanings, but both can be identified.

In Langer's theory, science is advanced by discursive thought which
is reducible to analytic concepts and to "facts." Langer points out that
the discursive use of symbols, which reaches its climax in science, is
only one way of knowing. There are nondiscursive ways of knowing,
like visual forms, forms in which the elements of the whole are
presented simultaneously as in paintings, images, metaphors, and
myths. As such, artistic meaning is not subject to tests of falsification in
the same way as are propositional statements.

Rather, artistic form is more comprehensible in terms of consistency, coherence, economy, and elegance. However useful the discursive symbols, one must turn eventually to artistic form for the expression of feeling. Langer's theory of art is an "imitation" theory in which artistic form serves as analog to emotion, just as discursive language serves as logical analog to the physical world (Dickie, 1971). Whatever the strength of the claim, it is undeniable that artistic meaning can sometimes conflict with literal meaning. It is entirely possible that inappropriate uses of metaphor or wrongly reconstructed events or omitted data can mislead an audience.

For example, Woodward and Bernstein's *The Final Days* evoked questions about its truthfulness. A controversy developed over whether the portrayed events were true and even to what extent the authors could know certain private happenings. Some participants contended that the authors had left out discordant details in order to intensify the drama about Nixon's disintegration. The credibility of the authors suffered because the book was too dramatic. Whatever the merits in this particular case, it is not difficult to see how literal truth may sometimes be sacrificed to dramatic form. John Keats notwithstanding, truth and beauty are sometimes incompatible.

Beyond the truth of the work itself is the question of whether the work is fair to the people portrayed. I have dealt with this justice issue in another place by connecting it to infringement of one's right to self-esteem (House, 1976). The trade-off between truth and justice in *The Final Days* is certainly debatable. Even liberal newspaper columnists have protested that the authors went too far in their portrayal of Nixon as a disintegrating person.

An evaluation can be seriously threatened if an element in it proves to be untrue or of questionable origin. What if, for example, in the Smith et al. (1976) evaluation of Outward Bound, one discovered that the person who wrote the excellent first-person narrative was not the person who actually experienced the travail? Somehow it would threaten the authenticity of the piece if the writer reconstructed someone else's adventures.

In fact, what if the trip into the Rockies were really based on three trips taken at different times by three different persons, and for aesthetic reasons, the author combined the three separate experiences into a single dramatic narrative? The advantage would be obvious. As it stands, the narrative powerfully conveys the feeling tone of the mountain experience—truth of feeling—in a way that three fragmented narratives could not do. The advantage would be a gain in the coherence of the piece and in its credibility and persuasiveness.

On the other hand, the narrative would not be literally true. Would the author be justified in taking such liberties? There would be a trade-off between literal truth and truth of feeling, between truth and beauty. As important as beauty is in evaluation, truth must take precedence when there is a conflict between the two. Ultimately, evaluation is not fiction, as necessary as imagery and form may be to conveying complex meaning. Trade-offs are possible between truth and beauty. One may omit some facts to make the report more coherent, more readable. But one would sacrifice only a little truth for a great deal of beauty. Truth is relatively more valuable.

For me the resolution revolves around the idea of the evaluative story. Liberties are permissible with the dramatic structure as long as the evaluative story remains unchanged. That is, did people go into the mountains and experience these things, although not exactly as the literal plot would have it? If people did not experience similar things or if the figurative language suggested feeling states that were different from those the mountain trip induced, then the license with the evaluation would be too great. The audience would be misled in a significant way and have a false picture of the program. Also, one would need to be told that the events were reconstructed. One could test the veracity by the internal consistency of the narrative, by its coherence with the quantitative analysis, and by its congruence with the reader's own experience.

Nor are quantitative studies immune from this conflict. Measurement and analysis techniques are often based on aesthetic criteria and sometimes result in inappropriate applications. Furthermore, the methodology sections in most studies are written from a reconstructed view of what happened rather than how the data were actually collected and analyzed. There should be a limit to such reconstruction, the limit being the point at which the evaluation story is significantly changed. For example, the audience may assume that standard precautions in data collection were taken when indeed they were not. Or the audience may assume a treatment occurred when, in fact, its implementation was questionable. Since in a quantitative study so much is assumed by the audience, and unspoken by the authors, reconstruction of what happened is a continuing problem.

To return to the initial example of the drunken driver study, was the researcher justified in employing potent images of the drunken driver?

The answer is a qualified "yes," if one accepts that the purpose of an evaluation or a policy study is to inform opinion and to lead to action. The qualification is that the image of the drunken driver must be congruent with the rest of the study, though not the only rendering the author might have chosen, and that the rendering must reflect properly the real world. Such renderings are essential to moral action. They speak the "vocabulary of action" that remains an obligation of the evaluator (House, 1973). Yet in those concrete instances in which truth and beauty conflict, truth is more important than beauty. And justice more important than either.

NOTE

1. Similar theories exist in aesthetics. The objectivism of Piaget's psychology has its analogs in both moral philosophy and aesthetics. In philosophy Rawls's (1971) theory of justice is predicated on an "original position" in which a "veil of ignorance" limits the knowledge and motivations that people choosing their principles of justice must have. People in the hypothetical original positions do not know their social position or particular talents. In addition, they are rational and not altruistic. In other words, self-interest has been reduced as motivation, and people presumably will act impartially. As in Piaget's psychology, the actor is conceived as an impersonal, abstract being without contingent motivation.

In the philosophy of aesthetics the corresponding position is called phenomenol objectivism (Gottshalk, 1962). One must view an object from the proper aesthetic attitude, which includes displacement of the practical and loss of awareness of self. In assuming this attitude one will be able to show objectively how certain features of the work cause certain emotions (Beyer, 1974). Contrasted to this view is the position that the meaning an object has is related to one's interest in viewing the object (Beyer, 1977).

6

JUSTICE

> Justice is the first virtue of social institutions, as truth is of systems of thought.
>
> John Rawls, *A Theory of Justice*

Consider a typical situation for the practicing evaluator. He is hired by a government to evaluate an educational program for disadvantaged students. How does he proceed? What does he look for? The possibilities are greater than might be suspected. He may administer a standardized achievement test and compare the scores to those of students who do not have such a program. He may create a special test, perhaps based on objectives, to assess certain areas of academic "deficiency." He may measure student attitudes, opinions, or self-concepts.

On the other hand, he may solicit teacher opinions, attitudes, and judgments about the program. He may observe how teachers and students behave in the classroom, in the halls, in the streets. He may record and analyze what teachers say about students, how they grade them, what standards they set. He may ask parents about the program, about the teachers, about the schools. He may examine parent participation in school activities or school efforts to involve parents.

AUTHOR'S NOTE: This chapter is an extensive modification of the ideas in "Justice in Evaluation," in G. V. Glass (eds.) *Evaluation Studies Review Annual*, Vol. 1, Beverly Hills: Sage Publications, 1976, and "The Role of Theories of Justice in Evaluation," *Educational Theory*, Vol. 29, No. 4, 1980. The latter was a response to Strike's (1979) critique.

He may solicit the opinions of employers about the content or results of the program. He may match program content against job skills or trace student job opportunities, or pay, or performance after the program. He may examine grades in later school years. He might ask subject matter experts or political leaders to judge the program. He may render his own judgments. He may hold a mock trial and have members of the public judge the program. There are many other things he might do.

What does the evaluator do? There are a number of influencing factors—his experience, his training, what the government wants, what the people in the program want, etc. One of these influencing factors is the conception of justice that the evaluator and the sponsor of the evaluation hold, usually quite tacitly. What the evaluator believes is right and the prevailing conception of justice significantly affect the evaluation.

Admittedly, the influence is complex and far from direct. The evaluation is not a deduction from the conception of justice. The connection is more vague, more implicit—but nonetheless influential for all that. The dominant conception of justice limits the approaches one takes, what activities one finds legitimate, what arguments count as significant. Conceptions of justice act more as broad frameworks of consideration rather than as internally consistent machines for deducing conclusions. They distribute the burdens of argument in particular ways.

Evaluation techniques and practices do not per se belong to a particular theory of justice, like utilitarianism or Rawlsian justice-as-fairness. For example, multiple regression is not per se utilitarian—but an evaluator who held that there were a few quantitative indicators of success would find himself using multiple regression over and over. Someone who held that the interests of various publics should be directly represented in an evaluation would find himself using interviews far more than would a utilitarian. It is not the technique itself that is utilitarian but the reasoning that leads to particular choices of what the evaluator should do.

The evaluator proceeds partly by intuition, and philosophy can sharpen the evaluator's intuitions and sensitivities. The evaluator's intuitions are not only of justice but of self-interest, and philosophy can sharpen the better intuitions by reflections on theories of justice. Not only can people justify evaluations by reference to conceptions and theories of justice, they do so often, albeit in the indirect manner suggested here.

The evaluator must choose. If he holds that increased standardized test scores will mean more schooling, a better job, more money, and presumably more satisfaction for the students—in short, that test gains are in their interest—he may well use that as the indicator of success for the program. If he believes that parental participation is central, or that the interests of the students are best represented by their parents' opinions, he will conduct a very different evaluation. He may still employ standardized tests. How the interests of the student are represented in the evaluation, and whose interests are registered will result in significantly different evaluations. That different interests be represented is a matter of democratic theory, but there are many conceptions of justice consistent with a democratic viewpoint. For example, a neo-Marxist evaluator may well search for inequalities in the school setting, whereas a political pluralist may strive to represent the opinions and values of many diverse groups.

Evaluation is by its nature a political activity. It serves decision-makers, results in reallocations of resources, and legitimizes who gets what. It is intimately implicated in the distribution of basic goods in society. It is more than a statement of ideas; it is a social mechanism for distribution, one which aspires to institutional status. Evaluation should not only be true; it should also be just. Current evaluation schemes, independently of their truth value, reflect justice in quite varying degrees. And justice provides an important standard by which evaluation should be judged.

In this chapter I outline three conceptions of justice—the utilitarian, the intuitionist/pluralist, and Rawls's justice-as-fairness—and relate these to current approaches to evaluation. I try to assess some of the weaknesses and strengths of the conceptions and arrive at an overall judgment as to which is preferable. As Strike (1979) has pointed out, there is no single approach to evaluation determined by one's theory of justice. However, I contend that one's theory does limit possible approaches to evaluation and is used to justify these approaches (House, 1979).

Utilitarianism

Utilitarian ethics, according to Rawls (1971), stipulates that a society is just when its institutions are arranged so as to achieve the greatest net balance of satisfaction as summed over all individuals. The principle of utility is to maximize that net balance of satisfaction. Utilitarianism requires that there be a common measure or index of satisfaction in order that quantitative calculations of utility can be made. In education, this common measure is almost always construed to be standardized test scores. It is the surrogate index of satisfaction.

The basic structure of an ethical theory is given by how it relates two basic concepts: the good and the right. In teleological theories—which utilitarianism is—the good is defined *separately* and *prior* to the right. The right then becomes that which maximized the good—be it satisfaction, excellence, or whatever. Rationality itself comes to mean maximizing the good, a concept with great intuitive appeal. Not maximizing the good is looked upon as at least inefficient, perhaps fuzzy-minded, and even irrational. It is in utilitarian ethics *immoral.*

In the systems analysis approach in education, for example, test scores are established as the index of the good. That which maximizes them is both the right and proper thing to do. The best educational programs are those which, of the available alternatives, produce the greatest gains in test scores. Experimental design, instrumentation, and statistics are means for efficaciously determining the "best" alternatives by logically and quantitatively relating the right to the good. Social worth becomes a matter of maximizing test scores. Most evaluation discussion revolves around the efficiency of the evaluation as a means for determining the certainty and magnitude of gain.

The effect of such a theory is to separate moral judgments into two distinct classes. The good, the "value judgments," are a separate class of judgments and can be prespecified without reference to what is right. Traditionally, the "right" includes the problem of the distribution of basic goods. In modern economics, heavily dependent on utilitarian thought, there is a very great emphasis on the production of basic goods but less attention as to how those goods are distributed. Attention is focused on increasing total production rather than on distribution of the goods. In utilitarian evaluation the emphasis is on increasing test scores, not on how those scores are distributed.

Utilitarian justice means that total net satisfaction is maximized. If someone has greater desires and expectations than everyone else, those must be considered, desire for desire, equally with someone with fewer desires. In a sense, if one has greater expectations, one is entitled to more. It is even possible to take away satisfactions from those with less in order to appease someone who "needs" more. This trade-off is one cause of the failure of modern economics in developing countries. The gross national product of a country may be substantially increased by new industries. However, the money or the industry itself is often tuned to meeting the rising expectations of the new middle-class desires while the expectations of those lower down remain unimproved. Increasing total wealth does not necessarily improve the lot of everyone. The trade-off of lower-class satisfactions for higher-class satisfactions is consistent with utilitarian justice. Total satisfaction is maximized.

Likewise in education and other social areas—the desires (needs, objectives, etc.) are often taken pretty much as given. We mount "needs assessments" to determine these needs as objectively and quantitatively as we can. In our measurement theory, based on individual differences, the needs are intrinsic and lie there waiting to be measured, prioritized, and balanced against other needs. If upper-class people have very great expectations for their children, all their desires enter in the needs analysis and demand satisfaction. Their fulfillment will be reflected in the common measure of achievement and all the basic goods and values dependent in society on those scores. Distribution across people is not nearly so important as the total sum. Maximize everywhere is the dictum.

Since it is only the final net score that counts, one person's loss may be balanced by another person's gain. It is just for upper-class students to maximize achievement scores and advance their social position—even though they put lower-class children to disadvantage. Everyone must be free to advance his own good; and since what is right is that which maximizes the good, upper-class actions are both right and good.

Since all desires are taken at face value and since expectations and desires are much higher in the upper social and economic classes, utilitarianism has an upper-class bias built into it as a system of justice. One man's desire for a Rolls Royce is just as valid a claim as another man's desire for a Ford. The greater demands of upper- and middle-class students are honored at the expense of the lower classes.

In utilitarianism it is essential that everything be conflated into one system of desires so that justice can be served. Everything must be reduced to a unitary measure so that comparisons are possible. The basic method of comparison is the classic utilitarian "impartial spectator." By being both impartial and sympathetic to all parties, the spectator (needs assessor) can organize all desires (needs) into one coherent system of desires (set of objectives). He weighs and balances the intensity of desires and gives them appropriate weight in the overall system (evaluates). An administrator or legislator (the ubiquitous decision-maker) then adjusts the limited means in order to maximize the satisfaction of those desires. The result is efficient administration with the highest possible maximum satisfaction.

The utilitarian evaluator's resemblance to the impartial spectator is strong. In modern economics and modern evaluation the impartial spectator relies very heavily on quantitative measures for his impartiality. Modern econometricians push for "hard data" to measure the effectiveness of social programs (Rivlin, 1971). These can be converted into the most efficient design for society. The ideal evaluator also sympathetically records desires through needs assessments and definitions of objectives. He assigns weights and impartially measures results.

All educational needs are conflated by the evaluator into one system by familiar research techniques. Rawls notes: "Utilitarianism does not take seriously the distinction between persons, mistaking impersonality for impartiality." But this reductionism is essential for utilitarian justice to determine what is good and right to do.

As I indicated in Chapter 3, the systems analysis, goal-based, decision-maker, and goal-free models of evaluation seem to be to be based on a utilitarian conception of justice. They all try to arrive at the greatest utility by maximizing a small number of variables, a goal set, a decision-maker's preferences, or weighing outcomes. They try to arrive at a judgment of overall social utility, which, in turn, leads to maximum happiness in society. As in economics, cost is a prime consideration since wasted money could be used elsewhere to increase happiness; that is, utility could be improved.

Utilitarianism assumes that the essence of rational behavior is the maximizing of individual satisfactions or individual utilities (Macpherson, 1966). Human essence is rational action which maximizes utilities. Since people's desires for all kinds of satisfactions are unlimited, and the means of satisfying them always scarce, the problem is to find the system that would employ the scarce means to produce maximum satisfactions. Maximizing utilities is the ultimate good.

Utilitarianism is based on the idea that everyone is trying to get the most one can. Maximizing utilities means that one finds an arrangement by which people get satisfactions with the least effort. This leads to problems of how to identify and add together the satisfactions or utilities that people obtain from different things, of how to compare them on a single measuring scale. This is necessary in order to say that one assortment of utilities is the maximum one, to say that one set of utilities adds up to a larger total utility (Macpherson, 1966).

Among the utilitarian approaches to evaluation, systems analysis tries to identify a critical set of variables like social indicators; the goal-based approach takes the program goals as given; the decision-maker approach identifies the key decisions of the decision-makers as critical; and the goal-free evaluator identifies the actual program effects. Each model takes a slightly different approach to maximizing utility.

Utilitarianism has been a brilliant and productive mode of thought. But by taking demands as they exist and by insisting on a common measure of welfare, it often favors the higher social classes at the expense of the lower. When the common measure turns out to be indicators like standardized achievement tests, the problem is compounded, for the tests themselves may be socially and racially biased; are based on a theory of individual differences; have been used historically for the explicit purpose of selecting people into and keeping them out of social groups (Karier, 1973); and may be used to legitimize inequalities. Utilitarian justice no longer coincides with many moral sensibilities.

Pluralism/Intuitionism

The second theory of justice is the pluralist/intuitionist theory. This theory asserts that there is an irreducible family of first principles which must be weighed against each other by asking which balance of the principles is most just (Rawls, 1971). There is no higher principle, such as the principle of utility in utilitarianism, which can be used for determining the weights of the ultimate principles. Hence, there is a plurality of first principles by which judgments of justice are made, and no explicit method or set of priority rules for weighing these principles against one another.

Most "common sense" notions of justice are of this type, as are most formal philosophical doctrines. Usually there are distinct groups of specific precepts which apply to particular problems of justice, like taxation or criminal behavior. These specific precepts are applied more or less intuitively within defined areas, some people balancing the fundamental principles one way, and some another. The relative weighting of specific principles can lead to the most intense debates, such as in freedom of speech, even when people agree on the funda-

mental principles. Custom and the interests of the parties involved lead
to different weightings.

Intuitive balancing of principles provides no way of judging the
justice of customary practices themselves, however. The intuitionist
hopes that people can agree on the principles once they are identified
or at least agree to some procedure for arriving at weights. At the same
time the pluralist/intuitionist claims there is no supreme ethical conception which underlies the weights. The complexity of moral facts is too
great to be encompassed by such a principle.

The origin and content of the principles of justice are different for
the schools of evaluation that I have labeled pluralist/intuitionist. In the
art criticism model of evaluation, the educational critic applies principles which he has arrived at through his own experience and training
in educational programs. Presumably, each critic would have his own
set of principles which he applies to a given situation in an intuitive
fashion. Like the art critic, the educational critic would arrive at a
composite judgment of the program or policy.

The professional model uses a set of principles which are often
agreed upon in advance. For example, *Evaluative Criteria* lists many
criteria suitable for judging English programs, another set for judging
math programs, etc. English experts or math experts apply these stated
criteria—and perhaps others—in an intuitive fashion. Each expert
balances the principles according to his own disposition.

Similarly, the Council on Program Evaluation (COPE) has a long list
of criteria which it used to judge university departments. These criteria
could, in fact, be subsumed under a few principles like quality of
research and teaching. The Council then arrived at a set of judgments
by intuitively balancing these principles. Usually, research was given a
very heavy weighting in these judgments. In both the art criticism and
professional models, the criteria, ultimate guiding principles, and
weightings are derived from educational professionals.

By contrast, the quasi-legal and case study models of evaluation
generally derive their principles and weightings from participation of
the people involved in the program or in making decisions about the
program. In the quasi-legal model employing a mock trial procedure,
the jury and judge determine what criteria and principles will be used in
reaching a decision. Exactly what principles are employed depends on
how the jury, judge, or hearing panel are selected. They may be
members of the public at large, as in a real jury, or decision-makers who
must take responsibility for the program at issue.

In many cases, such as in a "blue-ribbon" panel hearing, the panel may consist of prestigious members of the public or prestigious members of a professional subgroup generally thought to possess authority in that area, such as a group of tax experts or evaluators or decision-makers. For example, the joint Dissemination Review Panel in HEW reviews evaluations of federal programs to determine whether these programs should be "validated" for dissemination to the rest of the country.

Finally, among the pluralist/intuitionists are those who value participation of the people involved in the program. Generally, this participation consists of collecting the viewpoints and opinions of various people about the program or policy at issue. The evaluator faithfully records and portrays their viewpoints. In this manner, the principles, criteria, and weightings of the people involved are used to judge the program. Of course, in selecting and emphasizing some aspects and viewpoints at the expense of others, an inevitable occurrence, some of the evaluator's own principles come into play.

In portraying the judgments of various groups associated with the program, this latter approach is pluralist not only in the philosophical sense of judging on the basis of several principles but also pluralist in the political sense of representing different political interests. Of course, the judgments of the participants and the evaluator are almost always intuitively balanced.

The pluralist/intuitionist theory of justice is the most common-sensical of all, but it leaves the evaluation subject to whatever principles and weightings the judges, whoever they are, happen to employ. At one extreme, it threatens total command of the judging process by professional principles and at the other extreme, a complete relativism in which everyone's opinion is presumed to be as good as everyone else's. Neither extreme would seem to coincide with what most people identify as justice.

Justice-as-Fairness

The most recent of the modern theories of justice is that of Rawls (1971). Rawls has suggested two principles of justice by which social institutions and arrangements can be judged. Rawls calls his conception "justice-as-fairness." Unlike utilitarianism, "justice-as-fairness" assumes that there is always a plurality of ends and a distinctness of persons so that one cannot conflate all desires into one system. An agreement by which the good can be distributed and by which disputes can be settled is arrived at first. Then, once the principles of distribution are agreed upon, individuals are free to determine their own good and to pursue it—but always in accord with the agreed-upon principles which determine what is right.

In defining how these principles are arrived at, Rawls uses the hypothetical construct of "the original position." Assuming that all people are morally equal beings and are accorded fair treatment (and do not know what social disadvantages and advantages they will have in the actual society), what principles would they willingly agree to in order to define justice?

Rawls's general conception of justice is this: "All social values— liberty and opportunity, income and wealth, and the bases of self- respect—are to be distributed equally unless an unequal distribution of any, or all, of these values is to everyone's advantage" (Rawls, 1971: 62).

The specific principles of justice for institutions are these:

First Principle

Each person is to have an equal right to the most extensive system of equal basic liberties compatible with a similar system of liberty for all.

Second Principle

Social and economic inequalities are to be arranged so that they are both:

(a) to the benefit of the least advantaged, consistent with the just savings principle, and

(b) attached to offices and positions open to all under conditions of fair equality of opportunity [302-303].

It is clear from these principles that justice-as-fairness limits other ends. It puts boundaries around the things one may do. One does not take desires and aspirations as given. Rather, desires are restricted by the basic principles.

Justice-as-fairness specifically precludes imposing disadvantages on the few for the advantages of many. The priority rules for the two principles of justice specify that the first principle always has priority over the second. Basic liberties are to be maximized without regard to social and economic benefits. Only then may social and economic inequalities be allowed. According to the second principle, these inequalities are allowable *only* if they benefit the *least* advantaged in the society. Inequalities are not allowable if the least advantaged are not benefited. Nor can there be any trade-offs of basic liberties for social and economic advantages.

The second principle, the "difference principle," singles out the position of the least advantaged in society to judge whether inequalities are permissible. For example, if high salaries are necessary to attract people to positions that would benefit the least advantaged, then the inequalities may be permissible. (This judgment is in contrast to the "efficiency principle" of utilitarianism. The efficiency principle allows redistributions of primary goods only to the extent that giving to one social group does not take away from another group. This puts heavy emphasis on the existing order of things. A structure is maximally or optimally "efficient" when it is impossible to make some better off without making others worse off. In Rawls's scheme, justice-as-fairness is *prior* to efficiency as a principle in this conception. One maximizes the long-range expectations of the least-favored position subject to the restrictions imposed by the first principle.)

Assuming for the moment that one accepts Rawls's theory of justice, of what import is it to evaluating, if any? Clearly, the two principles are so abstract so as not to determine evaluation. On the other hand, as an important distributive mechanism, it seems reasonable that evaluation might attend to justice-as-fairness. The basic liberties protected by the first principle are political liberties, freedom of speech and assembly, liberty of conscience and freedom of thought, freedom of person and property, and so on.

In addition, the most important primary good, according to Rawls (p. 440), is self-respect. Without self-respect a person will not see that his own plan of life, whatever it is, is worth pursuing. He is cut off from a basic meaning in life. A major argument against utilitarianism is that some may be forced to give up their expectations in order to benefit the general utility. Having to involuntarily lower their expectations for the sake of others reduces their own basis of self-respect. This is not permissible in justice-as-fairness.

The first principle might be applied to evaluation in two ways: in what the evaluator looks for and in how the evaluation is conducted. The basic liberties are guaranteed by the first principle, including the right to self-esteem. For example, a major complaint of those who oppose testing in particular is that test scores lower the self-esteem of many children in school. Not only do critics claim that tests are racially and class biased, but radical economists (Bowles and Gintis, 1972-1973) contend that tests are used precisely for the purpose of legitimizing the hierarchial structure of the social-class system so that even the lower members of society feel they deserve to be where they are. A lowering of expectations is built in.

Whatever the general truth of these charges, in justice-as-fairness these are serious concerns and the proper concern of the evaluator. Often it is easier to determine the worth of a *particular* practice, and that is closer to the evaluator's actual job. For example, sending a child home with his I.Q. score pinned to his coat, now a practice in some large cities, may be repugnant to even die-hard testers. Other practices, such as beating children to raise test scores, are usually ruled out—even if they raise test scores dramatically. There are certain things that cannot be done in the name of the common good.

Applying the two principles presumably reduces, but by no means eliminates, intuitive judgments. After one has decided that self-respect is a right that takes precedence over other considerations, whatever the program or sponsors want, one is still faced with applying the principle. This entails a series of intuitive judgments, and the evaluator's job in applying criteria to specific circumstances remains a difficult one.

Nonetheless, choosing primary criteria to apply over most other criteria (unnatural though it is to those of us raised in an empirical tradition) provides a moral base that is more helpful than might first appear. Sometimes the insights are informative. For example, if everyone has a right to self-esteem, it also follows in a just society that those least advantaged cannot violate the self-esteem of those better off. Self-denigrating activities are not allowable. This assumes, of course, that the self-esteem of those better off is not based on the lowered esteem of those worse off.

If the information is injurious to the self-respect of the person involved, it should not be included in the evaluation report—no matter how it affects the good of the project. The rights of the individual are to be protected over the good of the project. Only in the case of trading off this right for another equally important right could this principle be violated. Of course, at issue in a project would be the *total system* of basic equal rights of all concerned. A despotic director infringing on the self-esteem of others would not have to be treated so gingerly. Trade-offs of basic rights are permissible.

After the first principle is applied fully, one turns to the second principle. The essence of the second principle is that social and economic inequities are just only when they are arranged so as to benefit the least advantaged in society. A "representative man" from the least-advantaged sector must prefer his prospects with inequalities to his prospects without them. The social structure is judged from a particular social position—that of the least advantaged. The disadvantages of those lower in the social structure cannot be justified by the advantages that may accrue to the rest of the society, as would be permitted in utilitarianism. Of course, this judging must be done consistently with the first principle. One cannot trade off basic liberties for social and economic benefits.

As with the first principle, the second principle might be applied in two ways: as a criterion for the program and as a criterion for the evaluation itself. In the Illinois Gifted Evaluation, we kept in close touch with the program staff and were quite fair on the basis of the first principle. In retrospect, the major weakness was that we did not investigate possible deleterious effects from grouping talented children together. We did investigate the effects on the gifted children themselves, but we did not investigate the effects on nongifted students nor consider the broader social impact on the class system. Admittedly, these are not easy questions to resolve, partly because they have not been asked often enough. But they should have been addressed more than they were.

In justice-as-fairness, inequalities in natural talents are recognized but are not regarded as necessarily entitling one to greater material expectations in society unless they are used to benefit those less well off. For example, one might allow greater recompense for physicians in compensation for the training they endure and in expectation that attracting more talented individuals to medicine would benefit those least advantaged as well as everyone else. But one is not entitled to great expectations simply because one has greater natural talents. In a sense, the contract arising from the "original position" is an agreement to share fortune and misfortune as in a family. Members of a family do not maximize their good fortune at the expense of the least-advantaged family member.

What difference might the second principle of justice make in an evaluation? Consider Coleman's equality-of-educational-opportunity study (Coleman, 1966), essentially a liberal attack on a social problem. Although not strictly an evaluation, Coleman's study was an attempt to assess the lack of equality of educational opportunity, a kind of needs assessment on which government policy was constructed. Coleman was presented with the problem without any clear conception of what equal opportunity meant. As Ennis (1975) notes, one's conception depends on what one means by "education" and what one means by "having an opportunity." Coleman chose education to mean academic education and among five conceptions of opportunity chose "equality of results" as measured by a vocabulary test.

The study presumed a single measure of utility. The mode of analysis was multiple regression analysis with background and school variables regressed against the test scores. From this Coleman reached the conclusion that schools were not redressing inequalities as reflected in test scores. Presumably, basic skills as reflected in test scores were what blacks needed for equality. Socioeconomic and racial isolation was deemed to be the primary problem and desegregation was seen to be the answer. Busing was the tactic.

As analyzed by Ennis (1975), much of this was implicit in the letter of transmittal which identified racial isolation as the major deterrent to educational opportunity and in the conception of equality held by Coleman and the government authorities. I would add that the conclusion also was implicit in the methodology of the study and the theory of justice within which it was formulated. Ennis (1973) noted that a causal chain of reasoning is only partly empirical; the other part is value. Values enter in determining where one might interfere to make a difference. Liberals might see busing as an answer but reject family interference while conservatives would approve neither. Ennis noted, "What he apparently did was to select factors for study, changes in which he thought (1) would not violate some set of values (at least mostly his), and (2) might make a difference. He then did an empirical study of these factors in an attempt to see which ones did make a difference."

By this approach the researchers determined the measure of utility and those factors they found acceptable for interference that might affect it. The empirical part of the study was in determining which of the predetermined factors would affect the predetermined ends. Even the analysis was subject to value judgments in the determination of which variables should be entered first in the stepwise multiple regression. By entering background factors first, the covariance attributable to background-school interaction was not attributable to the school. In addition, the residual error can be attributed to almost anything else, e.g., "luck" in Jencks analysis (Levin, 1972). I do not believe the Coleman study was poorly done; but even though highly quantitative, it was *necessarily* full of hidden value assumptions.

The Coleman approach closed off several other available policy options. It neglected entirely the attitudes, if not the interests, of the groups most intimately involved in favor of a general measure of utility. In this case, desegregation led to busing black children to schools of white ethnic groups who were only slightly above the blacks in social and economic status and to busing white children to ghetto schools. This threatened the ethnic whites' own precarious position. Coleman has now questioned busing (1975) and has said about his original study: "It is clear that for this purpose to be achieved, there should have been far greater attention to the reactions of whites with the economic means to move." The viewpoint of these people was not considered in the study.

There was even a greater omission, however: Neither was the viewpoint of blacks considered—and these were the people who the desegregation policies were supposed to help. Black viewpoints—or white ethnics' viewpoints—could conceivably have suggested alternative policies for social justice. Not only were the governmental policies removed from the influence of those most affected, the needs assessment study did not reflect their viewpoints and interests. However noble the intents of the policy-makers, the approach was heavy-handed in its paternalism.

In this case, those who paid the highest price for the social reform were the blacks and the white ethnics—the two least-advantaged groups in this setting. In a sense, the gain for the blacks was attempted at the expense of those who were most naturally antagonistic to them and who had the most to lose. The social groups who formulated and implemented the policy were substantially removed from being affected by it.

There was one additional injustice. Within the educational system, the costs of desegregation were borne most heavily by the least advantaged—the children, and particularly the black children who were subjected to the ravings of the racists. Even within its own terms, the original study proved inadequate because where desegreation did occur, test scores were not necessarily increased (Coleman, 1975). Apparently, important factors were excluded from the causal analysis. Finally, above everything, the approach kept control outside the hands of those at the bottom.

A pluralist/intuitionist approach to the problem might have collected the viewpoints of everyone involved. It would not have established predetermined ends nor eliminated alternative causal possibilities without inspection. In addition, a justice-as-fairness approach would make certain that the viewpoints of the least advantaged were given priority over the others. After the problem was examined from the viewpoint of the least advantaged, the next priority would be given to the second least advantaged—the white ethnic groups in this case.

Using Theories of Justice

None of these dominant theories of justice is entirely satisfactory as a basis for evaluation. Utilitarianism comes closest to being the official government philosophy. Where possible, government officials try to reduce everything to common measures of money. Cost-benefit analysis is the ultimate mark of this approach, and a concern about money is often a sign that the evaluator harbors this theory of justice. There is much to be said in favor of utilitarianism. It does provide a strong criterion by which public decisions can be made and justified. Its major weakness is that it tends to favor the upper classes over the lower and leads one to judgments that do not always square with one's moral sensibilities. Employing utilitarian measures often leads to oversimplification in results, as in the Follow Through evaluation.

The pluralist/intuitionist theory of justice is most consistent with every-day, common sense notions of justice. Most people employ multiple principles in arriving at judgments and balance these principles intuitively. The principles employed vary from person to person and from situation to situation. The principles used to judge the justice of taxation policies are not necessarily the ones employed to judge the justice of salary schedules. This squares with commonsense and everyday usage, but is it sufficient for evaluation of public programs?

Would one be satisfied in knowing that one evaluator would employ one set of principles but another evaluator a different set in evaluating a particular program, especially if the program were one's own? The very cornerstone of justice is the notion of consistency, the notion that similar cases be treated similarly. Consistency seems to be threatened by such an approach. At one extreme is the threat of relativism—that everyone's principles are as good as anyone else's. Hence, any judgment is as good as any other. This seems to make something of a shambles of evaluation. Politically pluralist approaches that use the judgments of involved groups as the ultimate criteria for the evaluation are threatened by this possibility.

At the other extreme of the pluralist/intuitionist approaches, principles derived entirely from professionals are not likely to gain full acceptance by the public. A teacher's notion of treating her students justly may not square with the parents' notion. Which does the evaluator employ? Few people would be willing to let those who run the railroads have sole control over how that should be done. Similarly, professional approaches to evaluation in which professionals evaluate other professionals, whether they are teachers, surgeons, or engineers, have lost credibility over the last decade. The public has lost confidence in the professionals regulating themselves. It would seem that people are not willing to leave judgments of justice, which are essentially decisions about distribution, entirely to others.

In the most modern theory of justice, Rawls has provided a theory which is more egalitarian than utilitarianism and more absolute and determinate than intuitionism/pluralism. Rawls thinks it squares better with common sense. But justice-as-fairness has its own difficulties as a theory. Many criticisms have been made of it. One of the most common is that the absolute priority of the first principle over the second means practically that the difference principle would never be applied. Others claim that even the smallest advantage to the disadvantaged would justify taking everything away from the advantaged.

Nor is justice-as-fairness always consistent with one's intuitive thoughts about justice. Justice-as-fairness provides only for consideration of the disadvantaged; it does not make special provision for their participation in deciding their own fate, a direction I find highly desirable. The most telling logical criticism for the evaluation of public programs is that the collective good cannot be derived from individual wants in the way that Rawls does. The individual good is not equivalent to the collective good, an idea I shall develop in the next section of the book.

Nonetheless, my own judgment is that justice-as-fairness is superior to utilitarianism as a theory of justice, which is not to say that utilitarianism is worthless. Justice-as-fairness is deeper in moral sensibility. I would prefer a pluralist/intuitionist conception of justice over either, but only one in which certain values are specified. I will argue in the next section that an appropriate theory of justice would take into consideration the values of moral equality, moral autonomy, impartiality, and reciprocity, as well as the aggregative principle of utility.

This judgment is not a universal denunciation of all utilitarian thought in evaluation. There are many instances in which utilitarian thinking is appropriate and does not lead us astray. For example, an evaluation of a plan to maximize use of hospital beds may revolve around the notion of efficiency to the exclusion of most other considerations. It is when there are other pressing considerations that utilitarian thinking goes awry.

Generally, as I have suggested at the beginning of this chapter, one's theory of justice does not determine the type of evaluation one does. There are too many other factors influencing an evaluation than that. One's theory operates implicitly and subtly. If one is a utilitarian, one will be led repeatedly back to considerations of utility and money. If one is a political pluralist, one will be led to portray the opinions of different groups about the program. If one is a Rawlsian, one will be led to considerations of the rights of individuals and the interests of the disadvantaged. If one is a neo-Marxist one will be led to uncover social and economic inequalities in the situation. One's implicit conception of justice is in the long run significant.

I suspect that each person's conception of justice is far more varied, idiosyncratic, situation-dependent, and incoherent than the great theories I have discussed here. Only a few people have the ability to articulate a coherent theory of justice; their names grace the backs of books. It is not necessary for the evaluator to subscribe to one of these grand theories (each of which is deficient) or to articulate his own. What is professionally responsible is for the evaluator to use these grand theories as signposts telling us where we are and where we want to go. They serve as guides for our direction.

Part III

PRINCIPLES OF EVALUATION

Thus to respect another as a moral person is to try to understand his aims and interests from his standpoint and to present him with considerations that enable him to accept the constraints on his conduct.

John Rawls,
A Theory of Justice, 1971, p. 338

7

DEMOCRATIZING EVALUATION

The Politics of Choice

Historically, in Western countries the liberal state preceded democratic government. The liberal society was conceptualized as a competitive market in which the individual was free to make the best bargain for himself in almost any endeavor. The basic liberal idea was that the social system be organized on the principle of freedom of choice. "Liberal democracy is the politics of choice" (Macpherson, 1965: 33).

> The essence of liberalism . . . is the vision of society as made up of independent, autonomous units who co-operate only when the terms of co-operation are such as make it further the ends of the parties. Market relations are the paradigm of such co-operation, and this is well captured in the notion that the change from feudalism to the liberal apogee of the mid-nineteenth century was one "from status to contract," and that subsequent developments reversed the process once again. Contract provides the model even for unpromising relationships such as political ones, where laws benefit some at the expense of others. The system as a whole is said to be beneficial to all, so everyone would agree in advance to its existence [Barry, 1973: 166].

Liberalism was indeed liberating. From the seventeenth to the nineteenth centuries, it freed people from custom and authority. It substituted impersonal contract and market relationships for status ones. Although the freeing-up process created great inequalities of wealth as a by-product, this inequality was perceived as an inevitable and reasonable trade-off. Inequalities were not new.

In these liberal societies, even government was made more responsive by placing it in a market situation. It was conceived as a supplier of political goods from which consumers selected their preference. Alternative political parties were held responsible to the voters by the procedure of elections. Thus, government was kept responsive to the interests of the electorate, but the electorate was by no means democratic. Initially, it was a small elite of wealthy, upper-class males. Choice in government was offered only to this elite, and government was responsive to this elite's interests.

Democracy came haltingly. Through the mechanisms of free speech and assembly, the lower classes demanded voting rights. On the basis of equal individual rights and equality of opportunity, they asked for rights and liberties similar to those attained by the upper classes. Within the logic of liberalism, it was unfair for them not to have a choice in government and thus represent their own interests. Once enfranchised, the lower classes used the vote not to overthrow the upper classes but to take a competitive position in serving their own interests.

The liberal form of democracy was substantially different from the nonliberal forms which later emerged in communist and developing countries. Both the communist and developing countries rejected the idea of the market society. The communist societies saw democracy as rule by or for the common people. The proletariat would rule en route to a classless society. There was little room for liberal freedoms.

Developing societies, by contrast, often rejected both the market and class-based ideas and saw democracy instead as rule by the "general will" of the entire people of a country. Instead of contested elections, a single political party often dominated government in its pursuit of the general will, there being little basis for competition of political parties in a traditional and nonmarket society. In these three distinct political societies, choice had a different meaning.

Thus equality was a fundamental idea, but in the liberal democracies it remained entwined with ideas of choice, competition, and the market society. Even though those liberal ideas became more democratized through extending the franchise to diverse groups and through extending the range of public decisions, the principle of choice also remained fundamental. As a basis for guiding evaluations in these liberal democracies, I propose the principle of *equality of choice,* a principle which combines both equality and choice.

Although consistent with the two fundamental ideas of liberal democracy, equality of choice is significantly different from the purely liberal position from which much policy and evaluation now tacitly proceed. The purely liberal principle of choice would require that choice be maximized without regard to its distribution. The liberal democratic principle of equality of choice requires not only that choice be maximized but that it be distributed somewhat equally. Liberal democracy becomes not only the politics of maximizing choice but the politics of distributing it.

Liberal Democratic Evaluation

The concept of a formal, public evaluation procedure to aid in making choices about public programs and policies is in itself derived from the liberal notion of choice. Insofar as it has reference to the lower classes or to every citizen, it is also democratic. Choices about programs and policies are often made on the basis of private preference and private interests. There is nothing in liberal evaluation (in maximizing choices) to prevent it from being used for private ends.

One can evaluate as easily for a king as for the public, and there is nothing in the liberal notion to prevent this. Indeed, evaluation for private interests would be encouraged. In its most strident form, the evaluator would evaluate in the interests of whoever paid for the evaluation. Such liberal evaluation would be judged by utility to its audience, whoever that audience might be. But evaluation of a public program transforms a choice into a deliberate *public decision.* Service to private interests cannot be the ultimate criterion for the evaluation. Utility cannot be the primary value. Liberal democratic evaluation would recognize a societal and public interest beyond the private interests of individuals.

All the major modern approaches to evaluation assume freedom of choice. They also assume an individualistic methodology, a strongly empirical orientation, and a free marketplace of ideas in which consumers will "buy" the best. All are liberal in that they are based on the idea of a competitive, individualist, market society. They differ considerably, however, in what choices will be made, on who will make the choices, and on the basis upon which the choices will be made. In other words, they differ in their democratic tendencies.

In practice, evaluation can be further democratized by extending evaluative choices to all groups and by extending public evaluation to all public choices. This can be accomplished by expanding the type of data collected, by focusing evaluation on higher levels of decision, by extending audiences and reference groups, and by extending choice to include the method of evaluation itself. These moves would be directed to advancing the principle of equality of choice in evaluation, just as equality of opportunity is advanced in the larger society.

The fundamental notion of equality is to take everyone (or one's designated group) as a single reference group. If people are treated differently, one must justify the different treatment by strong principles or reasons (Barry, 1965). Evaluation necessarily proceeds from a point of view which includes some particular reference group. The reference group is the range of people the evaluator takes into account in making his evaluation. More precisely, the reference group is the group of people whose interests cannot be ignored.

The reference group must be identified preparatory to the evaluation. It may or may not be identical to the audience for the evaluation. For example, the evaluator may direct the evaluation to key government decision-maker, yet hold a disenfranchised group as the reference group, the group whose interests are considered. The reference group need never have heard of the program or the evaluation being conducted in its interest.

The reference group can be very small, such as oneself and one's family, as when one buys a car. Or it may be very large, such as consumers, as in some public program evaluations. While the fundamental notion of equality would suggest taking every single person as the reference group, this would put a rather heavy demand on each evaluation. The proper reference group for an evaluation, I would suggest, are all those who are affected by the program or policy. This limits the range of consideration as a practical matter and allows special consideration for groups who are differentially affected by a program or policy.

Interests

Modern evaluation is not a social decision procedure unto itself but is part of a social decision procedure for allocating resources. It anticipates some kind of situation in which social decisions are made. In this process, the role of evaluation is limited to rational persuasion on the basis of common principles and values.

Evaluation entails manipulating facts and arguments in order to assess or determine the worth of something. A set of principles or values serves as the basis for making judgments. The criteria employed may be as few as one, such as the utilitarian's criterion of maximizing utility, or be a mixture of criteria with no previously determined priorities, as in the pluralist position.

In making political judgments in a liberal democracy, there are two types of principles or considerations: want-regarding principles and ideal-regarding principles. Want-regarding principles take people's wants or desires as given and suggest how these wants shall be satisfied or the want-satisfaction distributed, without making judgments about the wants themselves. Ideal-regarding principles, on the other hand, specify that some wants are better than others and should be encouraged by public action. For example, the desire for the arts may be considered more important than the desire for sports and hence be accorded public support (Barry, 1965).

It is characteristic of liberalism that public decisions are made primarily on the basis of want-regarding principles. Wants are accepted at face value for public purposes, with no judging of one as more worthy than another. Only want-regarding judgments are implemented publicly. Of course, individuals are free to pursue their ideal-regarding judgments in their private lives.

Liberalism considers as legitimate only those wants arising apart from the influence of the state. Since no people are considered to have better taste and judgment than anyone else, everyone's opinion is considered to be equal for political purposes. The only criterion of goodness becomes want-satisfaction (Barry, 1965). By contrast, non-liberal positions judge certain wants as being more important than others and as worthy of public support. A perfectionist or a Marxist believes that certain human wants deserve to be satisfied but not others. The ideals for judgment are included at the beginning. Sometimes the expressed wants themselves are questioned as to their authenticity. This suggests the possibility of nonliberal evaluation.

Within the liberal tradition, however, wants are taken as expressed, and the question becomes one of either aggregating or distributing want-satisfaction. Aggregative principles are those which apply to maximizing want-satisfaction, the key idea being the pursuit of one's "interests." Distributive principles include concepts such as justice, fairness, equity, equality, and freedom.

The basic aggregative principle is that of maximizing want-satisfaction. To say that one is included in the reference group for an evaluation is to say that one's "interests" have somehow been taken into consideration in the evaluation. A program or policy is in a person's interests when it increases his opportunity to get what he wants. In other words, "interests" represent generalized means to whatever ends a person may have. Presumably, one can protect or increase a person's interests, e.g., his wealth or power, without knowing what his ultimate ends are (Barry, 1965).

By this account, people can also mistake their own interests. They may want a program or policy which will not produce the result they expect, a situation where evaluation may be particularly helpful. Or they may deliberately choose a program or policy opposed to their own interests. Generally, the concept of "interests" serves as a useful guide to the amount and distribution of want-satisfaction, and hence as a practicable index for evaluation. It is often implicitly used in this fashion.

The concept of "interests" is also comparative. A program or policy is in someone's interest only when compared to another program or policy or compared to the status quo. People may agree on the results of a particular program or policy without agreeing on whether it is in a particular group's interest. Since people may deliberately or unconsciously compare the program to different competitors, the standard or class of comparison changes and ultimate judgments about the program's success may differ.

Much dispute in evaluation is over the class of comparison for the program or policy, and not over the actual empirical results. (See Glass's and Scriven's dispute over the utility of some instructional audio tapes in Appendix A.) Whether the program or policy is in the reference groups' interest hinges on choices of a comparison, a choice often concealed in the discussions of methodology.

Many leading evaluation theorists implicitly assume that the purpose of evaluation is to help decision-makers or the reference groups themselves determine the relevant interests of various groups (Cronbach, 1979). If the evaluation is to do this, the interests of the reference group must be represented in the evaluation somehow. The general principle is that the interests of all those affected by the program or policy should be included in the evaluation, although how this is to be done is open to question.

In a purely liberal evaluation, wants are taken as given, each want counting one as a candidate for satisfaction. There is no attention to the derivation of these wants by particular groups or social classes. Thus there is the apparatus of "needs assessments," which are usually collections of wants. Insofar as they require people to judge programs directly, they ask for immediate judgments of interests. These surveys are almost always class-biased because of their sampling of respondents and their methodology. They solicit information on instruments containing categories of middle-class professionals (House, 1973).

By contrast, nonliberal evaluations would be based on judgments about certain wants and interests. The most common deviation is that of the professionals who harbor strong sentiments about what an ideally educated person should be. Sometimes this ideal is in conflict with publicly expressed wants for education. An evaluation may incorporate many of the professionals' ideal-regarding judgments. Or the evaluator may be guided entirely by the notion of public sentiments. Of course, the professionals' judgment may be superior to the public's on many issues.

Another ideal-regarding possibility is to promote the interests of particular classes, such as the lower classes. Such an evaluation would be based on an explicit ideal conception of what society should be like, and the evaluation would incorporate values and criteria derived from this particular view of society. Certain things would be designated as important in advance. Nonliberal, ideal-regarding approaches do not necessarily promote choices.

The view advanced here is that of equality of choice. People should be given a choice so that things are not determined for them, even in their own interests, but choice should be distributed in such a manner that social groups and social classes have equal opportunities for making such choices. Lower social groups should be given an opportunity to determine the choices in their interest.

The Public Interest in Evaluation

If one is concerned with the interests of one or a few people, that is a "private" interest. While nothing prevents evaluation from representing purely private interests, it is difficult to see how the evaluation of public programs and policies can be so restricted.

Almost always, public programs and policies are concerned with the interests of a large group of people, such as the handicapped or disadvantaged or gifted. At the local level these may be the interests of a particular school or group of students in a town. This is a "special interest." Although many government programs concern special interest groups, even more common is a program or policy that involves the interests of two or more groups jointly. A handicapped program involves not only the students, but their parents and teachers and employers as well. These groups may be said to have a "common interest." In a liberal democracy most government programs are advocated by separate special interests but are the result of a coalition of common interests. Evaluators are usually faced with a program or policy representing several interests.

Evaluation itself may be conceived as a policy resulting from a common interest. Parties to the evaluation agree that all will gain from an evaluation. The evaluation will determine if the program at issue meets certain criteria. Even though one of the parties to the evaluation may not like the results, and may actually have its interests damaged by them, the evaluation as a whole can still be said to be in the common interest.

Finally, there is the "public interest." This is the interest that people have in common as members of the public, the "public" being not some definite persons but an indefinite number of "non-assignable" individuals (Barry, 1965). The public interest may or may not be stronger or worth more than a private, special, or common interest, but it is differently shared.

Suppose that two special interests, e.q., the automobile manufacturers and unions, reached an agreement in their common interest requiring an increase in the price of automobiles. What about the interests of those people not a party to the contract, particularly the consumers? The public interest covers the interests of those nonassignable members of the public who will be affected by such an action. In this sense, the membership of the public is not fixed but varies with issue and context. Often the public is identified with consumers, who generally want more and better goods for a lower price. However, it is not difficult to imagine an issue in which consumers may be in conflict with other segments of the public like environmentalists.

How then can the public interest be defined? The resolution is not as simple as an individual weighing and balancing his own net interest— several different individuals are involved. In this case, the public interest is often defined as the sum of all interests involved. This is equivalent to maximizing want-satisfaction without regard to distribution. An alternative is to advance only those interests that people hold in common (where shared interests exist) and to ignore divergent interests.

Different evaluation approaches represent interests in different ways. I have previously classified the eight major approaches to evaluation into two major groups—the utilitarian and the pluralist/intuitionist. The utilitarians try to arrive at an overall judgment of social utility based on a single dominant principle or criterion, that principle being the aggregative one of maximizing want-satisfaction.

The utilitarian group is further divided into a *managerial* subgroup which takes managers as its prime audience and/or reference group and a subgroup which takes consumers as its audience and/or reference groups. Within the managerial subgroup, the systems analysis approach construes social indicators, such as standardized test scores, as surrogate measures of social utility, which is equated with the public interest. Any social group's interest is presumed to be advanced by increasing its scores. Where interests conflict, all interests are summed. Presumably, maximizing test scores maximizes want-satisfaction. The public interest is further construed as the most score increase for the least money. The "best" program delivers this.

The behavioral objective approach represents interests in its definition of objectives. If the objectives are maximized, or the established minimums achieved, the public interest will be served. The evaluator measures the objectives. In the decision-maker approach it is presumed that the decision-maker's official position represents the public interest. The evaluator's task is to provide the public with information to improve its decisions. Whether the public interest lies in social indices, publicly expressed objectives, or decisions of public officials, all these approaches identify the public interest with the official managerial structure.

Evaluations based on these approaches differ as to whether they take the managers as only the audience or also as the reference group. If they take the managers as the reference group, they serve the interests

of the managers rather than the public. Unfortunately, this happens all
too often. Evaluations are conducted to serve managerial (special)
interests, which is unacceptable even within the theory of these
approaches.

The consumer subgroup sees the public as divided into producers
and consumers. Its audience may be either managers or consumers, but
its reference group is the consumer. The evaluator represents consumer
interests. The model is *Consumers' Union.* Again, the public interest is
often identified as best product for least cost.

The pluralist/intuitionist group evaluates on the basis of many principles, the priority of which is unspecified. It is divided into a professional subgroup and a participatory subgroup. The professionals believe
that those most knowledgable and informed about a field should have
most say in it. The public interest is best served by having experts
decide. Decision-making judgment is in a sense delegated to this group's
superior knowledge.

As long as the professional subgroups see themselves as advancing
the means of publicly defined ends, there is no necessary conflict. But,
of course, professionals have their own strong ideals about what an
educated person should be. Since the evaluation standards are often
professional ones, the standards may differ from public standards. In
this sense, professional evaluations may deviate, for better or worse,
from strict want-regarding principles and employ the professionals'
ideal-regarding considerations. In addition, these standards are difficult
to disentangle from the profession's own interests. Recently, there have
been many attempts, ranging from competency-testing programs to
medical review boards, to assert public demands in these evaluations.

Finally, the participatory group believes that the public interest is
best served by having people participate in the evaluation to some
degree. The quasi-legal approaches solicit the opinions of those involved
with the program and incorporate these, often verbatim, into the
report. The quasi-legal approaches allow participation by having
affected parties present proofs and arguments in quasi-legal proceedings. These approaches are not only pluralist in that several criteria are
used to evaluate but also politically pluralist in that several interests are
represented in the evaluation.

Power Concentration vs. Power Diffusion

It is instructive to compare two evaluation approaches that are extremely different in definition of the public interest, one a power concentration approach, the other a power diffusion approach. The power concentration approach is exemplified by the evaluation policy of the U.S. Office of Education over the past decade (McLaughlin, 1975; House, 1978b). It presumes that the public interest can be best defined by the central government. Representatives are elected, and they appoint a bureaucracy. The bureaucracy defines policy and makes authoritative determinations. It may engage a group of experts to help in this endeavor (Barry, 1965).

In fact, the federal government often acts as if it will decide which social programs are best and has used a variant of the systems analysis approach to evaluate public programs. Social indicators, almost always standardized test scores in education, are used as the index of the public interest. Power and decisions are concentrated in the central government officials, evaluators, and indices.

On the other hand, the power diffusion idea goes back at least to Hume who said, "every man must be supposed a *knave* and to have no other end, in all his actions, than private interest." On this thesis, no one is to be trusted with such power. There must be checks and balances, such as were built into the U.S. Constitution. The power diffusion thesis in education is perhaps best represented by Mac-Donald's "democratic evaluation," the most explicitly democratic of the participatory approaches.

In "democratic" evaluation, the evaluator collects quotations from program participants and faithfully represents their views in the report, which is written as a case study. The evaluator is a "broker" in exchanges of information accessible to nonspecialists. He represents a range of interests and has no concept of information misuse (Mac-Donald, 1974). The evaluator does not make recommendations but rather presents the information to audiences to use as they see fit. Ideally, the evaluator presents the evaluation report to the people from whom he collected the data and lets them veto information they do not wish included.

MacDonald's evaluation seems to envision a decision situation like direct democracy in which citizens discuss and decide issues face-to-face. This, in turn, is based on the classic view of liberalism in which individuals associate directly for their individual ends, without recourse to institutions or government. The individual's choice is maximized. The government, and, in this case, the evaluator, is only a referee.

This view of evaluation compares favorably on some political and moral ground to the approach of the federal government. I have criticized federal evaluation policy severely for failing to include divergent interests, for unfair treatment, and for technical deficiencies in execution (House et al., 1978). Even when properly executed, the supposition that social indicators really represent the public interest is dubious. More often, the evaluations represent special interests. Nor do the unilateral and often arbitrary actions of the government enhance the moral quality of the evaluations.

MacDonald's evaluation approach intentionally includes diverse interests, allows people to represent their own interests, and is based on an idea of mutual consent. MacDonald's concept of democracy seems to be close to that of government with the "consent of the governed," or, in this case, of the evaluated. There are, of course, other concepts of democracy, particularly those having to do with distribution of goods among social classes. Compared to federal policy, which has a way of imposing actions without consent or consultation, a consent-based approach has considerable appeal.

On the other hand, a power diffusion approach (for requiring consent does diffuse power) is not without its own problems. It is somewhat doubtful that direct democracy is possible in an industrialized, mass society composed of fragmented groups. Decisions are usually taken at the group or central level, which may require different information. Of course, one may argue that decisions *should* not be made at such levels, that bad decision-making results. One may also ask whether soliciting the consent of every person to the evaluation results may lead to a common interest among program participants but neglect the public interest. Will valuable information be excluded? Will the evaluation be biased toward the status quo and toward not taking action?

Practically, securing the consent of every participant necessitates very high negotiating costs. It may take an enormous amount of time and energy to negotiate with every person. In fact, several of these evaluations have been delayed and not completed because of this difficulty (Simons, 1977). If bargaining costs are too high, people refuse to participate and pass on unexamined work. Negotiating over results also introduces the possibilities of misuse by unscrupulous persons

(Elliott, 1977). One way of reducing negotiating costs is to bargain with representatives, but, of course, this begins again to concentrate power.

A final difficulty in such procedures is the information cost (Barry, 1965). In collecting and conveying information from groups to decision-makers, small articulate groups may be at an advantage. Large, amorphous, inarticulate groups, like the public or the lower classes, will find it very costly to formulate their viewpoints. Hence, even though total information available for decision-making increases, that information may well be biased toward special interests rather than the public interest. Power diffusion may actually enhance the influence of special interests (Barry, 1965).

Of course, all approaches to evaluation have difficulties. I emphasize these problems to demonstrate there is no panacea even in a democratically conceived evaluation. MacDonald's "democratic" evaluation is weak on representing social class interests but introduces an extremely important moral idea into evaluation—that of mutual consent. Mutual consent is manifested in choice. I would prefer that consent be exercised in the evaluation agreement rather than in the results, however.

Distributive Principles

It is inevitable that people's wants and interests conflict with each other, and necessary that some resolution of these conflicts be made. Whereas aggregative principles take into consideration only the amount of want-satisfaction for a reference group, distributive principles like equality, justice, and fairness are used to judge the way want-satisfaction is distributed among members of a reference group (Barry, 1965). Or, more accurately, the principles are used to judge the *procedures* by which allocative decisions are made.

Social decision procedures by which conflicts are resolved become critical in a liberal society. In liberalism there are few substantive matters on which everyone agrees, so that decisions cannot be expected on the basis of results or some ideal pattern of distribution, e.g., to everyone as equal share. Rather, they must be justified on the basis of the procedures used, of which public evaluation is one. Distributive principles usually apply to the decision procedures rather than to the decisions themselves. Evaluation I would conceive as a fact-finding or "value-finding" procedure preparatory to an actual allocation procedure. It is a decision procedure only in that it publicly determines a state of affairs on which other decisions may be based.

The fundamental notion of equality specifies that all people be considered as part of a single reference group. Assuming that the reference group has been narrowly or broadly defined, how are things to be distributed among them? A more forceful consideration is that of distributive equality. The "strong" interpretation specifies that a good is to be divided equally regardless of any personal characteristics of people in the reference group. The "weak" interpretation is that only *opportunities* for satisfying wants should be equal. The weak form, for equal opportunity rather than actual sharing, is the ideal held in liberal societies. Hence, it is easier to argue that the interests of all relevant groups should be included in an evaluation rather than that their interests should be equally met. Only opportunity is provided.

Inequality of opportunity arises from unfairness in procedures or in background conditions. When proper procedures are not followed or when irrelevant factors like race or social class affect decisions, then the procedure is unfair. Presumably, fair procedures and background conditions lead to equality of opportunity.

In evaluations, groups rightfully complain not only of their interests not being represented in an evaluation but also of biases arising from improper instruments, analyses, etc. Procedural and background fairness become extremely important in a social situation in which one has an opportunity to enter a competition for want satisfaction but in which one must compete against other interests to win.

How the distributive principles apply is dependent on the particular social decisions procedures employed. Barry (1965) identifies seven "pure" types of social decision procedures: discussion on merit, combat, chance, voting, bargaining, contest, and authoritative determination. Different evaluations anticipate different types of social decision procedures.

It is somewhat difficult to see how evaluation can feed into a decision procedure like combat. One may imagine combat as a metaphor for political maneuver and bargaining, but actual combat (imposing one's will by force) would be rare. It usually becomes either bargaining or contest. Likewise, chance as a determination procedure is rare. Voting can be imagined but is seldom used. That leaves bargaining, discussion on merits, contest, and authoritative determinations.

Both bargaining and discussion on merits may be part of negotiations. But bargaining narrowly conceived is a situation in which one party offers another an advantage or disadvantage in return for the other party performing some action. Much social decision depends on bargaining, but that is not evaluation's role. One can imagine an evaluation being used as a threat in a bargaining situation, but it is difficult to envision any moral basis for evaluation that uses threats and material inducements in its design. The role of evaluation should be limited to persuasion in the social decision process. This is a critical issue that marks the boundary between politics and morality, and one to which I will return. To have any moral authority evaluation cannot be conceived as bargaining. Its results are not purchasable by threats or inducements.

This leaves discussion on merits, contest, and authoritative determination as legitimate decision procedures that evaluation should anticipate. Discussion on merits sets out to reach an agreement on the morally right division of goods. Agreement is reached on the basis of what is in the public interest, what will produce the most want satisfaction, etc. There are no threats or inducements. If agreement is reached, then the parties have changed their minds about what they want. Even if one party had the power to change things, it would not want to. By contrast, in bargaining, each party tries to get everything it can by virtue of its power. Through discussion on merits each party becomes convinced that the solution is the correct one. This would seem to be the ideal social decision procedure for evaluation.

Sometimes the discussion on merits will hinge on a question of who is better at something. To settle this the original question may be replaced by a contest, such as a competitive examination. The original question of merit is not settled but is replaced by the question of the contest, which can be more easily, and perhaps more objectively, settled. Evaluations employing comparative experiments and planned variations are such contests. Since the resolution depends on comparative achievement, all parties must know in advance what the criterion of achievement is. And, of course, in order to be fair the result must be an accurate index of the quality which the contest is supposed to be measuring (Barry, 1965). Evaluators call this validity. For example, in the Follow Through evaluation, set up as a contest, there was considerable doubt as to whether the contest measured the quality it was supposed to. In this sense, it was unfair (House et al., 1978).

Finally, there is authoritative determination. When the parties cannot agree, they may call in someone to settle the dispute, someone all parties recognize as a legitimate judge. The parties set up an arbitrator.

In authoritative determination, the arbitrator determines the result on the basis of the merit of their cases, whereas in a contest, the contestants themselves decide the issue on the basis of the skills and competencies at issue. The determination procedure needs an arbitrator to decide the result, whereas a contest needs an umpire to see that the rules of contest are followed. Again, in Follow Through the federal government acted as referee, determining the rules, then acted as an arbitrator by declaring the winner. These are incongruous roles.

Although most evaluators would hold that discussion on merits in which all parties come to an agreement on the basis of the results is the ideal social decision procedure, perhaps most evaluations involve authoritative determination. The evaluator, or government officials, or a group of professionals declare the decisions. Of course, even in these situations, discussion on merits usually precedes such a declaration, although discussion is limited to a select group of discussants.

Adversary evaluations which incorporate a jury or judge actually model themselves after legal authoritative determination procedures, thus forcing resolution. Other evaluations, like some of the case study approaches, try to prolong and enlarge discussion on merits by prohibiting authoritative determinations on the part of the evaluators. Others encourage the evaluator to enter his explicit interpretation of events into the social decision procedure. Actual decision procedures are mixtures of these pure types.

In order to be seen as legitimate and as constituting equality of opportunity, these social decision procedures must be seen as being *fair*. A fair decision procedure enhances equality of opportunity. A fair evaluation enhances equality of choice. Fairness is a comparative principle (comparing one's opportunities to others') which applies to the decision procedures themselves.

Procedural fairness requires that the prescribed formalities actually be adhered to. In fair discussion on merits there are usually no such formalities (though there may be rules of discussion) except that there must not be coercion or inducements. Otherwise, the procedure degenerates into bargaining. In a fair contest, the rules, whatever they are, must be followed, and a fair authoritative determination must follow the procedures established for it. Background fairness is a refinement on procedural fairness and requires that the parties involved have a correct initial starting position. In authoritative determination, there is also the consideration of whether the arbitrator correctly applies the relevant rules. Correct application of a rule leads to consistency, a basic requirement for justice.

All these considerations of fairness lead to the "right" result in the decision procedure. Together they constitute equality of opportunity. In general, fairness of decision procedure is critical in a liberal society because procedures are all that people do agree on and not the results. Furthermore, when one agrees to such a procedure and accepts benefits arising from it, it is only fair that one continue to adhere to the procedure even in circumstances where it is not personally beneficial (Rawls, 1971).

Evaluation as a Moral Decision Procedure

Evaluation can be construed as a social decision procedure, although I believe more accurately that it is part of a complex mixture of decision procedures. This mixture varies from one social context to another. Evaluation rarely actually decides social issues, though it may. Most often it feeds into another decision procedure in which the actual allocation of goods is made. The way the evaluator envisions this ultimate decision procedure is important.

As the fact-finding and "value-finding" part of a chain of decision procedures, evaluation itself anticipates and takes on features of these procedures. Insofar as it is construed as a discussion on merits or a contest or an authoritative determination, it is subject to similar considerations of fairness. The extreme concern with methodology, with "due process" as it were, reflects the criticality of belief in proper decision procedures.

Much of the actual definition of "proper" methodology is derived from professional and technical communities. Through their methodologies, technicians try to eliminate "bias," that is to insure reproducibility of results. However, reproducibility of results does little to insure that the evaluation is democratic or morally acceptable.

Reproducible results may be reprehensible from a democratic or moral point of view. The positivist methodology, based on reconstructed physical science, misleads the evaluator here. It may be that the government official, anticipating a severe challenge to his authoritative decision-making, strongly urges the evaluator to employ his "hardest," most scientistic methods to bolster the government's authority. But the engaged evaluator will find, belatedly perhaps, that reproducibility is inadequate in this realm.

Democratic theory holds that in order to be acceptable, a policy must reflect and respond to the interests of the members of the community (Care, 1978). Democratic decision procedures are designed to absorb and articulate these interests. As a decision procedure in a democratic society, so must evaluation. But even this may be inadequate. Would a procedure that accorded every person an equal share or automatically assigned resources heavily to the lower classes be considered fair? I think not, at least not in a liberal society, though one may envision a society in which such procedures would be fair.

Not every procedure or policy reflecting members' interests is necessarily a moral one (Care, 1978). Such a procedure or policy may result from a bargain or compromise in which inducements or threats were employed. This is not morally acceptable for an evaluation that presumes to provide a basis for discussion on merits. How then is an evaluation procedure to be construed as fair or morally acceptable?

The answer again lies in choice, in giving the parties involved some say in the evaluation itself. Participation in the design of the evaluation procedure itself offers a way of establishing moral acceptability (Care, 1978). Moral acceptability I take to be closely related to moral autonomy and consent. One cannot impose one's will on someone else. Voluntary agreement to a decision procedure I take as morally binding one to that procedure even though one may not like the results of the procedure. However, not every agreement is morally binding.

Care (1978) has advanced the notion of "procedural moral acceptability" such that participating in an agreement makes the results of the agreement morally acceptable. When persons engaged in the agreement reach certain standards and fulfill certain conditions, the results are morally acceptable, as in following the rules of a game. Following Care I have outlined the conditions necessary to make an evaluation agreement a fair one (see Chapter 8).

In other words, the parties involved in an evaluation reach an agreement or understanding in advance as to what the evaluation will do. This agreement serves as the basis for judging the evaluation to be a fair one, just as adherence to the rules of a game make the playing of it fair. But not any type of evaluation agreement will do. The agreement may be only a bargain. In order to confer moral acceptability, the agreement must be reached under certain conditions which guarantee that participants will be able to identify their real interests in the matter. There are twelve such conditions necessary for a fair evaluation agreement.

Whether these conditions can ever be fully met is an interesting practical question. In any case, they provide a moral ideal against which an evaluation may be assessed. To the degree that an evaluation agreement fails to meet these conditions, it cannot be said to be a fair and morally binding agreement. Hence, it becomes suspect as a guide to the fairness of the evaluation itself.

Thus, a fair evaluation agreement is one possible way of insuring equality of choice. The agreement may be entirely informal and unwritten, yet it partakes of the "contract" idea. In a society conceived as a collection of independent, autonomous individuals who cooperate only for their own ends, the essence of liberalism, the contract is a means by which individuals voluntarily place themselves under obligation. The social contract is as firm a moral basis as liberalism has to offer.

FAIR EVALUATION AGREEMENT

A few years ago Daniel Stufflebeam, Wendell Rivers, and I contracted with the Michigan Education Association and the National Education Association to do an evaluation of the Michigan Department of Education Accountability system (House et al., 1974). As a panel of evaluators we knew our assignment would be very difficult politically no matter what our conclusions were. One side or the other would likely be unhappy, and perhaps both.

In two days of negotiating with officials from the associations, we attempted to protect ourselves as best we could by arriving at an explicit agreement with them. We were especially concerned with the degree of freedom we had to conduct our evaluation; we were also concerned that our work not be open to censorship by the associations if it proved to conflict with their interests.

As we discussed our assignment among ourselves, Stufflebeam was in favor of putting our concerns into a written agreement rather than leaving them unspecified and ambiguous. I was not enthusiastic about a

AUTHOR'S NOTE: This chapter was published as Ernest R. House and Norman S. Care, "Fair Evaluation Agreement," *Educational Theory*, Vol. 29, No. 3, Summer 1979. Reprinted by permission.

written document at the time since I felt that I would do as I thought proper anyway, document notwithstanding. Stufflebeam proved to be right on this issue. He wrote the agreement we eventually signed, and the agreement proved valuable not only in defining our relationship to our sponsors but also in demonstrating that relationship to outside audiences. (A copy is attached as Appendix C.)

I have come to the conclusion that such agreements are critical to an evaluation and that they influence to an important degree what happens in the evaluation. Stake (1976) has organized the opinions of various experts as to what should be included in negotiating such evaluation agreements. The question I wish to address in this paper is: what constitutes a *fair* evaluation agreement? that is, when is an evaluation agreement fair to the parties who are affected by the evaluation and to the evaluators themselves?

Fairness Characterized

Fairness itself, of course, is a long-standing subject of interest to those concerned with practices, systems, and institutions. In the context of the present discussion, fairness is to be considered as related to obligations that arise from expectations, such as those generated by rules or regulations, either explicit or implied. The *principle of fairness* holds that a person is obligated to do his part as defined by certain institutional rules when he has voluntarily accepted the benefits of an arrangement or taken advantage of its opportunities to further his interests (Rawls, 1971). The basic idea is that when a number of persons engage in a mutually advantageous endeavor according to rules, and restrict themselves in order to benefit all, those who have submitted to the restrictions have a right to a similar acquiescence on the part of those who have benefitted. One is not to benefit from the efforts of others without doing one's fair share. Violations of this principle are considered *unfair*.

Rawls (1971) put two restrictions on the obligations that arise from fairness thus understood. First, the background institutions must themselves be *just*. I will not discuss this restriction here, but its force may be illustrated in this way: if a slave fails to deliver his worldly goods to his master, as (let us say) they have agreed that he should, one would not necessarily view the slave as being unfair to the master since the general institution under which the agreement was made is patently unjust. On this view one cannot be bound to unjust institutions. The second restriction, according to Rawls, is that obligations arise from *voluntary* acts such as promises and agreements, even though these voluntary acts may be implicit or "tacit," as in the case of acceptance of benefits from an arrangement.

The obligations in question may be distinguished from "natural duties" which are independent of institutions and of social rules. For example, one may have a natural duty to help others who are in jeopardy, regardless of prior agreements or institutions. If one did not provide such help, people would not say one was being unfair. Perhaps "unnatural" would be a better term. Natural duties may override obligations of the sort I have in mind. At times, evaluators may have to resort to their consciences rather than to their contracts.

Even though obligations may arise from voluntary acts such as promises and agreements, these latter acts may be tacit. For example, one type of tacit agreement might involve material expectations for performing one's job. If one performs one's job according to certain expectations and one is not appropriately rewarded, one feels unfairly treated. The contents of the obligations are defined by the rules or promises which specify what one is to do. The obligations are owed to specific individuals cooperating in the arrangement in question.

The possibilities for misunderstanding in the evaluation of educational programs are many, and it is advisable to spell out specifics in evaluation agreements, even though complete specification may not be possible. Stake (1976) has suggested five major areas of concern for negotiation: the purposes of the evaluation, its audiences, the methods of inquiry including reporting procedures, confidentiality, and options for continuing negotiations. He offers a thirteen-point checklist of topics to be pursued in negotiating an agreement.

It remains, however, that an evaluation agreement might be reached that is not fair to the parties concerned, no matter how fully articulated or specified. The agreement might be unfair to some group involved in the negotiation or to some group affected by the evaluation itself. The fact that agreement is reached is not by itself a sufficient condition of its fairness. Thus we may ask: what are the conditions under which the fairness of evaluation agreements is secured, or at least contributed to?

Some Conditions of Fair Agreement

Norman S. Care (1978) has explored the question of what, in general, are the conditions under which policy agreements among persons are morally acceptable, and his investigation, without claiming completeness, yields a group of twelve conditions that must obtain for an agreement to be considered fair. These conditions are somewhat arbitrarily classified in such a way that some of them are viewed as applying to the persons making the agreement, others to the agreement itself, and others to the procedures employed to reach the agreement. In what follows I will elucidate these several conditions briefly, offer some remarks concerning their satisfaction in the case of the Michigan evaluation agreement mentioned above, and comment generally about their satisfaction in the context of evaluation agreements concerning the review and assessment of educational programs. The aim of doing so, again, is to secure a better understanding of what it is for an evaluation agreement to possess the moral dimension of fairness. There are, of course, other dimensions (or values) at stake in such agreements, notably efficiency and effectiveness. But in the present discussion attention is focused on the value of fairness only.

(1) *Noncoercion.* In the first place, then, fairness requires that the participants in the effort to reach agreement not be coerced. This is to say that the participants must not have special control or influence over each other. This, it may be noted, is in contrast to collective bargaining agreements in which the coercion of one side by the other is an integral part of the negotiations. But, in general, bargains (according to Care's view) are not necessarily fair agreements—even when such bargains are mutually acceptable to the parties to them.

Care's general account recognizes three types of coercion. First, participants must not be coerced by other individuals who have special power over them. Second, groups and factions must not form among the participants for the exertion of pressure. Finally, the participants must not be coerced by the circumstances in which they find them-selves. It is clear that one may be tempted by all kinds of "deals" when one is in desperate or even stressful circumstances. But the existence of such circumstances, in general, leads us to doubt the fairness of agreements reached in them.

I think it is accurate to say that the Michigan agreement was not coerced in any of these major ways. Neither the association spokesman nor the evaluators were under any pressure to make the agreement, though all parties found it desirable to do so. There was no coercion of one individual by another; there was no coercion of individuals by factions; and the circumstances of neither side were especially desperate. Both groups might have walked away from the project without serious damage to their interests. The associations did not need to have the work done, certainly not by this particular group, and the evaluators were not in dire need of work.

What about the more typical situation in which a government funding agency requires that an evaluation be done? Is this coercive? In most cases, I think not. Although the government agency may require an evaluation, this requirement is itself normally a part of a previous funding agreement between the agency and the recipient of funds. Indeed, fairness itself might require that the evaluation be done if it is called for as part of the original funding agreement.

The situation becomes less clear the more the government specifies the content of the evaluation agreement and designates who shall do the evaluation. The recipient may have little room to negotiate his own interests. Nonetheless, if provision for an evaluation is called for as part of the original funding agreement, and this is properly understood by the recipient, then the requirement is not unfair—unless, of course, the funding agreement itself is not fair. In this latter case we reach the circumstances ripe for coercion and hence for unfair agreements.

Suppose, for example, that a regional educational laboratory is desperate for funds. Perhaps its very existence is dependent upon securing a large government contract. It is much more likely in such circumstances to enter an agreement that its officials, and outsiders, would consider unfair. In evaluation the situation is more typically represented by the hundreds of small private consulting firms that do many of the evaluations for government agencies. Many of these firms are indeed in severe need of money, and they are much more susceptible to coercion in agreements than are more stable institutions.

In fact, the evaluations produced by these agencies are sometimes scandalous, and a major exposé awaits only an investigative journalist with time to spare. The deliberate government policy during the Nixon administration that directed some tens of millions of dollars to small private consulting firms was based on the idea that these firms would be "more responsive" to government agencies. At its best responsiveness has meant a willingness to negotiate important issues in the evaluation—an important and valid idea. At its worst it has meant a vulnerability to government coercion, i.e., a willingness to prepare the kind of study and produce the kinds of results a particular agency seeks. The results, I fear, speak for themselves. Unfair and coerced agreements will produce unfair and biased results.

(2) *Rationality.* A second condition of fairness is that the participants be rational. This does not mean that they must perform unusual mental feats, but rather that they be able to argue from one proposition to another, to give evidence for points of view, and to estimate the consequences of their actions (and take them into account). It seems obvious that people are rational to varying degrees, but, as Care speculates, it may not be necessary that participants be equally rational in order for an agreement to be fair.

Ordinarily, I think, the rationality of the participating parties is not an issue in making evaluation agreements. It may be that people are rational in somewhat different ways. For example, evaluators may typically favor means-ends reasoning and pragmatic arguments rather heavily. Other participants in the agreement may not find such reasoning quite as persuasive as do the evaluators. But I think there will not be significant differences in this area in most cases. (For an analysis of the kinds of reasoning used by evaluators, see Appendix A.)

(3) *Acceptance of terms.* A third condition of fairness is that the parties to the agreement must accept the operating rules that their procedure imposes upon their thinking. The "operating rules" at issue here are those that structure the effort to reach agreement, e.g., in familiar legislative contexts, Robert's Rules of Order, or, in other contexts, perhaps simply the mutually understood constraints of informal debate. In general, the more one has difficulty with the terms by which the effort to reach agreement is to proceed—for example, the more one feels artificially constrained or compromised by them—the less fair the agreement reached may seem to be. We may imagine cases, for example, in which evaluators feel that they should not have to negotiate the content of the evaluation with clients at all. In other cases parties to the proposed agreement may be willing to negotiate certain aims of the evaluation but not the methods. In the Michigan evaluation I believe the terms and procedures of the evaluation were acceptable to both sides.

(4) *Joint agreement.* A further condition of fairness is that the agreement be "joint." This is a difficult condition to formulate clearly,

but the intuitive point is that fairness requires that the agreement be viewed as something more than a coincidence among individual choices. Participants must realize that the achievement of the result requires the agreement of others, and that the result is to be an object of commitment to which allegiance is expected from all members of the agreement group. In other words, one cannot simply state one's position and wait for others to compromise. The agreement is to be thought of as the object of a group effort conducted by members of the agreement group, and not as something to which one may give allegiance depending on current mood. Construing the agreement as truly "joint" in this way may make the negotiations a serious and difficult rather than casual and simple business. Again, the satisfaction of this condition seems a matter of degree.

Generally this condition was satisfied, I think, in the Michigan case, though perhaps to a lesser degree than some of the others. Certain of the evaluators (particularly myself) waivered at times, between operating on their own private principles and committing themselves to a joint agreement. Indeed, one of the reasons I was originally less than enthusiastic about a written agreement was that I felt I would act on personal principles, and that others would do the same, thus making a written agreement beside the point. But I now see the joint explicit agreement as critical in defining expectations and obligations that will determine whether all parties feel they have been treated fairly.

Of course, even when a joint agreement is achieved, it is worth adding that we may still be able to imagine situations in which satisfaction of the conditions of fairness may be less important than the applicability of some other principle. For example, it may be less important to have a fair evaluation (based on contract expectations) than to have a just one, e.g., an evaluation noninjurious to the least-advantaged members of society, or not inconsistent with the cornerstone value of equality. There is an important philosophical question here, concerning whether an agreement satisfying such "procedural" conditions of fairness as those under discussion in this paper could still fail to meet independent substantive principles of justice, perhaps widely and deeply held, such as those just mentioned. This question is recognized here, and touched on below, but not resolved in this chapter.

(5) *Disinterestedness.* This condition is one of the first to come to mind when one reflects on fairness, yet it is perhaps the most difficult

to achieve in practice. In arriving at an agreement, one is not to pay excessive attention to one's own interests. One may advance one's own interests and arrive at a bargain or a compromise with someone else, but the bargain will not necessarily be a *fair* agreement. At the same time this is not to say that one should entirely ignore one's own interests. Rather, one must strive for what we ordinarily call "impartiality" in the attempt to reach agreement. There are various organizational arrangements meant to help achieve impartiality in judgment, and these have been recently discussed by Scriven (1976a, 1976b). On any account, this condition of disinterestedness seems clearly to admit of degrees of satisfaction.

(6) *Universality.* Closely connected to the condition of disinterestedness is the condition of universality. One attempts to arrive at a policy which will affect everyone equally, including oneself. This may be understood here as meaning that if the policy requires that people be treated differently, one would be willing oneself to occupy any of the different positions relative to the application of the policy. Again, the capacity and willingness to discern and pursue solutions which are "universal" in this sense seem a matter of degree.

(7) *Community self-interestedness.* Although one must avoid excessive self-interestedness as an individual, the participants in the effort to reach agreement must select a policy that is best for themselves as members of the group to whom the policy is to apply. Fairness allows self-interestedness of persons as members of the group (and perhaps in different positions within the group) on which the agreed-to result will have an impact. In evaluation this certainly must include the people being evaluated, even though they may not in fact be represented (for whatever reason) in the negotiation between the sponsors of the evaluation and the evaluators. Their interests too must be pursued.

These last three conditions of fairness seem closely related to each other. It may be that the three taken together—individual disinterestedness, universality, and community self-interestedness—provide an account of the moral value of impartiality. Care (1978) suggests that to deliberate impartially is to deliberate without excessive attention to one's own interests, to consider only universal solutions, and to choose in line with one's self-interests as a member of the group which is to be affected by the agreement.

I have argued elsewhere that impartiality is a necessary condition for fair evaluation and that objectivity is an insufficient condition (Chapter 4). If objectivity means an externalized public, repeatable procedure, it is entirely possible that such an objective procedure will be biased toward particular programs. For example, a test based on one curriculum may be biased when applied to a rather different curriculum, even though still objective in the sense mentioned (cf., Walker and Schaffarzick, 1974).

Whereas objectivity suggests a lack of attitude or a neutral attitude, impartiality suggests a capacity to balance (legitimately) different attitudes toward the object being judged. People being judged expect not a lack of concern on the part of their evaluators, but rather the capacity to recognize their concerns and to balance one against the other. For example, in a court trial one would not want a judge from another culture who was perfectly objective in applying irrelevant criteria. Rather, one would want a judge from one's own culture who employed relevant criteria but who was impartial. Care's three conditions, especially the condition of community self-interestedness, capture this feature for fair agreement procedures.

What about the Michigan agreement in this connection? How did it meet these conditions which Care associates with impartiality? One of the strongest protests of the Michigan Department of Education was that the evaluation was "biased" (Kearney et al., 1974). Regarding the condition of disinterestedness, I think the agreement was a fair one. Neither side pushed its own interests excessively. The associations' representatives did not control the evaluation process nor did they have any control over potentially negative results. The evaluators had no excessive self-interests represented that I could discern. The financial rewards were quite modest, and, in fact, the evaluators were aware that certain sanctions might occur if the results were negative toward the state agency. A considerable amount of personal publicity resulted from the evaluation, but the publicity may have been just as great if the results had been otherwise.

I also believe the condition of universality was reasonably met. We would have evaluated any other similar program in the same way and would have been happy to have our own programs evaluated in such a manner. Further evidence of this is that we were able to justify our procedures and results to our colleagues in evaluation rather success-fully.

The third condition of fairness (community self-interestedness) as it relates to impartiality is more problematic. It is true that the associa-tions' representatives were able to choose the evaluators they wanted and those they believed, as judged from previous work, might best represent their group interests, just as government agencies are usually free to choose evaluators for their programs. After reflection on the experience overall, however, I am not certain that the group interests of the Michigan Department of Education were sufficiently represented in the agreement, though such interests were by no means absent from our deliberations. For example, we would not allow an association official to be present in taking testimony unless a department official was also invited.[1]

The situation was made more complex by the fact that our evalua-tion was of the Michigan accountability system, which is itself an evaluation scheme in which (in our opinion) the best interests of the teachers and students in Michigan were not well represented. One of our main criticisms was that this evaluation scheme was not fair under some of the conditions I am elucidating here. Nonetheless, if our agreement is to be criticized on the basis of partiality, I believe it is most vulnerable to the charge of underrepresenting the interests of one of the parties most affected by the evaluation, i.e., the Michigan Department of Education. Failure to represent the interests of those affected by the evaluation is one of the most common evaluation flaws, especially when those affected are not parties to the agreement.

(8) *Equal and full information.* A further condition of fairness is that participants be informed of relevant facts and that they be equally informed. The idea is that some participants cannot be in possession of relevant information that others lack. I would suggest that typically this condition is not fully met. If the evaluator knows that few programs are able to raise standardized test scores under carefully controlled condi-tions, he is required by fairness to inform the client of this in the negotiations, assuming, of course, that it is a relevant piece of infor-mation. Likewise, the client or sponsor should not hide relevant facts from the evaluator. Negotiating a multivariate design with a lay group puts the latter at an uncomfortable disadvantage since they may have only a vague idea of what the multivariate procedures entail. The more

technical the evaluation design, the more difficult it becomes for nonevaluators to reach a fair agreement from their point of view. They enter a realm of mystification.

(9) *Nonriskiness.* Care also argues that the agreement must be "non-risky" from the standpoint of the participants' expectations regarding its implementation. For if the policy to which the participants agree cannot be thought of by them as indeed something that is to be implemented, then it is unclear what has become of their conception of themselves as participants in a joint effort to solve a problem *by agreement.* This condition may present special difficulties for an evaluation agreement because in general an evaluation may always entail some risks, especially for the persons being evaluated. But on the other hand one of the purposes of an evaluation agreement is to *diminish* the risks of the evaluation for those being evaluated by giving them some say in the evaluation itself and by spelling out some evaluation limits. For example, Scriven (1976a) proposes that evaluatees have the right to see a first draft of the evaluation report before it goes to the client and also the right to attach contrary points of view to the evaluation report itself.

Some of the most interesting work in evaluation theorizing is devoted to protecting the evaluatee from incompetent and arbitrary evaluations. While the risk to the evaluatee can be reduced, it would not seem possible in evaluation to eliminate it altogether. In the Michigan accountability system evaluation, for example, there were definite risks to all parties involved; I know of no way to *equate* them.

(10) *Possibility.* Another condition on the agreement is that it be possible to carry it out. While this condition may seem platitudinous, it is embarrassingly neglected by evaluators. It is all too common for evaluators to promise fantastic activities and timeliness for little money—and then not be able to deliver. I do not know what percentage of evaluation projects falls into this category, but it is quite high. Part of this inability is related to inexperience in evaluation and to too much desire for the contract. It is also not unknown for the other party not to be able to deliver on its promises, especially in providing access to data sources. When the agreement is impossible to fulfill, it is not a fair agreement. The other party is then left with commitments for which its expectations are not fulfilled. In the Michigan evaluation, both groups were able to do what they said they would do.

(11) *Count all votes.* For the agreement to be fair, the parties to it must have an opportunity to register whatever they wish to register in the final step of the agreement process. Care suggests, however, with contexts involving compensatory justice in mind, that it may not be necessary for everyone to have an *equal* vote in order to achieve fairness.

(12) *Participation.* A final condition on the agreement is that all parties to it be allowed to participate. Each must be allowed to "have his say" as defined by the procedures. In the Michigan evaluation, both of these last two criteria dealing with procedures were met. All parties to the agreement had a chance to participate and to register their "votes."

Reflections on the Conditions of Fairness

It is interesting, as Care has noted, that only some of the twelve conditions necessary for a fair agreement seem to be conditions on the procedures employed to reach agreement. By far most of the conditions discussed here pertain to the *participants* themselves. This is striking because most of us are tempted to think that a proper choice of *procedures* is what guarantees or justifies an evaluation's being fair. We are led to believe that if the procedures followed are somehow correct, the agreement must be satisfactory. But if the present discussion is on the right track, then apparently many of the conditions involved in fairness are outside the control of procedures in the narrow sense, just as the use of majority rule does not per se guarantee justice in a democracy. Things like the degree of coercion, disinterestedness, etc. of the participants are important influences on whether an agreement reached and the consequent evaluation will be a fair one. This is not to say, of course, that "anything goes" as regards procedures. If proper procedures are followed *and* the other conditions are met, then the agreement should be a fair one. Furthermore, there are various practices designed to reduce partiality, coercion, etc., and to achieve the satisfaction of the other conditions. The point is that procedures by themselves do not guarantee either that these conditions are satisfied or that the evaluation agreement is a fair one.

A second feature of these conditions is that their satisfaction seems in most cases to be a matter of degree. An agreement can be more or less fair, depending upon the degree to which the several conditions are met. There probably are no completely fair or unfair agreements, although the more fully the conditions are met, the more confident we are that the agreement approaches an ideally fair one.

Furthermore, there may always be a basic uncertainty about whether any agreement is fair. As Care suggests, many of the conditions in question here (e.g., disinterestedness, noncoercion) are of a type such that one can never be certain that they are fully satisfied in others or even in oneself. Scriven has suggested that although one can never eliminate bias completely, the object in evaluation should be to reduce it to manageable proportions. Similarly, although one can never be certain one is being completely fair, the object is to be as fair as possible.

What can be seen in the contract itself? In Stake's monograph (1976), several evaluators and administrators who commission evaluations have offered advice on the *content* of an evaluation contract. Some of this content (e.g., purposes of the evaluation, possibility of completion, participation, release of information, confidentiality, information provided by one party to another) pertains to the conditions necessary for fairness. Other advice is not relevant to the fairness of the agreement. Generally, the contract itself gives limited hints as to the fairness of the evaluation agreement.

For example, in the Michigan agreement (attached as Appendix C) it is evident that there has been a negotiation, that the audience and the issues to be investigated have been mutually agreed upon. The evaluators have maintained the right to release the report and the association officials the right to endorse or not endorse it. Resources, a delivery system, and access to data have been agreed upon. Finally, the evaluation procedures themselves are left ultimately in the evaluators' control, but the essential procedures have been mutually defined.

So from the agreement itself one might reasonably suppose, if not strictly infer, that such conditions as those of rationality, acceptance of terms, joint agreement, possibility, and participation have been met. However, not much can be said, based solely upon the document, about the conditions of noncoercion, disinterestedness, universality, community self-interestedness, equal and full information, nonriskiness, and counting all votes. The fact that the evaluators have the right to release their report without censorship is important, for it helps eliminate the problem of self-interestedness on the part of the association officials if the latter had censorship control over the report. Such a procedure in this case reduces but does not eliminate the possibilities of bias. There are other places in which biases can still enter, such as in the self-interestedness of the evaluators. Of course, one can also look for confirmation or disconfirmation of bias in the final evaluation report and in the evaluation procedures themselves.

How Binding Is the Agreement?

This is a difficult question, and may remind us of the problem in jurisprudence of whether citizens have an absolute, prima facie, or no (moral) obligation to obey the regularly established laws of their community. But most evaluators recognize that there is a time when even a fair evaluation agreement should be broken. For example, in difficult situations, such as those indicating malfeasance, when it is a case of breaking a contract or following one's conscience, Stufflebeam says:

> I believe the evaluator should not be the sole decision maker if he has previously agreed to limit his report to certain defined audiences. Instead, I think he must reopen the negotiation of the contract and seek to reach agreements with the other parties concerning whether the information should be released and then should honor such agreements. Of course, there are times when questions of basic morality such as emerged in the Watergate mess present themselves. Then I think the evaluator must do what he believes, based on his own conscience, must be done for the welfare of society and in consideration of the interests of the persons to be affected by the release [Stake, 1976].

I believe Stufflebeam's position represents the consensus of evaluation experts, although not all would agree. Ralph Tyler says, "No one individual's conscience should be accepted as valid. The way in which information will be treated should be part of the contract" (Stake, 1976).

The philosopher's point of view, as represented by Care (1978), is that if the conditions of fairness have been met "as far as one can tell," then one has good reason to accept the results of the agreement. However, it is conceivable that one's rejection of it might be "rational and right" when the satisfaction of conditions such as those discussed above is in question. The less confident one is that the conditions are fully satisfied, the more one may be justified in reserving the right to reject the results of the agreement. In any event, rejection remains a very serious matter, not to be taken lightly or without due cause. Fairness is at issue.

My own interpretation of when one has the right to break a fair agreement is similar to the opinions above. The question of fairness typically arises in the context provided by voluntary agreements entered into for mutual advantage. But where the claims of fairness and justice conflict, justice has priority. For example, if fulfilling a fair agreement means that one must commit an unjust act, then the agreement must give way. Likewise, the claims of fairness are secondary to the claims of natural duties, such as the duty of helping another person who is in jeopardy.

Admittedly, not everyone agrees on specific principles of justice. Within evaluation itself there are several conceptions, as I have indicated elsewhere. The Rawlsian conception would suggest that the principle of fairness operates within the bounds of two principles of justice. Since these principles are very broadly defined, I would not expect much of the actual detail of an evaluation agreement to be determined by them. There are possible areas of conflict, however. For example, if an agreement required the evaluator to violate the self-esteem of someone being evaluated, then the evaluator would have to be unfair in not meeting the terms of his agreement as opposed to being unjust, for self-esteem is a primary good in the Rawlsian conception of justice. In the utilitarian conception of justice, one could not violate the principle of maximizing the net satisfactions in society.

In summary, fairness is an idea that pervades evaluation, almost always at the intuitive level of consciousness. Here we have been concerned with understanding what conditions must be satisfied for an evaluation agreement to be considered fair. Among these conditions are: noncoercion, rationality, acceptance of terms, joint agreement, disinterestedness, universality, community self-interestedness, equal and full information, nonriskiness, possibility, counting all votes, and participation. A fair agreement is binding unless it is in conflict with our natural duties, or with more important moral principles such as those of justice.

NOTE

1. Stufflebeam reports that prior to the time when we signed the evaluation agreement, he went to the Michigan Department of Education, accompanied by his dean, to inform them of what was going on, to ask for their cooperation, and to solicit their point of view. The Michigan officials were upset that the evaluation was being done but said they would cooperate and that they were glad Stufflebeam was involved. Philip Kearney, then Deputy Superintendent of Michigan, warned that Stufflebeam's relationship with the state department might be affected, depending on how the evaluation turned out. It was. In this sense at least, the interests of the Michigan Department of Education were represented in the evaluation (private correspondence).

POWER AND DELIBERATION

Weaknesses of Liberalism

The question of how the public interest and the interests of all parties are to be represented in an evaluation is critical. Utilitarian approaches assume that the public interest is represented by indices of welfare and that governments should take strong actions based on these decisions. Modern welfare liberals believe in a concentration of power within the government, a power wielded on behalf of the public interest or the interests of special groups the government is trying to help such as the disadvantaged.

Since utilitarianism allows the trade-off of lower-class wants for those of the upper classes, total want-satisfaction being the criterion, this approach can be undemocratic, particularly in its failure to represent the interests of those less well off. There is no necessity in this, but in maximizing want-satisfaction, federal policy has not been concerned enough with distribution. Efficiency has been preferred over justice.

The most democratic of the evaluation approaches, the participatory approaches, are pluralistic in two ways. In the first way they bring to bear a mixture of several principles or values rather than a single criterion, as in a strictly utilitarian approach. Second, they represent several different interests, ideally the interests of all those concerned with the program or policy. To the degree that they are responsive to the interests of members of the community, one might consider them democratic (Care, 1978).

Yet even the pluralistic approaches can be criticized in the same way that political pluralism is criticized. Pluralism has been attacked for discriminating against certain kinds of issues. Only the issues advanced by a legitimate group ever emerge for consideration. If an issue is not the special interest of a legitimate social group, it tends to be overlooked. It is difficult to advance issues of the common good, issues that relate to the welfare of the whole society, because there is no particular group to advance these issues. In fact, perceiving society as the aggregate of individuals or groups makes it difficult to identify what the common good is.

In the "referee" version of pluralism, the government acts as a referee, letting individuals work out their own problems but making certain that individuals follow the rules. This is similar to the role of MacDonald's "democratic" evaluator who is a broker between individuals in exchanges of information but who does not directly interfere or make recommendations himself.

The referee version of pluralism has been criticized for favoring strong individuals over the weak and for solidifying the power of those in incumbent positions (Wolff, 1968). For example, as this role operates among regulatory agencies in government, the neutral regulators deal only with the leaders of various interest groups and not with the rank and file members of those organizations. Hence, it is often the interests of the executives, the union leaders, the most influential farmers, etc., which are represented.

The referee's actions in response to the strong often help the leaders consolidate their positions and thus play a conservative rather than a neutral role. Although the rationale of the approach is that every individual's interests will be represented, the free play of opposing forces leads to the domination of the strong—or so the criticism goes.

A similar criticism is made of the "vector sum" version of pluralism. This version conceives of groups rather than individuals as the basic units. The individual represents his interests through his group. Various groups operate to get the government to act on their behalf. The role of the government is to be responsive to these group interests. The eventual action and direction of the government will be determined by the vector sum of these group pressures.

This is similar to the role of Stake's "responsive" evaluator. The evaluator is responsive to groups in and about the program, and the evaluation takes the shape of these shifts in pressures. The evaluator responds to the group interests, opinions, concerns, etc., in the conduct of the evaluation. Like the referee version of pluralism, the vector sum version sees competing claims as legitimate but does not try to decide among these claims.

The criticism against the vector sum version of pluralism is that not every group's interest is considered (Wolff, 1968). The distinction between a legitimate and illegitimate group is a very sharp one, and there is no obligation to respond to "illegitimate" groups. Organized groups are usually recognized as legitimate, but unorganized ones are not. Those with organizing resources and skills are best represented. This also favors smaller groups who can get themselves together more easily. So in practice established groups are favored over emergent ones. Disadvantaged groups that have interests but little power are not recognized. In government action, this version often acts as a brake on social change—or so the criticism goes.

In summary, the participatory approaches to evaluation are significantly more democratic than many other liberal approaches. They offer more choice on a greater number of issues to a wider public. They represent the interests of many groups. However, they are deficient. They have not entirely escaped some of the difficulties of liberalism in general and of pluralism in particular.

Nor would I exempt my own suggestion for a fair evaluation agreement from this criticism (House and Care, 1979). Although offering moral acceptability to participants in theory, such an agreement is likely to be concluded in practice only by the evaluator and sponsor. One of the conditions of a fair agreement is that the parties to the agreement consider the interests of all those who are to be affected by it, but this is an admonition, not a guarantee.

Power and Interests

Most criticisms of liberalism are criticisms that not all interests are equally represented in considerations, usually because an imbalance of power prevents their representation somehow. Lukes (1974) has codified these objections. Liberalism, he says, takes men as they are and applies want-regarding principles to what they prefer. Their policy preferences are manifested by political participation (as in the partici-patory evaluation approaches).

The pluralists assume that "interests" can be understood as actual policy preferences. A conflict of interests is equivalent to a conflict of preferences. Liberals are opposed to the idea that a group's interests can be unarticulated, unobserved, or that people may not be aware of their own interests. As conceived by liberals, interests are "subjective" inter-ests as seen by the parties themselves.

Corresponding to this conception of interests is the liberal view of power, which focuses on individual behavior in making decisions on issues over which there is observable conflict of subjective interests. These interests must be expressed as policy preferences as revealed by political participation (Lukes, 1974). Of course, in utilitarian evaluation approaches participation may be limited to a "needs assessment" designed to collect wants. In pluralistic approaches, interviewing captures more complex policy preferences.

Another conception is that of the reformists. They assert that many conflicts and issues never arise because of imbalances in power. Many issues never reach the decision stage because they challenge the interests and values of the decision-makers. So they are suppressed. There is a conflict between the interests of the decision-makers and those whose interests are excluded from the decision process.

In the reformist view power would entail the capability to define issues and submerge conflicts, not simply to decide conflicts once they arise. Interests are still conceived as subjective interests that can be articulated and observed. Some interests simply never have the oppor-tunity to surface. Hence, the reformists have a wider concept of "interests" than do the pluralists. The reformists consider as legitimate interests not only the policy preferences of those included within the political system but also the preferences of those partly or wholly excluded from it.

The third view of power is that of the radicals. They assert that even the reformist view is too methodologically individualist. Power consists of collective forces and social arrangements, as well as of individuals realizing their wills in the face of the resistance of others. Actual observable conflict is not the only indicator of power since power may be exercised in such a way as to determine what a person wants. Conflict may not be observable. The social system may actually shape what a person wants, and these wants may be opposed to the person's best interests. A person's perceived subjective interests may not be his "real" ones.

Hence, conflicts can be "latent" between the interests of those exercising power and the real interests of those excluded. There *would be* a conflict of wants or preferences *if* those subjected to power became aware of their own interests. To assume that a lack of grievances represents a genuine consensus is to rule out the possibility of a false or manipulated consensus, in the view of the radicals.

Generally, liberals, reformists, and radicals would concur that power should not prevent the representation of interests, conflicts, and issues. They disagree as to the extent that the current social structure actually permits such representation. Both reformists and radicals point to interests that are rarely included within liberal evaluations.

Against the liberal notion they would contend that many interests are excluded from evaluations, particularly the interests of the powerless. The powerless are not able to articulate their interests because they do not have equal opportunity. Covert grievances are ignored. In addition, real decisions are never the subject for public evaluation. Evaluators are left to evaluate only that which decision-makers allow them to, and this will be consistent with the decision-makers' own interests. If the ideal is to represent the interests of all those affected by the program, this ideal is seldom attained or approximated.

Empirically, there would seem to be considerable evidence to support these contentions. Few evaluations represent the interests of any but the sponsors and the most articulate and organized groups. Issues are often defined in advance of the study, thus preventing other issues from arising, and those issues that do arise usually grow from overt conflicts. Even where evaluators conscientiously try to ascertain the interests of disadvantaged groups, they are often not able to do so. For example, in an evaluation involving a bilingual program, we were never able to get Latino parents to meet with us to express their views. There was no problem soliciting the views of the middle-class Anglo parents (Amarel et al., 1979). Assuming that the evaluator knows their interests puts him in a paternalistic position.

Adopting and implementing the radical position is problematic. It requires that the evaluator recognize that people's subjectively perceived interests and wants may not be in their "real" interests. Defining "real" interests is a major difficulty. One definition is that real interests are what people would want and prefer, were they able to make the

choice. Or more precisely, policy X is in A's interests more than policy
Y if A, were he to experience the results of both X and Y, would
choose X as the result he would rather have than Y (Lukes, 1974: 34.)
Real interests are often associated with choice under conditions of
autonomy.

Now it is indeed the case that a person may mistakenly want a
policy that would damage his own interests. In fact, evaluation is a
method for telling whether a program or policy has certain results.
Ordinarily, one wants the *results* of a program or policy rather than the
policy itself (Barry, 1965). Thus it is possible to judge someone's
interests for him better than he can for himself. Of course, this may
also be a dangerous course of action.

Judging someone's interests for him may promote a policy he would
reject on other grounds. In addition, the person may deliberately
choose a policy he knows not to be in his interest simply on the basis of
principle. Even judging the interests of someone on the basis of what he
would want if he knew the results does not fully meet the radical
criticism, however. The wants themselves may be suspect. Thus, it is
difficult to find even a radical definition that would identify what
"real" interests are, although one can see how apparent interests may
be mistaken.

Now in the face of these difficulties, the classical liberal solution is
to "settle" for wants and perceived interests as given. The position I
have taken is that "real" interests may be discovered through a particular form of participation, one which gives the individual choice under
conditions of autonomy (Care, 1978; House and Care, 1979). This
moves toward defining "real" interests or what the individual would
choose autonomously, the radical position, but retains individual choice
itself. The individual can discover his real interests through participating
with others in deciding the evaluation. Real interests are those arrived
at in such a process. This does not satisfy an infallible identification of
real wants but at least provides a method of challenging perceived ones.
Hopefully, the two converge.

Power and Authority

There are several definitions of power. Essentially, A has power over
B when A affects B in some significant way (Lukes, 1974). The

definition of power involved in the last section was that A has power over B when A affects B in a manner contrary to B's interests. Other definitions would tie power entirely to authority and consensus and hence dissociate it from conflicts of interests. Power would then be exercised with legitimate authority.

The definition of power used here, however, differentiates it from authority. Power may involve imposing one's will on someone without his accepting it as legitimate. Authority means that B complies with A because either the content of A's command or the procedure by which A reached it was legitimate. Figure 3 illustrates these differences. Hence, power may or may not be a form of influence, depending on whether sanctions are used, while authority may or may not be a form of power, depending on whether a conflict of interests is involved (Lukes, 1974).

In this conception power is set against influence. Power occurs where there is a conflict of interests. If sanctions are employed, then power becomes coercion (threat of deprivation) and force (no choice) and is not based on authority. One has imposed against the other's will. If sanctions are not involved, then power may be a form of influence. That is, it is exercised within the bounds of agreed-to authority. B complies because A is reasonable, even though there is a conflict of interest. This is legitimately exercised power.

However, there is a problem here from the radical's point of view. The conflict of interest may be latent. B may endorse a policy and see it as legitimate by mistakenly seeing it in his interest. This is power exercised in the form of "manipulation." B doesn't realize what he is doing. This is an important point of departure for the radicals. B is confused over his wants and real interests. Liberals take B's acceptance at face value. Here it is classified as influence not based on authority.

Finally, where there is no conflict of interest, A is exercising only influence over B. This is legitimate consensus authority exercised in terms of B's own values. Influence takes the form of inducement, encouragement, or persuasion. However, of the forms of inducement, only persuasion is open to the evaluator.

The only form of influence or power that evaluation may legitimately use is that of persuasion (Chapter 4). A would cause B to act or think in a certain way because B accepts A's reasons. B would see A's utterances as authoritative because the content is legitimate and reasonable in terms of B's values or because it was arrived at through a

FIGURE 3 Conceptual Map of Power

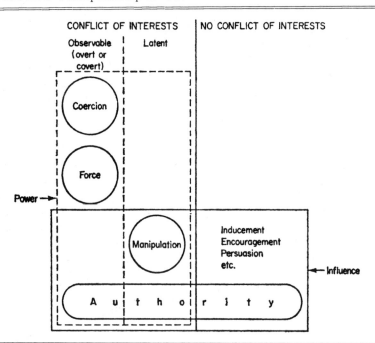

Note: Adopted from Steven Lukes, *Power: A Radical View* (London: Macmillan, 1974), p. 32. Reprinted by Permission of A D Peters & Co Ltd.

legitimate procedure. Force, coercion, manipulation, and inducements are outlawed.

In the sense that A causes B to do or think something he would not otherwise do or think, rational persuasion is a form of power. But in the sense that B autonomously accepts A's reasons for doing so, and changes his mind, it is not against B's will. Hence, it is not power. Rational persuasion is caught between a definition of power based on causality on one hand, and one based on reason and autonomy on the other (Lukes, 1974).

Presumably, radicals would be willing to exercise power over someone in his own real interest, assuming a conflict between A and B's preferences. At the other extreme, one might believe that any or most forms of control of A over B are illegitimate, making B's autonomy an absolute priority. In the first case, an evaluation would proceed by identifying B's real interests and the programs and policies that may lead to it, without B's cooperation. This threatens paternalism, but is the way many government evaluations proceed. Again, presumably, radicals would select different measures of real interests than do government evaluators, but their approaches and techniques, e.g., systems analysis, might be similar. At the other extreme, evaluators would make no recommendations and would try to keep their influence at a minimum. This threatens anarchy, and there are also a few evaluation approaches that advocate this line. Most evaluations fall between these extremes in influence and power but most gather around the paternalistic pole.

What the radical perspective does suggest is that evaluators should be more concerned about the total institutional structure within which the program or policy under consideration is operating and be concerned about the total social context within which the evaluation itself operates. The evaluator cannot rely solely upon the definition of the problem and situation as presented to him by the sponsor or decision-maker. To do so would be to reinforce the status quo, certainly a value position as tangible and as arbitrary as any other, and possibly to advance the interests of the sponsor or decision-maker over those of other people. Such a posture for the evaluator would hardly seem to be either democratic or moral. It makes evaluation a form of force, coercion, or manipulation.

Deliberation

The essence of the reformist and radical critiques of liberal approaches is that power relationships in fact determine what decisions are made. One way of testing such claims is by comparing actual evaluation deliberation to the way such deliberation should occur. Most people would concur that evaluation issues should not be determined by who has the most power. If issues are to be decided entirely by power relationships, there would be little need for evaluation other than as a means of legitimizing decisions that are made on a power basis. Some would contend that this purely legitimizing function is what evaluation does do, but few would contend that this is the role evaluation should play.

Every evaluation approach entails a significant role for evaluation within the decision process. However, every evaluation anticipates a somewhat different decision situation, and this different anticipation accounts in part for the differences among approaches. For example, the managerial approaches envision a few key decision-makers absorbing the results of the evaluation and, interacting with their constituencies, taking decisions which affect many people over a wide area, as in a federal program. The managerial evaluation techniques are geared to providing such an aggregation and summary of data that decision-makers can indeed make such decisions. While power relationships are not totally irrelevant, they are not expected to overwhelm the evaluation.

At the other end of the power concentration spectrum, the participatory approaches envision a decision situation in which participants within the program absorb the evaluation results and come together to discuss and decide, perhaps face-to-face, what decisions will be made. The evaluation information should be comprehensible to such a group, a demand quite unlike that faced by managers.

From the managerial perspective the critical problem is to make the evaluation results credible to physically and psychologically distant audiences. This is done by "objectifying" the data—turning them into reproducible numbers through the authority of social science methodology. In the power diffusion approaches credibility is a different problem. For those quite familiar with the program, the evaluation results are credible if they do not conflict with their experience of the program. The problem is to make the evaluation comprehensible so participants can understand it and relevant so they can act upon it. Again, it is presumed that power relationships will not sweep the evaluation results aside nor distort them for ulterior purposes.

Other evaluation approaches envision quasi-legal deliberations in which adversaries are made equal in power, deliberations in which professionals discuss results among themselves, or situations in which individual consumers act in a market situation. Each of these anticipated decision situations imposes different demands upon the evaluation. What the evaluator anticipates actually shapes the data and the evaluation. But all of them presume that power will not invalidate the evaluation.

What kind of decision situation *should* evaluators anticipate? First, in evaluating public programs, the evaluator should anticipate a *collective* decision, not merely a private, individual one. Even if there is one major decision-maker, he will take action only after a process of deliberation with others and on the basis of publicly justifiable considerations.

An evaluation may be conducted for an individual's private interests, as in the purchase of a car, and up to a point the evaluation process is the same. But it is a fundamental error to construe public evaluation as merely individual evaluation. Public evaluation entails public criteria and values. It must anticipate collective decision processes. A collective decision process is not the same as an individual weighing and balancing criteria in her own net interest. Construing public decision procedures as equivalent to individual procedures writ large is a fundamental flaw of utilitarianism. Selecting the best means to a given set of ends for an individual cannot be the same process when the ends are plural. That necessitates a collective decision process, and for evaluation this means a procedure of discussion on the merits.

There are two polarized schools of thought about such collective deliberations (Barry, 1973). One school holds that one should enter such collective deliberations in order that one might represent one's own interests. After all, one knows one's own interests best and should advance them. Hence, deliberation is a summation and consideration of all group interests.

The other school contends that such a deliberation for the purpose of making social decisions is catastrophic. If each person pursues her own interests, there is no way of arriving at a just decision. Discussion on merit will degenerate into simple bargaining about who gets what. Compromises will be based on coercion and power, not on what should be done. Deliberation under such conditions degenerates into a compromise among interests (Rawls, 1971).

This school contends that the basis of discussion should be a discussion on merits in which each person participates because she has an important contribution to make to the discussion. The discussion is improved by the presentation of alternative views. In such deliberation the discussion hinges on common principles or premises. Each person must adopt a wider viewpoint and be totally disinterested. An exchange of opinions checks partiality. The deliberators must all assume a totally disinterested role or else there will not be just decisions. Such is the pure view of deliberations on action.

Now there is no doubt that self-interest must be somehow restrained if one is to have a rational deliberation in which evaluation results play a role. But such a pure deliberation procedure is so far removed from situations in which people do take action that it seems beyond reach. In the fair evaluation agreement preceding the evaluation, we have suggested certain restraints on interests, but not their elimination. In a deliberation on evaluation results with a view to action, it would seem impractical and perhaps unwise to exclude considerations of people's interests altogether.

An intermediate position between these two poles is that those who share power are capable of carrying on arguments and deliberations based on principles which have themselves as the object of decision (Barry, 1973). But if other groups with distinctive interests are excluded from power, their interests are also likely to be excluded from the coverage of the principles used by the groups in power. Equalized sharing of power is propaedeutic to power relationships not determining results.

In other words, participants can represent interests and still discuss a rational decision on the basis of principles—provided there is some rough balance of power among the participating groups or individuals. At the same time, those excluded will not find their interests well represented. The more equality of power is approached, the more there will be equality of consideration for interests (Barry, 1973).

I propose this modified position be used as a standard for deliberation of evaluation results rather than the pure position in which it is assumed that those deliberating will have equality of power and no interests, i.e., that they will be "disinterested." I propose that the evaluator anticipate eventual deliberation on evaluation results in which the issues will be decided by rational discussion on common principles but not determined by power relationships.

It then becomes the evaluator's obligation to represent *all* the relevant interests in the evaluation. Generally, it will be the interests of the powerless which are underrepresented. If the evaluator is not to serve the dominant power interests in a partial, if unconscious, manner, he must make certain that all interests are represented in the evaluation. The modified position of impartiality, rather than disinterestedness, also allows specially affected minorities who have a greater stake in a program or policy to have a greater influence on the decision since the minority can represent its interests in both the evaluation and the deliberation. This is particularly important because many programs and policies affect people in highly differential ways. The pure deliberation process does not allow such special considerations since representation of interests is not allowed. All participants are disinterested.

The evaluator then should strive for an evaluation in which all relevant interests are represented and anticipate a deliberation of evaluation results in which interests are represented but which is not determined by power relationships. A disinterested, detached evaluation has the anemic characteristic of being irrelevant since it does not represent the interests of those most concerned. What people really desire is an impartial evaluation, one in which group interests are represented, in which groups are treated fairly, and in which the evaluator is not excessively promoting his own interests (see Chapter 8). In this sense, objectivity is insufficient as the basis for an evaluation.

Now, of course, power relationships do exist and play a role in all decisions. The evaluator does not expect his evaluation to totally determine the actual allocation decisions. There are too many other legitimate factors that arise in the eventual deliberation situation. Those who are to take action must weigh and balance the consequences in light of their own interests. The role of the evaluation is limited to informing and persuading the participants of a certain state of affairs.

The evaluator must anticipate a deliberation situation which is not determined by power. What if the evaluation feeds in impartial reports reflecting all interests and some interests are continually ignored? What if decisions are usually taken on the basis of power rather than con-sensual deliberation? To that degree, the radical critics of liberalism are correct. Power really decides the issues, and evaluation is only cosmetic.

Collective Determination of Choice

Implicit perhaps in the notion of deliberation is the idea of collective determination of choice. It is possible, or at least imaginable, to determine matters without resorting to deliberation. One can imagine each individual making up his own mind and voting on an issue without engaging in any discourse with his fellows. The sum of individual decisions would simply decide the issue. No deliberation need occur. Yet there seems to be something fundamentally deficient in such a procedure, in fact something unnatural. Somehow dialogue is needed to justify if not to persuade.

Nothing in the theory of liberalism prohibits a procedure without deliberation. The summing of individual preferences and private interests does not require dialogue. Private interests can be expressed through market mechanisms. Yet there comes a time when it seems necessary to identify the common interest by collective determination. Perhaps the fundamental weakness of liberalism is that individuals are not really separate atoms cooperating with each other only for or even primarily for self-interest. They are members of and products of the society in which they live. They are always embedded in a community and involved in reciprocal relationships.

Liberalism is methodologically individualist in that it reduces all values to states of consciousness in one or more separate individuals. Values are either simple, involving the state of consciousness of one person, or compound, involving the separate states of consciousness of several persons. It does not allow for reciprocal values, values involving a reciprocity of consciousness between two or more people. Reciprocal values are involved in collective choice and in maintaining and being a part of a community of people.

Wolff (1968) calls such a collective deliberation upon goals a "rational community." It is an activity in which politically equal rational agents come together to deliberate with one another for the purpose of arriving at a consensus on collective goals and actions. This is achieved through discourse. The underlying guiding metaphor is that of community.

All discourse involves a reciprocity of consciousness between the participants, but the reciprocity may be between a master and his slave or between a ruler and his subjects. These are reciprocal but unequal. The achievement of rational community requires not only a discourse but a discourse among equals. Free dialogue requires an uncoerced reply. Power relationships distort discourse. Each participant in a rational community must recognize his fellows as rational moral agents and acknowledge their rights to reciprocal equality in the dialogue (Wolff, 1968).

Rational community requires mutuality of awareness of participation. When people come together and experience reciprocal awareness, they have a sense of community. This is in contrast to the classic liberal view of individuals cooperating solely in an instrumental fashion for advancement of their own ends. Community and reciprocity are not fundamental values of liberalism. Liberalism does strive to establish reciprocal obligations through the notion of the social contract.

This conception of deliberation for action is similar to other such conceptions, such as that of Habermas (1973). Habermas envisions a deliberation for action in which those who are to take such action engage in practical discourse conscious of their common interests and knowledgeable about the circumstances and possible consequences of their action. The aim of such discourse is to reach consensus about what they should do.

Theory or scientific understanding feeds into such practical discourse but is always insufficient for determining what the participants should do. Only they can weigh the risks and consequences of their action for themselves. In Habermas's terms neither "theory" nor "enlightenment" can legitimize action. This can be done only through practical discourse.

Similarly, the conception of deliberation advanced here is one in which the audiences for the evaluation are informed by the evaluation results but are not commanded by them nor by the evaluator's recommendations, if these exist. Those who are to act on the results must deliberate among themselves as to what to do. In this deliberation power relationships are excluded, but participants are aware of their interests. These are the circumstances the evaluator should anticipate. He should not anticipate participants acting on his results without deliberation nor a power figure using the results to her advantage. The results are to be used in practical discourse, and the evaluator does his best to achieve that.

The Moral Basis of Evaluation

In sum, I propose that four values serve as the moral basis of evaluation: moral equality, moral autonomy, impartiality, and reciprocity. The fundamental notion of equality is that all people are to be taken as members of the same reference group and are consequently to be treated equally. Moral equality suggests that each person has an equal right to advance his own interests for satisfaction.

Second, moral autonomy suggests that no one should impose his will on others by force or coercion or by other illegitimate means. And no one should be imposed upon against his will. This value is intimately tied to the concept of choice, a basic liberal principle. Presumably, moral autonomy has not been violated as long as an individual chooses what to do (though some would consider this an insufficient criterion). Moral autonomy manifested in choice is rooted in the methodological individualism of liberalism, the primacy of the individual, and the tradition of the social contract.

Third, the conflicts of wants and interests are to be settled *impartially,* that is, by having all interests represented and none favored by whatever decision procedure is employed. Properly understood, impartiality is a moral value. Sometimes, particularly in evaluation, impartiality is confused with objectivity, the pressures for justification of the evaluation forcing such a confusion. Objectivity is easier to demonstrate and may be one way of indicating impartiality, but an objective procedure can be highly partial to a particular interest. That is, one may have an objective (reproducible) procedure that is highly biased. A reproducible result is insufficient to demonstrate impartiality.

The fourth value that I have suggested should provide the moral basis for evaluation in a liberal democracy is not as closely and as necessarily related to liberalism as the first three. Perhaps this is liberalism's greatest moral deficiency. This is the value of reciprocity on which a sense of community depends. One can argue both that reciprocity and community are implicit in human affairs and that they should be.

Liberalism sees society as a collection of self-interested individuals, each pursuing his own end. There are no necessary or obligatory relationships among them other than voluntary ones established for instrumental purposes. Contractual arrangements are introduced to provide some basis of mutual obligations. On the basis of equality, autonomy, and impartiality, each person could advance his own interests, consistent with not imposing on others, and could join with others in settling conflicts among interests impartially. Yet what about the losers in such a procedure? One is intuitively uneasy. The first three values permit the totally disinterested and uncaring attitude of each to all. Each can equally advance his interests for impartial allocation with no sense of responsibility beyond the carrying out of the agreed-upon procedures. A deal is a deal. Winners have no responsibility for losers.

Our moral intuitions rebel at such a conception. In fact, people in liberal democracies often have a strong sense of unease around the social losers. Their presence is disturbing. One way of dealing with this guilt is through altruism, the call beyond duty. This is reflected in heavy voluntary donations to charity in the most liberal countries like the United States. Although liberalism makes slight and reluctant provisions for the losers, people often feel intuitively that they are somehow responsible. Intuitively, most feel they are members of a community. Only a rather weak sense of community can emerge from correctly carrying out rules.

The notion of reciprocity is an ancient idea based on humanitarian ethics: "Do unto others. . . ." Humanistic ethics requires that there be no privileged positions among people. Reciprocity suggests that the relationship among people is one of symmetry, of treating others as one would be treated. Partly this reflects a refusal to take advantage of others even when one has a chance to do so. Whereas equality only entitles one to enter the race for one's interests under fair conditions, even assuming that life is such a contest, reciprocity makes the winners partly responsible for the losers. There is a reciprocal balance between the claims of oneself and the claims of others, between self-interest and altruism.

Arguments based on the principle of reciprocity often result from transpositions of points of view. Sometimes such arguments adopt the point of view of an impartial third party (e.g., an evaluator) in order to eliminate considerations such as status and wealth, which might upset the symmetrical relationships (Perelman and Olbrechts-Tyteca, 1969). This is the relationship to which evaluators should direct their efforts.

> Thus to respect another as a moral person is to try to understand his aims and interests from his standpoint and to present him with considerations that enable him to accept the constraints on his conduct [Rawls, 1971: 338].

The Underlying Conception of Justice

In its most abstract form, the rule of justice "requires giving identical treatment to beings or situations of the same kind" (Perelman and Olbrechts-Tyteca, 1969: 218). This provides for consistency of action, a requirement of justice, but does not specify what the categories of people, treatment, and situations are. The concept of justice must be manifested in a conception of these relationships.

Among the ancients, Plato thought that justice consisted in "rendering to everyone his due" (Diggs, 1974). Society consisted of classes of people (farmers, artisans, warriors, rulers, etc.), and each of these elements should be in harmony. Each should "receive its due" just as elements were harmonized within individuals. For his part, Aristotle conceived a just constitution as one that was in the common interest rather than in the interests of the rulers.

However, the modern conceptions of justice began with the liberalism of Hobbes. Unlike ancient and Christian philosophers, Hobbes conceived humans as self-seeking animals who used their intelligence to advance their own egoistic ends. Influenced by the natural science of Galileo, Hobbes believed that human behavior could be explained by mechanical principles, each person being mechanically geared to seek self-satisfaction (Diggs, 1974). Hobbes constructed a mechanistic epistemology of the senses to explain such behavior.

Since society was a collection of self-interested individuals, a strong sovereign was necessary to check such strong self-interest. Each individual would see it as a "natural law" that all should band together to protect their lives. This was motivated by individual self-interest. The common interest was the sum of individual interests. The state was an instrument for self-satisfaction. Justice consisted in obeying the laws of the sovereign. Hobbes's view was a full expression of methodological individualism. The individual came prior to society itself.

Following Hobbes, Locke reinterpreted "natural law" as including the liberty of each person to do what he wills, as long as it is not specifically proscribed by law and as long as it does not infringe on another person's life or will. These liberties became known as "natural freedoms." Each person had an equal moral right to freedom—a right negatively construed as not being subject to another person's will. The only moral obligation was to natural law or to reason. Even civil laws had to be moral. Government had to be derived from the consent of the governed. The state itself existed to protect liberties. Injustice was infringement on natural liberties. Locke transformed Hobbes's self-interested individualism into individual autonomy.

Hume tried to derive morality from observation and experience but concluded this could not be done. He drew the primary distinction between facts and values. Since morality was practical, it must involve motivation and be derived from values, whereas reason can only determine facts from observations. For Hume justice consisted in living by social conventions that were only conventions but that promoted private and common interests.

Rousseau, on the other hand, expanded greatly on Locke's notion of individual autonomy (Diggs, 1974). Moral legitimacy cannot derive from force or coercion. People are what their government makes them, and moral liberty consists in following laws that one prescribes for oneself. Liberty consists in participation, in actually making and following the laws, not simply in being free from another's will. The participation of all citizens results in the formation of the "general will," which expresses the common interest. Where special interests are in conflict, the common interest takes precedence. The worst injustice is violation of one's autonomy. Rousseau's view is a full expression of moral autonomy.

All these theories of justice required that the common good be supported in opposition to special interests (Diggs, 1974). The common good was generally taken to mean the benefits that one shares with others, as opposed to the ones that only benefit oneself. The objective of government was seen as the common good, and government serving only special interests was unjust (Diggs, 1974).

Implicit in the idea of serving the common good was the notion of impartiality. In particular, justice required impartial administration of the law. No one should be favored. All theories required impartiality — assuming just laws and institutions already in place. All persons should be treated alike when there were no relevant differences. So underlying these liberal theories of justice were the values of equality, autonomy, and impartiality.

However, Diggs (1974) notes a conservative drift in these theories. Aristotle had distinguished between distributive and commutative justice. Distributive justice was concerned with distributions of wealth and other goods among people. Commutative justice was concerned with transactions between people, especially with rectifying the wrong treatment of *one* person by another, as in a trade or a theft. Hobbes rejected distributive justice altogether, so that justice came to be identified with performance of covenant, with commutative justice. Philosophers following this tradition continued to ignore distributive justice.

In the nineteenth century amidst increasing accumulations of industrial wealth, considerations of equal rights seemed inadequate. Distributive justice became a primary concern. Conformity to law or convention seemed conservative as a theory of justice. Attention to what would promote the interests of all became more pressing.

These theories took two directions, one in which the state was called upon to check dominant interests and one in which every interest was given a voice (Diggs, 1974). In contrast to the liberals, who assigned the state a mimimal role in society, the organic theorists, mainly Hegel followed by Marx, saw society as a natural organism and institutions as objectified embodiments of human reason. One could not define human nature apart from the society in which an individual lived, as Hobbes had done. The individual's life was shaped by the social order. Society was conceived as an organism with the individual as a constituent part. The social order was to be judged by its contribution to freedom, i.e., natural self-determination. Marx, in turn, was not enthusiastic about considerations of distributive justice (Diggs, 1974). Rather, he tended to equate justice with the common good. He wanted a social order in which people were free to develop their potentialities.

These theorists reasserted the way humans were bound to their community and the role of the state in shaping individuals. One can discern the ideas of community and reciprocity here. Eventually, these ideas served as the basis for radical critiques of liberal notions. The social order shaped individual wants and interests. In fact, the state had a responsibility for doing so, for making men better.

On the other hand, the utilitarians, such as Bentham and Mill, followed the liberal tradition of methodological individualism. Following Hume, they thought that institutions were merely habits and the embodiment of unreason. Institutions must be subjected to reason. Since rational behavior for one individual consisted in selecting the action that most efficiently promoted the individual's goals, then rational behavior for society consisted in selecting the action that most efficiently promoted societal goals (Diggs, 1974). The methodological individualism of the utilitarians led them to equate collective decision-making with individual decision-making.

Based on the presumed motivation of self-interest in pursuing pleasure and avoiding pain, the utilitarians concluded that providing the most pleasure or happiness for the greatest number of people was the societal goal. Any action that accomplished this was just. Justice consisted in maximizing happiness or want-satisfaction. This became the dominant liberal social philosophy of the twentieth century.

The most recent liberal conception of justice is that of Rawls (1971). Rawls applied the device of the social contract to ask what principles of justice would free, equal, and rational persons, concerned with their own interests, agree to under conditions of fair agreement. Theoretically, each person would be free to advance his claims and to accept or reject the principles, i.e., he would have autonomy. Furthermore, since in Rawls's "original position," no person knows exactly what his social position will be, he cannot bias the results in his interest. Each person has an equal bargaining position.

From this hypothetical situation Rawls logically derives two principles of justice to which everyone would agree. The first principle guarantees equal rights and liberties to all, in the Lockean sense. The second guarantees fair equality of opportunity. Most originally, the second principle states that inequalities can exist only if they are in favor of the least advantaged people in the society. The "difference" principle, it seems to me, is an attempt to introduce the value of reciprocity into the social structure, an idea absent in utilitarianism.

The second principle, in effect, makes the rest of the citizens partly responsible for the least advantaged members of society, something utilitarianism does only in the somewhat gratuitous form of altruism. Rawls's position is methodologically individualist in that he derives his principles of justice from a priori deductions about what individuals would want. From individual considerations, conclusions are drawn about the collective good. Self-interested individuals are the starting point, as in Hobbes.

Many criticisms have been made of Rawls's theory, but one of the most telling is that the collective good cannot be derived from individual wants in such a fashion. In order to decide what principles should apply to a society, one must look at the society as a whole. The individual good is not equivalent to the collective good (Barry, 1974). For example, everyone may want a car, but that is not to say that a society with cars is the best society. One must consider the total society and not only individual wants.

Rawls's theory is an improvement over utilitarianism in that it is distinctly more egalitarian. It advances the value of reciprocity, albeit somewhat indirectly. Nonetheless, it has many logical problems and tends to be paternalistic. None of the theories of justice seems totally adequate as a basis for evaluation.

An appropriate theory of justice would take into consideration the values of moral equality, moral autonomy, impartiality, and reciprocity, although exactly how these are to be balanced against each other is hard to say. Rawls (1971) calls the theory of justice in which there are several competing principles but no a priori order of priority the "pluralist/intuitionist" theory. There is an irreducible family of first principles that have to be weighed against each other and no explicit priority rules for doing so. The weighing is intuitive, though one may be able to describe how one did so in a particular situation.

In the conception of justice I am proposing as the moral basis of evaluation, the four values, or principles based on the values (such as choice), serve as first considerations which must be weighed and balanced against each other in a particular situation. Only when they conflict in a particular concrete situation is it possible to say that one is more important than another (Barry, 1965). None has absolute priority over the others. They may be traded off against each other. There is no single overriding principle. Which principle is most important can be determined only by choices in instances where they are in no conflict (Barry, 1965).

Admittedly, this is an incomplete and rough sketch of what an underlying theory of justice should include. Other values more commonly recognized, such as efficiency, must be included in a full theory, but it is the moral values that are most often overlooked as considerations. If the evaluation of public programs is to be valid, it must contribute to justice in the larger society.

Part IV

META-EVALUATION

But we must also recognize that human beings are capable of bringing to consciousness the interpretations, evaluations, and standards that they tacitly accept, and can subject them to rational criticism.

Richard J. Bernstein,
The Restructuring of Social and Political Theory, 1978, p. 236

10

THE OBJECTIVITY, FAIRNESS, AND
JUSTICE OF
FEDERAL EVALUATION POLICY

Federal Evaluation Policy

In 1965 Senator Robert Kennedy insisted that an evaluation rider be attached to the Title I (compensatory education) section of the Elementary and Secondary Education Act. He felt that the schools were partly to blame for the low achievement of the students and that the new federal funds would not be used to good advantage. The purpose of the reporting requirement was to inform parents, particularly poor parents, how well their schools were doing. Educators would be responsible to their constituencies. Eventually, mandated evaluation was to spread to nearly all federal social programs.

In the same year President Johnson introduced to the federal government the Planning, Programming and Budgeting System (PPBS), already

AUTHOR'S NOTE: This chapter was published as "The Objectivity, Fairness, and Justice of Federal Evaluation Policy as Reflected in the Follow Through Evaluation", *Educational Evaluation and Policy Analysis*, Vol. 1, No. 1, 1979, pp. 28-42. Copyright 1979, American Educational Research Association, Washington, DC. Reprinted by permission. Helpful comments were provided by Gene Glass, Elizabeth Hutchins, and Rochelle Mayer. The work was supported by the Ford Foundation.

extensively employed in the Pentagon. Health, Education and Welfare Secretary John Gardner established a new office entitled Assistant Secretary for Program Evaluation (ASPE). This office was headed by William Gorham, who had had extensive experience in the Department of Defense. His deputies were Robert Grosse and Alice Rivlin. The goal was to "develop programs that could be stated, measured, and evaluated in cost benefit terms." These events are recorded in McLaughlin's (1975) excellent history of the Title I evaluation.

Whereas Kennedy was concerned with the responsiveness of the schools to poor people, the ASPE group was concerned with identifying the most *efficient* approaches to educating disadvantaged children. Operating from a "systems analysis" perspective, ASPE would identify the most effective programs so that allocation of resources would be more efficient. The ASPE approach assumed that one define a "production function" for education, that is, precisely define how a set of inputs, like money or particular programs, were related to a set of outputs, like test scores. One could then specify that only the most efficient educational approaches be used.

The first few years of the Title I evaluation did not please ASPE. The evaluations were done at the local level, and the results were almost uniformly positive. What is more, without a common measure of output across programs, one could not do cost-benefit analysis to determine which of the programs were most efficient. Partly to this end and partly to counter the negative effects of the Coleman report, Rivlin and Wholey of ASPE prepared the TEMPO study, which was conducted by a division of General Electric. The purpose was to see what quantity of resource yields what quantity of gain in a specified test score. The results were disappointing. The study could not discover gains in test scores. Even worse, Moynihan, then on Nixon's staff, used the results of the study to oppose further increases in school aid.

What went wrong? The ASPE staff reasoned that their approach was all right but that the data supplied by the school districts in the study were unreliable. They moved to centralize control of evaluation activities. They would collect their own data to ensure reliability. As a consequence, the Title I national surveys were begun. In addition they decided to convert the Follow Through program, originally a service program to continue the education of Head Start children, into a planned variation experiment.

The national surveys were conducted in 1968 and 1969. The 1968 survey results were as disappointing as the TEMPO study: no gains in test scores. The 1969 survey results were never made public. Secretary Finch of HEW was led to say that educators didn't know how to educate. President Nixon used the results as a reason to block an increase in Title I funds.

The ASPE group was disappointed but undaunted. Alice Rivlin argued that the problem was that social services were not organized properly to answer ASPE's questions of effectiveness and efficiency. Social service programs should be organized to answer the evaluator's questions. Rivlin's solution was for the government to assume more control over program inputs and design as well as over evaluation. Social programs should be designed as planned variation experiments.

The Follow Through program was organized to answer ASPE's questions, organized as a massive experiment. Follow Through classes had control groups to which they could be compared. The idea of planned variation was introduced. If local districts could not design programs innovative enough to produce gains in test scores, then special programs would be used to introduce planned variation into education. Natural variation was not good enough. In the Follow Through program, "sponsors" with special models of practice distinctly different from that of the public schools were brought in to implement new programs. Planned variation supplanted natural variation.

Although the Follow Through program was not perfect for ASPE's purposes, according to Rivlin, it was the only program to come close to meeting ASPE's requirements. "Despite its shortcomings in experimental design, Follow Through is significant as the first major attempt on the part of the federal government to try out different educational approaches in a reasonably systematic way" (Rivlin, 1971).

Federal evaluation policy, as revealed in Rivlin's *Systematic Thinking for Social Action,* took the following form: The key decisions in social services would be made at the higher levels of the federal government. Social services were not now efficiently organized and not much was known about producing such services. The only true knowledge about them was a production function specifying stable relationships between inputs and outputs, and the only way to such knowledge was through experimental methods and statistical techniques. "Information necessary to improve the effectiveness of social services is impossible to obtain any other way" (Rivlin, 1971: 108). In using such techniques, it was possible to agree on goals and on a few outcome measures like test scores. The end of evaluation was efficiency in the production of social services.

In the Rivlin philosophy there was a parallel between producing social services and producing manufactured goods. Similar techniques of analysis would apply, and social programs should be organized to produce data for the analysts. The federal analysts would learn what was correct. It was not necessary to have experience or contact with the programs in order to evaluate them. Furthermore, making this evaluation approach work was a matter of tough management and expertise. Only strong centralized government could do the job.

Such was the dominant evaluation philosophy in the U.S. federal government over the last decade. To find out how it worked in practice, one can examine the Follow Through evaluation.

The Inception of Follow Through

Follow Through began as a program to provide educational services to disadvantaged students in the early years of schooling. In 1967 as a result of funding difficulties, the program received only $15 million rather than the $150 million expected. Within HEW the ASPE group saw this as an opportunity to convert Follow Through into a planned variation experiment to find out "what works." Haney (1977) and Elmore (1976) have documented these events.

In 1967 William Gorham, then Assistant Secretary of HEW for Planning and Evaluation (ASPE), organized the White House Task Force on Child Development. The Task Force staff work was done by members of Gorham's group, including Alice Rivlin (Elmore, 1976: 159). The Task Force work was carried out within a tight budget imposed by the administration. So the emphasis shifted from expensive service programs to less expensive research and development.

The Task Force made twenty recommendations. One called for the use of federal funds to learn how to make education more effective. Another suggested the use of Follow Through to evaluate major variations in compensatory education. The Task Force report concluded that the "one fact that stands out . . . is our lack of knowledge about effective ways of raising the educational attainment of students" (Elmore, 1976). Follow Through would redress a matter of ignorance.

With the full cooperation of the Follow Through administration, the Bureau of the Budget, and ASPE, Follow Through became a planned variation experiment. To Congress and to local sites already operating, however, Follow Through was still defined as a community action and social service program, as it was for parents of the children.

For those developing the early childhood models of good practice, the "sponsors," Follow Through was a development program. One of the original sponsors claimed that the whole idea of planned variation was "mystifying" to the sponsors themselves. "The meeting in Washington of prospective sponsors to present their various orientations to curriculum, the idea that evaluation could be done by a third agency . . . and the assumptions that each sponsor had a complete package to present—all created a feeling of bewilderment and even madness" (Weikart and Banet, 1975). There were few if any distinct and fully developed early childhood models ready for implementation, an assumption of the planned variation idea. Out of necessity the program became one of development for those chosen as sponsors.

During the next several years new sponsors and new sites were added opportunistically to build political support for the fragile program. The big city mayors wanted sites so they got them. California wanted to be a sponsor so it was so designated. This strategy succeeded admirably in securing political support. By the midseventies the Follow Through annual budget had risen to $60 million. But it resulted in grossly mismatched comparison groups within the experimental design that had been chosen for the evaluation. The OE administrators were not too concerned about this, however, since they felt that the test score gains from the early childhood models would be so huge that mismatched control groups would make little difference (Egbert, 1977).

The evaluation got off to a shaky start with a contract to the University of Pittsburgh in 1967. For some reason the Pittsburgh group reported only pretest scores in their final report. The evaluation was reinitiated in 1968 with a large contract to Stanford Research Institute (SRI). The course of the evaluation can be divided into three phases, each phase named after the official inside the Office of Education (OE) and the contracting group outside who most clearly shaped the evaluation during that period. The three phases are the Egbert/SRI phase, 1968-1971, the McDaniels/Huron Institute phase, 1972-1973, and the Evans/Abt Associates phase, 1974-1977.

The Egbert/Stanford Research Institute Phase: 1968-1971

This phase of the evaluation was shaped primarily by Robert Egbert, Director of Follow Through, Richard Snyder, the chief of evaluation, and SRI. It was marked by a relatively expansive notion of what the evaluation should be, punctuated by attempts, usually abortive, to respond to the criticisms of various constituencies.

In Kansas City in February 1968, ninety-one sites were assigned to the sponsors largely voluntarily. In June, SRI was hastily awarded a large evaluation contract in a manner later criticized by the General Accounting Office. At that time, at least theoretically, the evaluation was fairly expansive in what it would investigate. The official list of evaluation criteria was broad (U.S. Office of Education, 1969). It included comparisons of cognitive and affective development, comparisons of children who had been in Head Start; extent of parent involvement; effect on parent attitudes, extent of medical, dental, psychological, and social care; evidence of changes in school programs and responsiveness to low-income children and parents; evidence of attitude changes of participants and their community; and evidence of coordination of community service.

The SRI plans clearly recognized this broad responsibility. "The overall purpose of the evaluation is to assess the impact of Follow Through on pupils, parents, school personnel, members of the community, and the school as a social institution in those settings where Follow Through programs are initiated" (Stanford Research Institute, 1972: 2). SRI also took on as a primary purpose the description of the programs being evaluated. Nevertheless, in the fall, SRI began administering only cognitive tests at forty-seven sites.

In Atlanta in October 1968, the annual Follow Through meeting exploded with protest, primarily from minority groups. They charged that SRI evaluators had a biased view of the program and "were insensitive to the parental and community involvement aspects" (Haney, 1977: 27). The Follow Through administrators were shaken by the virulence of the protests. New minority sponsors were funded, and institutional change became a primary goal for SRI to assess.

As a result SRI initiated several case studies of communities, but these did not fare well (Krulee, 1973: 246-251). The staff was isolated from the rest of the SRI staff, who had backgrounds in psychology and did not understand the case study approach. Gradually, these studies were cut back to "a more realistic level" (Krulee, 1973: 248). A few case studies were eventually reported, but they had no effect on the overall evaluation. According to SRI, each community seemed to be different so generalizations for policy purposes were difficult to make.

By 1971 (after so much fanfare at the earlier Atlanta meeting), the evaluation of institutional change effort was quietly abandoned.

Growing from the community studies as a separate study were the parent interviews, subcontracted to the National Opinion Research Center as an autonomous activity. Sixty thousand interviews were done. These continued for years but had no effect on the final evaluation results. Meanwhile, SRI continued with cognitive testing.

In April 1969, at a meeting in Pajaro Dunes, California, the sponsors themselves attacked SRI's evaluation efforts. They felt that the evaluation was "seriously biased" in its heavy reliance on cognitive measures since many sponsors did not have gains on these measures as a primary goal. "Specifically there was the impression that the cards were stacked, through reliance on measures of cognitive change for those sponsors that were behaviorally (i.e. cognitively) oriented and against all other sponsors" (Krulee, 1973: 219). The resentment had been building for some time, and even the behaviorists agreed with it. The sponsors again emphasized the institutional change goals. SRI publicly recognized the criticisms as valid and promised to redress them.

Three months later, at Palo Alto, the sponsors again emotionally charged SRI with undue slowness in developing noncognitive measures, community studies, parent interviews, teacher interviews, and classroom observation. The SRI staff was split on these issues. Some felt the community studies were not sufficiently "neutral" to use as information. Nonetheless, the sponsors pushed SRI to move in that direction.

As usual, the most emotional issue was that the evaluation was too narrowly focused on conventional cognitive measures, which sponsors thought would judge them unfairly. They were somewhat reassured by SRI's intentions of expanding the scope, though still anxious that they might be judged on the measures then being collected. Partly as compensation, the sponsors were allowed some money to assess their own programs. This pattern of strong criticism followed by assurances, but not much change, was characteristic of all three phases of the evaluation.

SRI did attempt to develop nonstandard measures that would better reflect some sponsors' goals. SRI solicited cognitive test items from sponsors and received 1500 items, the strategy being to develop a pool of test items to reflect objectives common to all sponsors. These items were reduced to 600 and arranged, along with a standard test battery, into 22 forms of eight tests (Haney, 1977: 182). In administering the tests SRI quickly ran into logistics and cost problems. Similarly, SRI tried to develop noncognitive instruments, but after field testing, rejected them as being too unreliable. The SRI staff admitted that it had not clearly recognized the limitations of existing tests nor the difficulties of developing new ones (Haney, 1977: 195). Efforts to develop instruments sensitive to individual sponsors' goals were abandoned.

In 1970, the results from the first data collection showed no positive Follow Through effects and was not publicly released. In May, an OE panel reviewed the evaluation and chastised SRI for failing to compare the models or to evaluate against specific goals. A series of ancillary studies was conducted, none of which had any effect on the ultimate findings.

In February 1971, the Office of Education again asserted its priorities for the evaluation. Richard Fairley, Director of Compensatory Education, visited SRI and complained that SRI's nonstandardized pupil achievement results could not be put into grade equivalents. Fairley's plan was to identify the best sponsors and mandate the use of these models in Title I. This plan required a standardized measure.

Throughout 1971 there were investigations of the Follow Through evaluation by the General Accounting Office, HEW, and even Nader's Raiders. In the summer, both Egbert and Snyder resigned from their positions. In November, Garry McDaniels was appointed Follow Through evaluation director. In four contract years, the Office of Education had spent $12 million on the evaluation.

The McDaniels/Huron Institute Phase: 1972-1973

Under McDaniels's guidance the Office of Education took more direct control of the evaluation. Four months earlier, Laurence Lynn, head of ASPE, had recommended to HEW Secretary Richardson, who was astounded at the evaluation cost, that the program be returned to experimental rigor. The recommendation was drafted by Michael Timpane and Joan Bissell of ASPE (Elmore, 1976: 291-292). McDaniels concluded that new instrument development should be curtailed. He awarded a sole source contract to the Huron Institute led by David Cohen and Marshall Smith. In a memo Smith advised that McDaniels obtain a consensus within OE on the long-term objectives of the evaluation and formulate a design to "maximally" meet the objectives (Haney, 1977: 45).

Jane David of the Huron Institute designed a sampling plan to "maximize the potential for valid comparisons" among sponsors and between Follow Through and non-Follow Through classes and to determine how effective Follow Through was. David's rationale for sampling called for separating the effects of the sponsors' treatment from the effects of the sites. This would be accomplished by including several sites per sponsor. "If a large number of different projects are included for a given sponsor then we can be fairly confident that the remaining biases are not strong." The confounding of model and site effects would be unlocked. This design would prevail.

McDaniels's new request for proposals called for assessment of impact on only a narrow range of the original goals. Faced with mounting costs and scandals, he drastically narrowed the scope of the evaluation in what Haney (1977) called a "funneling effect." The new data analysis contract was let to Abt Associates, who were certain they could employ new statistical techniques to handle the messy and complex data collected under questionable conditions. The basic purpose was to determine "which of a number of different approaches is most effective, under what conditions." SRI retained the data collection.

Working with sponsors to specify their objectives and models was no longer part of the evaluation. In the reorganization McDaniels farmed out tasks to different groups. The Huron Institute drew the sample, SRI continued the data collection, Abt Associates analyzed the data, and a panel appointed by the Office of Education selected the instruments. Instrument development was given the lowest priority although McDaniels offered the sponsors money to work on their own instruments. This softened the blow for the sponsors considerably.

McDaniels convened an OE panel to determine the set of common measures on which the models would be compared. The Metropolitan Achievement Test was chosen because it was "deemed desirable for comparison purposes to have a single instrument which could be used at several grade levels" (Epps, n.d.). The MAT also had adequate psychometric properties. The Raven's Coloured Progressive Matrices test was chosen because the MAT was so narrow and because the Raven's was difficult to coach and hence could not be taught by sponsors. The panel expressed reservations about both tests.

Even stronger reservations were expressed about the two noncognitive tests, the intellectual Achievement Responsibility Scale and the

Coopersmith Self-Esteem Inventory. The panel felt that "no really adequate measures exist in these areas" (Epps, n.d.).

Discontent soon surfaced again. At the annual Follow Through meeting in Denver in October 1972, the parents led the revolt. The parents claimed that they had had no real role in decision-making, planning, or in the evaluation, in spite of appearances (Haney, 1977: 60-61). They insisted that parents be required to evaluate sponsors annually. Their written document said, "We are tired of others deciding when a program is 'not good' or 'good' for us based on their concept of 'data' and their concept of what is 'wrong' with our children and what is needed to correct these 'wrongs.' " It continued, "The burden of being able to measure the kind of program we want should be that of the experts—rather than to design a program that they know how to measure." They demanded that parents be involved in the interpretation and collection of data (Steering Committee, 1972).

The sponsors wrote a supporting document sympathetic to the parents' concerns. Although the flare-up was similar to the one at the Atlanta meeting earlier, the Atlanta meeting had produced some immediate, if temporary, changes. This time there were no attempts to address the criticisms. Haney notes that the evaluation had been effectively isolated from stakeholder politics by this time. In fact, this was the last annual general Follow Through meeting, so there could be no more flare-ups of this type. The sponsors continued to meet periodically, however.

In 1973, two ancillary studies begun earlier were reported. In studying classrooms, Soar (1973) had found that there was not a high degree of consistency within models. Stallings's (1973) study was unique in that it attempted to describe empirically what some of the models were like, an original goal of the evaluation. Although finding systematic differences between Follow Through and non-Follow Through classes, Stallings also found that the models were not unitary treatments. These ancillary studies had no effect on the final evaluation.

Although the McDaniels/Huron Institute phase lasted only a few years, dramatic changes were wrought in the evaluation. The Office of Education took firm control, the scope of the evaluation was drastically reduced to a few standardized outcome measures, and the whole evaluation was transformed from a political to a technical enterprise. The Huron Institute supplied the technical expertise and rationale for the changes.

The Evans/Abt Associates Phase: 1974-1977

The last phase marked the technical execution of the evaluation design by Abt Associates and the complete dominance of the evaluation by the Office of Education. Garry McDaniels was replaced by Eugene Tucker, and the entire evaluation was transferred from the Bureau of Elementary and Secondary Education to the Office of Planning, Budgeting, and Evaluation (OPBE) in January 1974. The real decisions were made by John Evans, Director of OPBE.

When he was in the Office of Economic Opportunity, Evans had been primarily responsible for the Westinghouse/Ohio evaluation of Head Start. In many ways the early evaluation of Head Start was similar to that of Follow Through. The Head Start study was an "impact" study concentrating on gains in the test scores of children, though there was not the planned variation aspect. The Head Start Research Council had fought against the design of that study, making the same criticisms that would be made later when the study was completed (Datta, 1976). They complained about the insensitivity of the design, the difficulty of finding control groups and of controlling biases statistically, the lack of adequate measures of personal and social development, the lack of knowledge about the actual programs, and so on. Evans's group argued that the information was necessary for decision-making and that the biases would cancel each other out. The study was conducted and showed no differences between Head Start and non-Head Start classes. The findings were highly controversial and were used by Nixon to block further increases in funding.

In a move to centralize evaluation operations inside the Office of Education, Evans was brought into the Office by James Abert, Deputy Assistant Secretary of HEW for Evaluation and Monitoring. Both Abert and Evans believed in impact evaluation, i.e., that the effect of a program be judged by its impact on children's test scores (McLaughlin, 1975: 110).

Evans wasted no time confronting the sponsors. At a meeting in Clinton, Michigan, in October 1974, in response to a sponsor push for measuring institutional change, Evans said:

> Evaluation is a horse race; a comparative evaluation of the relative effectiveness of various approaches. . . . It is mushy policy to say that all models made a fine effort, so "take your choice." . . . We agree that the ultimate effects of Follow Through should be that

ten years hence its graduates should have a different life style, with fewer on drugs or in prison. But the problem is, how do researchers deal with this? We have to use the evidence we have, as a proxy chain for these longer term effects.

Decisions, even though largely political, may be influenced by evidence. Congress is often irresponsible in not facing issues. It responds to parents on the steps of the Capitol. But there is still some power in evidence. However, if we find that parents and kids are enthusiastic but the evidence is anecdotal and not persuasive, it would be irresponsible for us to tell other communities to consider the model. Arbitrary judgments will have to be made as to what evidence is compelling enough. The problem is allocation of scarce resources [Report of Fourth Annual Follow Through Working Conference, 1974].

Some of the sponsors at the Clinton meeting suggested that the Office of Education consider alternative evaluation approaches such as anthropological approaches. On this Evans was firm: "I don't agree. The other methodology has a low status as regards quality of evidence. The drift of the social sciences is towards greater rigor. We don't voluntarily embrace inferior approaches." Once again the sponsors protested the narrowness and invalidity of the measures to no avail.

Meanwhile, Abt Associates was proceeding with the analysis of the data. The first two Abt Associates reports were published in 1974 and 1975. The results were not pleasing to OE officials. The reports showed that the effects of each model differed dramatically from site to site. This might make it impossible to say that one model was best. Furthermore, Cline and his colleagues at Abt Associates reported that because the sponsors' samples differed from each other in all possible ways, "we cannot compare effects across sponsors" (Haney, 1977: 212).

The Office of Education response to this news was unequivocal. A new request for proposal (RFP) for data analysis was prepared, and the primary question of the RFP was to compare sponsors to each other directly. Abt Associates replaced Cline as project director, saying that they could compare sponsors. They bid on the new RFP and won the contract the second time to do what they said couldn't be done the first time. Major analysis decisions were to be made only with the concurrence of the OE. Dropped from the new analysis plan was an overall comparison of Follow Through and non-Follow Through. The Office of Education had decided it did not want that comparison, which would certainly show no difference, and concentrated entirely on comparisons of models.

In May 1975, a cost analysis contract was let to Resource Management Corporation to ascertain the costs of each model. When the comparative gains were determined by the main evaluation, the costs could be used to determine the cheapest, most cost-effective model. This analysis was confounded by the fact that each sponsor received the same amount of money per child whereas local site funding varied greatly.

When the sponsors were shown the results of the third Abt Associates report (though not the chapter comparing the models to each other), they were once again upset with the narrowness of the evaluation as well as Abt Associates's descriptions of their models. They organized a protest meeting in Washington in April 1976 and presented Abt Associates and the OE with a long list of criticisms challenging the validity of the evaluation. As usual, Abt Associates promised to do more statistical analyses.

The fourth, final, and major Abt Associates report was accepted by the Office of Education in April 1977. It explicitly compared the early childhood models to each other. The sponsors roundly condemned it. The large intersite variation had forced the Abt Associates analysts to be more cautious in their findings. Each model had good sites as well as bad ones. In fact, the variation within models was so great that the analysts refused to say that one model was better than another, though one could look at charts to see. The analysts said that so-called "basic skills" models were better.

When confronted by a reporter about the primary finding of overwhelming intersite variation within models, John Evans said the variation was "frustrating" but suggested the answer was "not that the world is crazy or that the sites are radically different," but that the models "weren't uniformly well implemented." "When a sponsor is paid to implement a model," he said, "the sites ought to be relatively homogenous." The Office of Education would launch an effort to understand "the puzzling wide site variations" (Education Daily, August 10, 1977). The idea that the same model in different settings would have different outcomes was apparently not an acceptable conclusion.

The Logic of the Evaluation

Each evaluation has a logic of its own, the possibilities of which I have indicated elsewhere. The logic of the Follow Through evaluation was ultimately shaped by the systems analysis approach that has dominated federal policy for a decade. This paradigm searches for the most efficient program and requires that both outcomes and costs be compared in a fairly precise manner. This entails a few common quantitative measures on which the models can be compared to each other.

Follow Through began with a broad set of social goals that it sought to accomplish. Sponsors and parents kept trying to push the evaluation back to those goals but the evaluators and Office of Education ultimately succeeded in reducing the outcomes to a few common measures on which scaled comparisons could be made. For example, even after the program was redefined as an experiment, theoretically, the evaluation could have examined the consequences of each model on a broad scale in each of the nine areas of impact, including institutional change. This might have been accomplished through pragmatic reasoning, judging a model by its many effects.

That was not the reasoning that guided the evaluation, however. Once the dominant question became "which model works best," the pursuit was to determine the model that gave the most effect for a particular cost, not to determine the overall effects. Determining the "best" model forced the evaluation into means-ends reasoning. Given the ends in sight, which model accomplishes it most or with the least cost? That model would be the best.

This is called technical rationality, and it is most prevalent in economics. Inside the federal government it was promulgated by ASPE, OPBE, and the Office of Management and Budget, all of whom had a hand in the Follow Through evaluation. It assumes that rationality consists of lining up clearly defined alternatives and choosing among them in terms of their effect on the particular objective one has in mind. The idea of a planned variation itself is a manifestation of this idea. One must assume that there are both clearly defined ends and means and a cause and effect relationship between them. The evaluation forced the Follow Through program into the technical paradigm.

It was necessary to specify what the ends and means were. Planned variation assumed that there were clearly definable means, i.e., models. The sponsors, as well as the Soar and Stallings studies, indicated this was not so, but the evaluation assumed that it was so, ignoring this conflicting evidence. Models were established by definition, by naming them.

The definition of ends was even more problematic. The program was justified on the basis of pursuing a large number of social ends. But direct comparison would become impossible or at least confusing if a large number of indicators were used. The paradigm assumes simplicity. Comparisons could be made only on common measures, and the fewer of those the better. SRI began with standardized cognitive tests and, reacting to sponsor protests, tried to develop a pool of common test items sensitive to sponsor models. These special tests did not yield standard grade equivalents and became logistically and financially impossible. In fact, there were not a few simple goals in common among sponsors.

With McDaniels's arrival, the OE solved the problem by fiat. It prescribed a set of common ends, four outcome measures. The rationale for employing the Metropolitan Achievement Test was that it could be used for comparison purposes. At his meeting with sponsors, Evans recognized that, ultimately, one wanted to improve the life chances of disadvantaged children but argued that tests were the best proxy measures for success. Cognitive test gain was the dominant end in sight by the evaluators at the beginning and remained so at the end.

Given the necessity for comparing the models to each other, it was also necessary to use quantitative measures, which test scores are. Quantification allows the model effects to be scaled, thus maximizing differences among them and making comparisons seem easier, or at least more legitimate.

Follow Through classes were compared to local control classes by analysis of covariance. That the analysis of covariance technique did not fit the reality of the program very well created problems, particularly for those familiar with the models, who could see that the fit between the quantitative techniques and the classes in the field was not a good one. It was nonetheless employed to facilitate the desired comparisons. The concern for maximizing differences through quantitative techniques was explicit in David's rationale for the sample and in Evan's rationale for quantitative techniques.

Throughout the evaluation both the ends and the models were severely reduced so that comparisons could be made. The sponsors themselves had developed more than sixty instruments to measure their models. And these are reported in an OE volume. But in the final Abt

Associates report there were thirteen models compared on four tests which yielded eleven subscores. Even this was too complex to make easy comparisons. The models were reduced to three types and the outcome measures to three matching indices.

The application of statistical techniques left the analysts with a set of results difficult to interpret. In addition, the results had not come out clearly. There were bad sites even with "good" models. Yet, by contract, the analysts had to compare models. Their solution was to define a set of model types and to apportion the outcome measures across these types. By labeling the models "basic skills," "cognitive/conceptual" and "affective/cognitive," they created a set of types people could readily interpret, rightly or wrongly.

But the outcome measures were clearly biased toward the so-called "basic skills" models. What to do? The analysts also labeled the outcome measures as basic skills, cognitive, and affective, implying that the measures matched the relevant types. In fact, some of the measures did match the "basic skills" models well, but the other measures did not match the other equivalent types. This after-the-fact classification provided a way of interpreting the results in easily recognizable, if wrong, categories and disguised the bias of the measures toward certain models.

The classification of models was accomplished by definition with little empirical justification. Earlier classification had defined the models in quite different ways—by degree of structure, by emphasis on home learning, by program orientation, etc. Sponsors were forced into the new categories. Labeling those models that emphasized the mechanics of reading and mathematics as "basics skills" gave that category public acceptance. But the labels are misleading. For example, reading was not included as a "basic skill" measure.

Challenging the ends-means reasoning through attacking the narrowness of scope, the measuring instruments, the statistical techniques, the definition and classification of models and measures, and the interpretation of results was to challenge the very logic of the evaluation itself. The sponsors and others did this repeatedly. After the final Abt Associates report, a panel of independent evaluators critiqued the evaluation and found it so severely wanting on these counts as to render invalid many of its conclusions (House et al., 1978).

Equally disturbing to some proponents of the evaluation was the intersite variation within models. It should not be there. The Office of Education had defined it out of existence in the first Abt Associates report by funding a new data analysis. To the credit of the Abt

Associates analysts, they recognized it as their primary finding in their final report. In other words, the models did not have uniform effects at every site.

Evans was upset by this. It would be a "crazy world" if every site were so different that the same models would have different impacts. He attributed this variation to sponsor failure to implement. Otherwise, it would be more difficult for the Office of Education to prescribe particular programs or to decide on the allocation of scarce resources.

Objectivity

The evaluation is ultimately defended by its objectivity and the need to make decisions. Since decisions must be made, it is better to make them on the basis of objective data than subjective information, even if the evaluation is flawed. This argument rests upon the presumed objectivity of the instruments, the sample, and the statistical procedures. It is a very special definition of objectivity.

Objectivity is often equated with agreement among observers. Agreement is accomplished by having externalized, specified procedures for observation. By this definition objectivity is achieved by having observers agree on what they see—replication of observation. What a number of people agree on is accepted. Anything not commonly observed is presumed to be merely subjective. This is the quantitative notion of objectivity, and it is closely identified with the objectivist epistemology of systems analysis. It was a guiding concept in the Follow Through evaluation.

In various phases of the evaluation, outcome measures were rejected as being "unreliable." Reliability is nearly equivalent to the quantitative notion of objectivity, being based on replications of observation. This is close to what Evans called "rigor" in his discussion with the sponsors. Reliability can also be mathematically represented.

SRI abandoned the noncognitive measures and, to a certain extent, the case studies of institutional change because of their unreliability. Abt Associates dropped its implementation scale for that reason. The Huron Institute drew a sample with several sites per sponsor on the presumption that biases would be eliminated by repeated observations. The Office of Education chose the standard test battery on the presumption that it met the psychometric requirements of reliability. That outcomes should be reduced to make comparisons was a requirement of the approach; reliability was a major way of making the decisions.

(Interestingly, Abt Associates also abandoned "number of days absent," a highly reliable indicator, on grounds that environmental factors in the community could have determined absence. By the same reasoning, substantiated by their own results, they could have eliminated the tests. This is the criterion of validity, not of reliability. That is, they argued that absence was not a good indicator of the effects of the models, just as the sponsors argued that the tests were not either.)

In its extreme form, the quantitative notion of objectivity, called intersubjectivism, becomes operationalism: everything must be jointly seen and specified to be considered "true." Scriven (1972) remarked that this notion of objectivity is a major philosophical error. It confuses the method of verification with "truth." Scriven contended there is another notion of objectivity that depends on the quality of the idea rather than on the number of people holding it. He called this the qualitative sense of objectivity. In this sense, being objective means being free from bias or distortion.

Scriven cited the incident of an evaluator of television receivers attaching a mechanical instrument to the television to measure decibel gain even though decibel gain is not highly correlated with picture quality. The naked eye will judge picture quality better. The technician does this because one can attain higher interjudge agreement on an instrument reading, even though naked eye reliability is also achievable at a lower level. In other words, reliability has replaced validity. One uses more reliable instruments even though they are less valid.

The same is true of the Follow Through evaluation. The evaluation is defended às being objective because it uses reliable instruments, even though the instruments were possibly invalid for the purpose to which they were put. In other words, the evaluation was objective in the quantitative sense that its findings are replicable ("stable" in the words of the Abt Associates analysts) but the evaluation was biased toward models that were favored by the tests. For example, the MAT reliably measures punctuation and shows the Direct Instruction model, whose materials are keyed to punctuation, to do very well on this part of the test. This result is replicable but does not necessarily imply that Direct Instruction is the best model.

The second sense in which the evaluation is claimed to be objective is that it employs a statistical procedure which may be more or less correctly performed. The validity of the mathematics is open to public inspection. This makes the evaluation appear objective but it begs the question of whether this was the appropriate mathematical technique to employ. Both the formulation and interpretation of results are at issue even if the mathematics are impeccable. In this evaluation the formulation, interpretation, and mathematics are all questionable (House et al., 1978).

So the ultimate defense of the evaluation is its objectivity, but its objectivity melts away upon inspection. The measures turn out to be reliable but of questionable validity. (Some are also unreliable.) The statistics are more or less proper but sometimes inappropriate, the interpretation from data questionable. The evaluation is replicable, reliable, and invalid.

Identifying objectivity with externally specified procedures has another effect. It tempts the evaluator to disclaim responsibility for his findings. The findings are the result of his objective instruments and procedures. How can one be held liable? This is called "objectivism" (Polanyi, 1958). It is not surprising that the Abt Associates analysts, wrestling with the paradoxes of their task, were occasionally tempted to disclaim responsibility. In fact, the parceling out of specific tasks by the Office of Education reduced the responsibility that any one group could feel toward the evaluation.

All this is not to abandon the concept of reliability. It is certainly a useful concept. But it should not be used to the exclusion of validity. For example, the evaluation might have used psychologists to interview children about their general mental health and have obtained more valid information in the affective realm. Objectivity (in the quantitative sense) is insufficient justification. An evaluation can be objective but biased.

Fairness

There are two senses in which the Follow Through evaluation was unfair. First is the way in which the outcome measures favored certain models over others. The classification of both the models and the outcome measures into "basic skills," "cognitive/conceptual," and "affective," and the matching of the measures to the models on this basis, gave only a semblance of fairness. It was, in fact, much easier for the basic skills models to score on "their" measures than for the others. For example, the OE panel which chose the Raven's because it could not be taught as correct" no model did better than comparison groups on it. But since it was included in the cognitive measures, it looked as if the cognitive models were specifically responsible for scoring well on it.

The second sense in which the evaluation was unfair concerns the understanding that the sponsors had with the evaluators and the Office of Education. The sponsors were repeatedly led to believe that the evaluation would be responsive to particular goals they were trying to achieve. The original list of evaluative criteria was broad enough to accommodate the sponsors. On this basis they agreed to cooperate. As early as April 1969, at Pajaro Dunes, they began to protest the heavy reliance on standard cognitive measures. SRI promised to develop new cognitive and noncognitive measures. It tried but failed.

If one makes an agreement with someone else, either tacitly or explicitly, and one lives up to one's promises but the other side does not, then one feels unfairly treated. The sponsors protested repeatedly and were reassured, but in the end the evaluation was based primarily on conventional cognitive measures. It is this feeling of being treated unfairly which accounts for the outrage at the evaluation that so many sponsors have expressed. They feel betrayed.

There are certain conditions that an evaluation agreement must meet to be considered a fair agreement. In Chapter 8, I outlined thirteen such conditions, such as noncoercion, full information, and no excessive self-interest. One of these conditions is "possibility"—that the agreement not be based on something one party cannot carry out. Clearly, SRI agreed to something that it could not do. In this sense, the original agreement was unfair and was so perceived by the sponsors.

By the time of McDaniels's redefinition of the evaluation, it was clear what the evaluation would do. McDaniels's actions, and many later by the Office of Education, were taken unilaterally, without serious negotiation. The Office of Education no longer accepted the previous agreement nor even the desirability of having one. They could do what they wanted, subject to political constraints.

The sponsors were not entirely without blame in the matter. From 1973 on, it was clear what the final evaluation would entail, though not what the conclusions would be. They continued to cooperate and to accept large sums of money from the government. On the other hand, they had a huge investment in their models by that time. Some had been involved in development work for five years, so withdrawal became unacceptable. They continued to protest and to hope for the best.

In fact, the circumstances that the sponsors faced came close to being coercive. If the government had negotiated the kind of evaluation it conducted as part of the original agreement, and this evaluation were fully understood and accepted by the sponsors, then the evaluation agreement would have been a fair one. Changing directions in midstream, when the sponsors had an investment, was quite another matter, however. At the very least, the understanding should have been renegotiated.

Fairness was also at risk in another way—through the lack of impartiality. To deliberate impartially is to deliberate without excessive attention to one's own interests, to consider only universal solutions, and to choose in line with one's self-interest as a member of the group which is to be affected by the agreement. Although the Office of Education met the first of these two conditions, it fell down badly on the third, acting in line with the interests of those to be affected. It did not attend properly to the sponsors' complaints. Hence, the evaluation lacked impartiality.

It is not enough that an evaluation be objective, it must also be impartial. Externalized, repeatable procedures can be biased. Whereas objectivity suggests a lack of concern or a neutral attitude, which the evaluation definitely had, people being evaluated expect impartiality—a concern expressed in balanced judgments about the interests in the program being judged. The sponsors correctly perceived both the lack of concern and lack of impartiality. If the first part of the evaluation suffered from lack of possibility, the last part suffered from lack of impartiality. All this is to say that not only was the evaluation unfair, the evaluation *agreement* was unfair.

Justice

The Follow Through evaluation fits well the utilitarian philosophy of justice, from which it is partially derived. Utilitarian justice strives to achieve the greatest net balance of satisfaction in society summed over all individuals. Utilitarianism requires a common measure of satisfaction so that calculations of utility can be made. In education, this measure is construed to be standardized test scores, which serve as proxies for other ends, as both Rivlin and Evans have indicated.

In utilitarianism, whatever maximizes the "good," i.e., test scores, is the "right" thing to do. So the correct early childhood model is the one that maximizes test scores. Not maximizing the good is immoral. Rationality itself is construed as selecting the best among a set of alternatives. Experimental design, instrumentation, and statistics are methods for determining the "best" alternative. In intent, the Follow Through planned variation experiment was a splendid manifestation of utilitarian ethics.

There are some problems with utilitarianism, however. In maximizing total satisfaction, it is permissible to trade off the satisfactions of some for increased satisfaction for others. In practice, those so deprived often turn out to be the powerless, the lower classes. Also, someone must make these assessments of satisfaction. This often turns out to be the government or an administrator. Utilitarianism in practice is often paternalistic.

These elements were operating in the Follow Through evaluation. Ultimately, the Office of Education decided what issues should be addressed and whose concerns should be heard. Disadvantaged groups protested as they saw the evaluation operating against their interests. The first protest came from minority groups at Atlanta. Minority members charged that the evaluators were insensitive to both parental and community involvement. In response to this protest several minority sponsors were funded and SRI began the community case studies of institutional change. Within a few years, the institutional change studies were abandoned. There were no studies looking at the larger community. In the data reduction effort in the second phase, most minority sponsors, being small, were not included.

Interviews with parents emerged as a separate strand and were subcontracted to the National Opinion Research Center. Sixty thousand interviews were conducted over several years, but no one seemed to know their exact purpose. Presumably, they were to record parent attitudes about the program and provide demographic information. No one seemed to be able to figure out what to do with the data or how to interpret them. When the Abt Associates analysts tried to include some of the information in their third report, one of the sponsors said it was too "personalistic" (Haney, 1977: 269). The parent data were not mentioned in the final Abt Associates report. Haney (1977: 270) reports that these data were much more complimentary of Follow Through.

In the original Follow Through design, parents were supposed to play an important role in decision-making and in other important aspects of the program. Except for the few models that emphasized their participation, they were effectively excluded from the program in any but a symbolic way, and this was true of the evaluation as well. Their last major protest was at the Denver meeting in 1972, where they claimed they had been excluded and asked that they be allowed to evaluate sponsors. They said they were tired of others deciding what was wrong with their children and what a good and bad model was. They were tired of experts measuring only what they knew how to measure. Nothing came of their protest, in spite of the fact that they were the only ones who could be said to represent truly the interests of their children.

The other powerless groups excluded from the evaluation were the teachers. In a few auxiliary studies, like Soar's and Stallings's, teachers were observed. But mostly they were sent a questionnaire by mail. Again, since they were not accepted as full participants, no one quite knew what the questionnaire was for. At one time, it was proposed that the teacher data be used as demographic data showing conditions of implementation. Again sponsors complained about the use as measures of implementation. Little was done with the information after that.

In retrospect, the least powerful members of the program—the minorities, the parents, and the teachers—were effectively excluded from the evaluation. In the first phase, matters were decided by collaboration of the Office of Education, the evaluators, and the sponsors. In the second phase, matters were decided by the Office of Education and the evaluators. In the third phase, the Office of Education decided the critical issues.

In the utilitarian framework this is a just situation because once it is determined which model produces maximum gain in test scores and once that model is implemented, total satisfaction in society will be increased. If the interests of the excluded are sacrificed, that is the price one must pay for progress. One must be tough, make "hard decisions."

On the other hand, there are those who reject utilitarianism and say that the interests of all those affected by the evaluation should have a say in it. Their interests should be directly represented. There are even those who say that the interests of the least advantaged should be a major concern. That Follow Through was a program designed to help the disadvantaged intensifies the issue. From these perspectives the evaluation was unjust.

Federal Evaluation Policy Reconsidered

The Follow Through evaluation was a culmination of a decade of a particular policy, and perhaps came closest to incorporating that policy. In view of the fact that the evaluation was biased, unfair, and unjust (in addition to costing $50 million), it is time seriously to question that policy.

Federal evaluation policy has been based on the systems analysis approach. Its major audiences are managers and economists. It assumes consensus on goals, on known cause and effect, and on a few quantified outcome variables. Its methodology includes planned variation experimentation and cost-benefit analysis. Its end is efficiency. It asks the question, "What are the most efficient programs?"

As articulated by major proponents like Rivlin and Evans, it assumes there is a direct parallel between the production of social services and manufacturing. The same analysis techniques will apply. The only true knowledge is a production function specifying stable relationships between input and output. The only way to such knowledge is through experimental methods and statistical techniques. It is possible to agree on a few output measures. The issue is efficient allocation of resources.

The key decisions will be made at higher government levels, and tough management can do the job. The ultimate justification is utilitarian—to maximize satisfaction in society. To maximize, one must know which programs are most efficient. This can be done only by comparing alternatives, for which one must have a common measure of output. This is a job for experts.

There are places where this approach can be applied successfully. But the United States as a whole is not one of them. The approach can be successfully applied where there really are only a few goals and outcome measures. This is likely to happen where the audience for the evaluation is very narrowly defined and agrees on a few criteria of comparison. It also helps if the criteria can be represented by a reasonably valid quantitative indicator. (For successful applications of this technique, see Glass's evaluation of a training tape for educational researchers [Glass, 1972] or Herbert's [1975] evaluation of an elementary mathematics curriculum for the National Institute of Education.)

For a broad-based social program in a pluralistic society like the United States, almost none of the assumptions of the systems analysis approach applies. Asking "which early childhood model of education is best for disadvantaged children in every place in the United States" results in misleading evaluations. Clearly, it is not true that there were a few agreed-upon goals or outcome measures for Follow Through. Consensus was achieved by government fiat. It is not true that there were distinct alternatives or that cause and effect were known or easily determined. The models accounted for only a small fraction, far less than 10%, of the variance on the government-selected measures.

It is not true that there is a stable production function relating inputs and outputs. At one site one model will do very well and at another will do very badly. It is not true that test scores are "hard data"—like number of bottles produced per hour. The effects disappear in a few years. Models do not have uniform effects across sites. This makes suspect government prescriptions of models. Neither do models transfer easily or faithfully from one site to another.

It is not true that producing social services is like manufacturing goods. One produces physical artifacts; the other does not. It is not true that the only way to knowledge is through experimentation and statistics. There are many ways to knowledge. It is not true that nothing is known about education. Practitioners know a great deal, although their knowledge may be tacit.

It is not true that collecting very large, and costly, amounts of data will eliminate biases. It is not even true that managers and economists are the only major audiences for the evaluations. With every large evaluation of this type, the newspapers seize the results and interpret them quite differently than do the experts.

In large-scale social programs, there will be many groups pursuing highly divergent interests. An evaluation of the program should somehow represent the interests of these divergent groups. This probably means multiple criteria and multiple methods of data collection. It means that information cannot be neatly summarized into one simple quantitative scale. It will most certainly mean that the program will have different outcomes and satisfactions for different stakeholder groups. These groups must somehow be represented in the evaluation, and there are various ways of doing so. There are at least eight other approaches to evaluation.

Perhaps the major error of the systems analysis approach was to mistake objectivity for impartiality. As Elmore noted:

In its early, naive formulation PPBS put the "very special staff of experts" at the elbow of the policymaker (the President, the cabinet officer, the agency head). Their advice would be objective and dispassionate, based on hard analysis and uncontaminated by narrow bureaucratic interests. Because of its objectivity, the advice would be regarded by policy makers as superior to other kinds of advice and therefore would play the determining role in policy formation [Elmore, 1976: 23].

The analysts thought objectivity was sufficient to ensure superiority and influence. More often it meant irrelevance. Objectivity sought to deal with interests by excluding them. What is needed is impartiality which deals with interests by including and balancing them.

11

A CRITIQUE OF THE APPROACHES

Throughout this book, I have discussed and criticized various approaches to evaluation. This chapter is a brief summary of the advantages and disadvantages of each approach. Any approach can be appropriate or inappropriate depending upon the circumstances of its application and the corresponding validity of the assumptions on which it is based. Even when an approach is appropriate, the individual evaluation may be good or bad, accurate or inaccurate, coherent or incoherent, fair or unfair, democratic or undemocratic, just or unjust, useful or useless, efficient or inefficient. If an approach is applied to a situation in which it is inappropriate, the possibilities of a poor evaluation are multiplied.

One way of undertaking this task of summary would be to list the standards and principles developed in this book and to judge each model by each criterion. This would be too tedious, however, and also misleading. It is only individual evaluations embedded in concrete circumstances that can actually be judged. The basic approaches themselves only have certain tendencies. For example, the systems analysis approach has a tendency to neglect the interests of some participants in the program, but there is no necessity in this. Hence, criticizing the systems analysis approach as inherently undemocratic overstates the case, even though there is a structural weakness in that direction. If one has a map that emphasizes, or even distorts, some features at the expense of others, one will not necessarily get lost. If one has an evaluation approach that emphasizes reliability of data at the expense of representing relevant interests, one will not necessarily conduct an undemocratic evaluation.

This chapter is structured somewhat more loosely, more like a casual discussion of the strengths and weaknesses of each approach, as befits the subject. I have either conducted or thoroughly criticized each particular type. I will bring these personal examples to bear in illuminating my critiques.

Systems Analysis

No evaluation approach has been criticized more severely in this book than has systems analysis, particularly in the chapter on federal policy. This is because systems analysis is the dominant, officially sanctioned approach and because its advocates make strong claims that this is the only scientific approach. What makes these claims embarrassing is that they are epistemologically naive and innocent—vestiges of a discarded positivism. Of course, not all make such extravagant claims.

There is no need to dwell at length on the fallacies and limitations of systems analysis. The approach, as outlined by theorists such as Rivlin (1971) and Rossi et al. (1979), assumes the viewpoint of government managers and economists. Information must be gathered on the planning, monitoring, impact, and costs of a program—all clearly for management purposes. In a sense, this is a realistic view since most evaluations are of government programs, but unfortunately, the approach is too often politically and morally deficient. It excludes the interests and concerns of those participating in the program, particularly those lower in the social hierarchy. The Follow Through evaluation is an excellent example of how the interests of the poor, the parents, and the teachers were substantially ignored.

At its worst, the systems analysis approach leads to scientism—the view that the only way to the truth is through certain methodologies. Objectivity is equated with reliability, with producing information from only certain types of instrument. Impartiality and validity are sacrificed. In reducing everything to a few indicators so that one can demonstrate reliability, do cost-benefit analysis, and discover the most efficient programs (and thus maximize utilities), the outcomes of complex social programs are narrowed to a few quantitative measures. Generally, the systems analysis approach is applied far beyond its appropriate domain.

Sometimes, however, the systems analysis approach is appropriate, as when the outcome measures can reasonably be reduced to a few possibilities and to simple cause-and-effect relationships. For example, if one is concerned about the number of hospital beds in a community, a quantitative indicator seems appropriate. Yet one would not want to use this as the sole measure of health care. Or, if the purpose and only purpose of "performance contracting" is to raise student test scores, it makes sense to use test scores as the measure of the success of the program. (For an in-depth discussion of tests and their relationship to evaluation and policy, see Baker and Quellmalz, 1979).

One way of strengthening the systems analysis approach is to broaden the number and types of indicators used. For example, in evaluating the impact of a new mathematics program, Herbert (1975) constructed dozens of special scales that measured abilities that mathematicians judged were indicative of high-level thinking, as opposed to the items on standardized tests. In a fairly classical control group design, both the special tests and standardized ones were administered to show that the program was better than traditional materials on the special tests and no worse on the standardized ones. Without the special tests the developers would have been justified in claiming invalidity for the evaluation. Herbert also conducted a number of side studies to eliminate alternative possibilities that other factors, such as better teachers, were not responsible for the results. This was a well-reasoned study. Unfortunately, many systems analysis studies are thick-witted, mechanical applications of stock methods. Good systems analysis studies are being done. What they have in common is that they are well-reasoned, and they don't try to pull elephants through keyholes.

Behavioral Objectives

The behavioral objectives approach to evaluation is the most familiar, and, if a vote were taken, probably the most popular among practicing evaluators. It is the most commonly advanced idea for evaluating. There are also wide-spread criticisms contending that specification of objectives is not really helpful to teaching or curriculum development (Atkin, 1968; Stake, 1973). These criticisms have reached a crescendo, but the objectives approach continues to be popular.

Underlying the objectives approach is the assumption that education, or whatever the social activity, is really a technology, a body of techniques that leads to prespecified ends. Waks (1975) suggested that two doctrines underlie this model—the "doctrine of technical planning and evaluation" and the "doctrine of behavioral specification." The first holds that if one's ends or goals are confused, one cannot apply techniques appropriately. The goals must be precise and exhaustive. To specify correct action a full set of objectives must close the "evaluation space," thus precisely determining outcomes. The second doctrine is that of behavioral specification, from which the approach gets its name. It holds that the behavioral objectives must be behaviorally specified, that is, measurable. Taken together, those two doctrines point toward an evaluation that defines success in terms of prespecified and measurable objectives rather than in terms of values actually obtained.

Waks's basic criticism is that "acting with purpose" is not equivalent to "taking means to a well-defined end." A social activity, like teaching, can be coherent and effective by relying on cultural traditions, training, experience, and socialization of teachers. None of this requires specification of objectives in behavioral form. The teacher is a participant in a whole way of life and manner of acting and thinking, according to Waks. Since the teachers have myths, history, traditions, and habits to rely upon, they do not need a "flux of goals" to provide meaning or direction. In addition, by removing goals from the background of practice and shared understanding in which they are actually used, behavioral objectives advocates introduce an artificial element into the teaching situation. Lists of objectives, stripped of context, make actual teacher behaviors look aimless. Replacing context-bound behavior with "artificial" objectives can seriously distort actions.

Other criticisms of the objectives approach are more practical. Who really defines the goals? Whose interests do they represent? Are the goals really a full set of the behaviors desired? How can the goals be reduced and measured? By whom? Are important outcomes neglected by the prespecification of objectives?

If one looks closely at the definition and specification of goals, one will often find that they were chosen and specified arbitrarily. The lists of goals are seldom exhaustive, and the means of selecting the most important goals are suspect. Defining the expected outcomes of a social program is much more difficult than it appears.

For example, in the Michigan Accountability system—a well-financed and sophisticated attempt to define objectives and objective-referenced tests for different grades in the state of Michigan—the specification of objectives was always somewhat arbitrary. For fourth grade math, more than four hundred objectives were identified. Yet testing for all these would take weeks of student time as well as hundreds of thousands of dollars in test development and administration. The list of objectives was cut to thirty-five or so, but the selection was arbitrary (House et al., 1974).

In Michigan the initial testing was done with norm-referenced tests, developed by major publishers, but since these did not correspond well with the state objectives, objective-referenced tests were developed. Five test items were developed to measure each objective. There is a great controversy over these kinds of measures. Some contend that the objectives-based tests are superior while others claim that they are invalid (Popham and Ebel, 1978).

On the positive side, objectives approaches to evaluation have a great deal of face validity. Should not a social program be held accountable for what it claims to do? These claims, after all, are the basis for public funding of the program. The evaluation has an obvious legitimacy by taking as given enunciated program goals and objectives. It resolves the evaluator's dilemma in a most straightforward way. This, after all, is what they *said* they were going to do. This prima facie claim has great appeal to the program developers themselves, especially at the beginning of their program when they have great aspirations for their own endeavors.

Another advantage of the objectives approach is its highly definable technology. First the evaluator does this, then this, and so on. The steps are worked out in great detail (Morris et al., 1978). This has appeal to the great number of novices who conduct evaluations every year. No other approach to evaluation has such an elaborate technology. Normally, like the systems analysts, the behavioral objectivists follow "scientific" procedures, although they have not been quite as insistent on this as the systems analysts.

All in all, in a technological society, the objectives approach to evaluation has a great deal of appeal, as indicated by its ubiquity. It was, in fact, derived from an industrial psychology, task analysis tradition. As with much technology, its difficulties lie in both its philosophical and practical dimensions. When one thinks seriously about it or tries to apply it, certain faults appear.

Decision-Making

A great advantage of the decision-making approach is that it focuses the evaluation—a very important practical concern for the evaluator. For any evaluation one might reasonably collect an enormous mass of information, so some selection is necessary. The decision-making approach does this by employing the criterion of utility. Which information will be most useful? The decision-making theorist's answer is the information which is most useful to the decision-maker. Decision alternatives should be outlined, and information relevant to them should be collected.

For example, in the evaluation of the Illinois Gifted Program, there were five parts to the program—demonstration centers, reimbursement centers, training programs, research projects, and administrative support. The demonstration and reimbursement centers absorbed most of the $4 million annual appropriation, and the effects of these projects were unknown, though it was believed that the demonstration centers were effective and the reimbursement centers were not. As an aid to decisions anticipated by the state administrative staff, by the state advisory council, and by the state legislature, we focused our evaluation on the areas of heaviest investment and least knowledge, discovering that the demonstration centers were less effective and the reimbursement centers were more effective than was commonly believed.

This information resulted in a restructuring of the demonstration centers and an addition of a million dollars to the reimbursement part of the state program. It was anticipated in the evaluation that there would be reorganization, reallocation, and basic funding decisions made by the three decision-making groups. Different versions of the evaluation information were presented to the three major groups, and yet a fourth version to the general public. Information about the research projects (believed to be ineffective and changed without data) and the training programs (on which other information such as dissertations was available) was not collected, nor was information on the operations of the state staff itself, since we could not see how that information could reasonably be used (House et al., 1971).

Of course, questions arise immediately. Why should the decision-maker, who is usually identified as the program administrator, be given so much preference? Does this not put the evaluator at the service of top management and make the evaluator the "hired gun" of the program establishment? Does this not make the evaluation potentially unfair and even undemocratic? The answer is that these are potential weaknesses of the decision-making approach.

The decision-making theorist might answer this criticism by responding that the decision-maker is the one who really makes a difference, thus employing the basic notion of utility of information again. In the long run, one must admit that while utility of information may be an important criterion for evaluation, it cannot be the only criterion. One would not want a useful evaluation that was also untrue or unfair. Utility must be balanced against other considerations.

As a practical matter, there are various ways of guarding against the evaluation's being used in an unethical way by decision-making powers. One way is to define the decision-making groups more broadly. Another is to protect informants against retaliation or action by higher authorities. Still another is to supply the same information to groups outside the decision-making circles. Still, the problem remains that information provided for decision-makers gives a strong management slant to the evaluation. It is not surprising that this approach to evaluation is the most popular with administrators.

For example, in the Illinois Gifted Evaluation, the top decision-makers were highly satisfied with the evaluation. One may well ask, however, about the people in the programs and in the school districts. Were their interests and concerns well served? There is no automatic answer to this question. One must examine the actual evaluation and its circumstances to find out. But the evaluator's position at the elbow of the decision-maker always leads one to wonder.

A second set of problems arises when the evaluator tries to define the specific decisions to be served. Decisions are not usually expressed in clear alternatives, and, in fact, it is often the case that the decisions to be served do not emerge until after the evaluation is done. Also, the decisions change shape dramatically over time. Decisions that determine the fate of a program are often not those anticipated by the evaluator. In other words, it is much more difficult to specify and anticipate decisions to be served than it would first appear.

For example, the Guttentag-Edwards approach uses a sophisticated scaling procedure to arrive at a set of decision-maker preferences, but the procedure is highly dependent on how the alternatives are defined by the evaluators. Only the top decision-makers are included in the preference polling. One may well wonder why the decision-maker's subjective value preferences should carry such weight. Patton's approach is to narrow the search to the most likely information user and to ask the "right" questions for that user. These questions would be those on which data can be collected, to which there is more than one answer, which the decision-makers feel they can use, and whose mode of utilization they can specify. All these are criteria of utility.

In spite of these difficulties, the decision-making approach provides a valuable insight into evaluation. It stresses the importance of the utility of information. Evaluation information is meant to be used. Connecting evaluation to decision-making underlines the purpose of evaluation. It is also practically useful to shape an evaluation in reference to actual decision-making considerations. Even if one cannot define precisely the decision alternatives, one can eliminate a number of lines of inquiry as being irrelevant. This is a beneficial discipline for those who approach the task from a research perspective. In other words, the decision-making approach underscores evaluation as a *practical* activity. The danger is in being a pawn of the decision-maker.

Goal-Free

The goal-free approach is one of the most talked about and least used approaches for evaluating social programs. Its purpose is to reduce bias, in particular the bias introduced by the evaluator's familiarity with the program goals and fraternizing with program personnel. Bias is, obviously, introduced by social contact. The evaluator is expected to ascertain all program outcomes and not just the ones intended by the program personnel. Consumers' Union regularly evaluates consumer products without reference to the producer's goals or intentions, yet the approach is rarely pursued with social programs.

The first difficulty is the lack of a highly specifiable technology for the evaluation. There is a sense in which "looking for all outcomes" defies a programmed approach. Scriven sees the evaluator as a hunter, a detective, an investigator armed with a variety of techniques but not with a lock-step technology such as the behavioral objective approach offers.

The very reasoning of goal-free evaluation is a bit strange to evaluators. They are mostly trained in an ends-means logic: "Here are the objectives. Have they been achieved?" Goal-free reasoning is more pragmatic: "Here is the program. What are its effects?" The traditional notion of objectivity for evaluators trained in the social sciences is quantitative. To them, objectivity means employing measures that are replicable, i.e., have high reliability. The goal-free notion of objectivity is qualitative—stay independent of various influences that might bias one's judgment.

To a certain extent, Scriven has tried to answer the demand for a methodology by constructing checklists that programs must meet. Critics respond that he is merely substituting his own criteria, his own hidden goals, for those of the program. He denies this. To understand his reasoning, it is helpful to think of evaluating a physical product like a car. In evaluating a car one can specify what functions a car must perform and evaluate the car according to these characteristics. The car must be cheap, get good gas mileage, have a good repair record, and so on. There is nothing arbitrary or even subjective about these physically ascertainable qualities, and the evaluator does not need to know the manufacturer's intentions to evaluate the car. One can apply this reasoning to social programs. Yet, is a social program the same as a physical product? Can its functions be determined without reference to the intentions of the program? In some ways, yes, and in some ways, no. (For a challenge to Scriven's position that offers theory-based evaluation as an alternative, see Hogben and Simpson, 1978.)

These difficulties are reflected in actual evaluations. Welch (1978) used an external panel to judge some instructional materials produced by a curriculum development project. The criteria employed were product criteria. The project was judged by the quality of its products, but the developers were unhappy with the evaluation because it did not reflect the processes of the project nor the growth and development that occurred in the project staff and institution. Changes in the college and development staffs were not reflected in the quality of the products. Both the evaluators and program personnel were uncomfortable with the methodology. There was no recognition of multiple audiences for the evaluation nor the possibility that different audiences might value the products differently.

The second major difficulty, other than methodology, is the social interaction. The outcomes of social action programs, and indeed their conduct, are highly ambiguous and subject to many different interpretations. In everyday life, when we try to interpret and understand the ambiguous acts of others, a common and necessary occurrence, we do so through the concept of the person underlying these actions. We presume that there is a stable structure called a person, and this structure serves as the context for interpreting actions. We know what a particular act means because we interpret it as derived from the person we know (Perelman and Olbrechts-Tyteca, 1969).

A primary feature of the person is his intention. We interpret an act mainly through what we presume to be a person's intentions. The same act may be differently construed given a different presumption of intents. Moral judgments are based on the intentions and morality of the agent as opposed to the morality of the act. Since intentions are presumed, one can only listen to the agent's expressed intentions and look for corresponding acts. Some philosophers, in fact, believe that ambiguity of behavior, necessarily interpreted by intentions, is what distinguishes the human sciences from the natural sciences.

The relevance to goal-free evaluation is this: Goal-free evaluation prohibits the program personnel from expressing their intentions to the evaluators. This means that the evaluators must judge the actions free from the context of the person and the person's intentions. In addition, the program personnel do not know the intentions of the evaluator. He remains an enigmatic figure. Both the evaluator and program personnel find this breach of social contract shattering. Only the most secure egos can stand up to such buffeting.

So although the argument for goal-free evaluation may make sense, the evaluator is faced with an unknown methodology and ambiguous evaluation situation, and the evaluatees with the prospects of inimical evaluation by a stranger with whom they cannot communicate. Few goal-free evaluations have been done. It is significant that in the one I conducted, the person who contracted the evaluation and set it up inside was a good friend of mine with whom I had worked for years. Even so, I was anxious about how to proceed, and the personnel in the program were anxious about my not understanding their intentions.

All in all, it is not that Scriven is wrong about the bias of being informed about the program intents. The bias is deeper than expected. Rather, it is that such fraternization may be socially necessary to allow an evaluation to proceed at all. My later attempts to conduct a goal-free evaluation have been rejected by potential clients.

Before goal-free evaluations can be widely employed, certain conditions must obtain. Either a prior relationship of trust has been established somehow, or the authority relationships are such that the program personnel cannot block the evaluation. This can happen by the evaluators and program personnel being far removed, such as Consumers' Union and General Motors, or both being subject to higher authority. Alternatively, trust-building tactics might include using other approaches in conjunction with goal-free evaluation. Evaluation has been construed in this book as a social process, and goal-free evaluation illustrates just how true this is.

Art Criticism[1]

This approach is worthy of serious consideration as a way of evaluating. The basic idea is bold and imaginative. Alternative methods of evaluation are needed to complement the scientific evaluation of social programs, and the long traditions of criticism that have graced the arts would seem to be a rich source of ideas. Yet the difficulties in establishing educational criticism as a legitimate mode of evaluation are formidable.

Its virtues are that the evaluator can draw upon his own experience and intuitive reasoning to judge what is happening and express these judgments in language and concepts that nonexperts can understand. Its difficulties are in legitimizing these judgments and controlling potential biases that might arise in the evaluation.

In Eisner's (1979) conception, criticism will increase awareness and appreciation, and it has three aspects—the descriptive, the interpretive, and the evaluative. In the first, one renders the "relevant qualities of educational life." In the second, one "accounts for" the events and their consequences by social science theories. In the third, one judges the educational processes according to educational criteria. It is the latter, according to Eisner, that separates the critic from the social scientist.

The mixing of social science concepts and theories into the criticism mode of evaluation is curious. It is easy to see how the critic might "render" the classroom setting in artistic categories and also evaluate it, but how social science concepts can be introduced in between is a puzzle. The examples of educational criticism provided in Eisner's book are no help since the evaluative categories are highly personal rather than scientific.

The two procedures for determining validity are the extent to which the criticism "forms a coherent, persuasive whole" and the empirical checking of the criticism against the phenomenon. A third interesting notion that the real question is not whether it is true but whether it is useful is introduced but not explored. It is not difficult to imagine a "useful" criticism that meets neither of the validity criteria. All in all, the discussion of validity is incomplete and must eventually be rethought. To be fair to Eisner, though, validity is a primary problem for all approaches to evaluation.

Eisner recognizes the limited extent of the analogy between art criticism and evaluation when he notes that one can examine a sculpture or a painting to see what the critic sees, since the art work itself does not change over time. A classroom, however, does change. Eisner's conclusion is that the classroom will not change in key features. One might expect a slightly different slant on this and on other issues if the evaluator's background were theater, music, or literature rather than the visual arts.

There is also a difference between the evaluation of a classroom and what an evaluator normally does. The evaluator usually evaluates an entire program rather than a single classroom. The analogy perhaps is with a review of an art exhibit rather than a single painting. In addition, in spite of Eisner's argument for the stability of the classroom (a point on which he is correct), the program evaluator is ordinarily looking for change rather than stability.

The issue of validity leads into the deeper questions of evaluation. What criteria does the evaluator employ? On what values do they rest? How are they justified? Eisner contends that the evaluator-critic must apply "educational criteria," but he seldom specifies what these are. He suggests that the criteria will come from an examination of the history and philosophy of education and from practical experience. He does pose two questions: Are the children being helped? Are they acquiring habits conducive to further development? These are certainly good questions, and the answers depend very much on one's theory of education and personal preferences. Eisner faces up to this directly: "Without some view of what counts as education, one is in no position whatsoever to make judgments about the educational quality of the process of schooling or their consequences" (Eisner, 1979: 44). It is clear that Eisner himself holds a notion of education as development (Kohlberg and Mayer, 1972).

What about those who do not hold a similar view of education? Are they subject to the evaluator's values? As a critic and expert, does the evaluator have the authority to make judgments based on his expertise? If so, does he make explicit the bases of his value judgments? Eisner is ambivalent on these issues, but their resolution is fundamental to the manner in which the critic functions. In our own evaluation, apparently the program administrators found us personally credible after a few hours' interview. Does the sponsor find a compatible critic? What about the people evaluated?

The three examples of educational criticism included in Eisner's book give one pause here. They are conducted by his students and are strongly judgmental. The first begins this way:

This classroom is almost a caricature of society.

The curriculum is served up like Big Macs. Reading, math, language, even physical and affective education are all precooked, prepackaged, artifically flavored [p. 229].

The second example assumes the first person narrative of an elementary student, but the narrative is very much limned by the values of the critic. The third reaches the conclusion that the teacher is leaving teaching because of parental pressures to structure the curriculum, although it is not clear whether alternative explanations have been explored. All three examples pose the interests of the students against the presumed efficiency values of the parents and the society.

It is not unusual for an art critic to advance controversial views—the reader can choose to ignore them. In fact, the reader can choose to read only critics with whom she agrees. A public evaluation of an educational program cannot be so easily dismissed, however. Some justification—whether of the critic, the critic's principles, or the criticism—is necessary. The demands for fairness and justice are more rigorous in the evaluation of public programs.

The final problem for the criticism approach to evaluation is this: Who is the audience for the criticism? One reads a review of an art exhibit or a play to decide whether to attend. One reads a criticism of an art work to increase one's understanding and appreciation. Whose appreciation is to be improved here? Eisner's direct response is that one does criticism for teachers who might find feedback on their teaching useful. However, the examples provided raise doubts about whether teachers would find such criticism acceptable. Of course, criticisms done for doctoral dissertations might differ considerably from criticisms conducted in actual evaluation situations.

In summary, the idea of evaluation as criticism is a bold idea worthy of exploration, and potentially an important one. Eisner's book is the logical starting place for such an endeavor. From a practical standpoint, our own educational criticism went rather well. Although the difficult issues of validity, values, and legitimacy must be worked out more fully, they are not insurmountable. The task now must be to push beyond these initial formulations.

Professional Review

As more occupations have become professionalized, professional review procedures have become increasingly important. There is a presumption in the professions that only members of the profession are qualified to judge the activities of their peers. Almost no one outside a profession would hold that this is true, perhaps even though holding that it was true for his own profession.

There is a recent trend for the public to challenge the right of professionals to control their own affairs. Consumers have demanded places on the boards of health care facilities, on advisory panels, and on school governing bodies. There is a belief that professionals will not police their own operations very vigorously. Doctors, it is believed, will neither privately challenge nor publicly testify against other doctors.

Public disenchantment with professionally controlled evaluation is reflected in the declining credibility of accrediting agencies. At one time it was sufficient for an institution to be accredited by the proper agency for the public to be assured of its quality—but no longer. Parents are not always convinced that the school program is of high quality when it is accredited by the North Central Association. In addition, political control of accrediting activities is shifting to state governments. Amateur reviews, such as those by Nader, are becoming more frequent, though they present problems of their own.

Certainly, the public is justified in questioning some of the evaluation procedures. Visits by accrediting teams are highly variable, and their rigor depends on the members of the team. These are often chosen by the institution evaluated. The institutions themselves often view the visitation as an unwelcome and even illegitimate intrusion into their affairs and sometimes use the occasion as a public relations opportunity rather than a chance for genuine self-study. If the evaluation is not taken seriously, the accrediting agency has little power over the institution.

On the other hand, as a result of public pressure for accountability, professional reviews are increasing in number. Many state departments of education and state boards of higher education are conducting their own accrediting visits rather than relying on private agencies to do so. Although the review procedures are usually similar to those of the private accrediting agencies, the threat of state disapproval and consequent withdrawal of funds are taken more seriously.

Another example is the popularity of internal professional review systems within universities and colleges. Universities have always evaluated individuals for promotion or for tenure, but the new systems evaluate programs, departments, and administrative units. Many were initiated as a way of circumventing direct intervention by boards of higher education as well as of making internal decisions and reallocating funds in hard times. A prevalent attitude is that it is better to have the institution itself conduct evaluations of its units rather than have an external agency do so. Many higher education authorities themselves use professional review procedures.

One might expect, however, that criteria used by the professionals within an institution will differ substantially from those employed by public overseeing agencies like boards of higher education. The content, as well as the rigor of the evaluation, is sometimes called into question. For example, the Council on Program Evaluation (COPE) at the University of Illinois, on which I served for three years, used quality of instructional program, research, service, contribution to other campus units, value to state and society, and future expectations as criteria for assessing departments.

In the actual Council deliberations, however, the quality of the research, as manifested in such things as national rankings, tended to overwhelm all other criteria when a university department was evaluated. Such would be the case, I suspect, at all major research universities. Even though indicators of the other criteria were seriously considered, nothing could compensate for a weak research program and nothing could negate a strong one, in the view of the Council.

One would suspect that a state board of higher education, since it is responsible for allocating funds to state universities, would be relatively more interested in costs and credit hour production than in quality of research. Even if both groups used the same set of criteria, the weightings of the criteria might differ dramatically in the final judgments. It is not difficult to see how the professors in this case might consider themselves the best judges of the quality of the departments while the overseeing board might consider itself the guardian of the public interest.

Even within professions there is strong disagreement over who should and could render judgments. Within the COPE operation, some departments, such as the physics department, felt that professors from other departments were not competent to pass judgment on their department. Some of the toughest internal political battles were over the Council's competence in judging other departments. Defenders of the COPE procedures argued that there were activities, criteria, and competencies that the professors shared as professors. Even though people from outside a department might be incapable of judging the content of the research, members of the Council were competent to judge how the quality of the research was regarded by other physics professors around the country. They were also competent as professors to judge the quality of instruction and so on. The interdisciplinary evaluation of departments continued even though it was sometimes conducted after lengthy and extensive negotiations and at the insistence of the top university administration.

In the conduct of professional reviews, the actual review procedures take on considerable importance. They are the means by which people determine whether the evaluation is fair. For example, in the early days of the COPE system, dozens of departments were reviewed without any recommendations being made to disband a unit. Suddenly—or so it seemed to those affected—the Council recommended the abolition of the College of Communication with some of its constituent parts assigned elsewhere and some disbanded.

This action created an enormous furor. The chancellor received more mail than at any time since men and women were assigned to co-ed dormitories. During registration, opponents of the recommendation collected ten thousand student signatures opposing the move. A rallying point for opponents was not the substance of the evaluation report so much as the unfair treatment of the unit. Other units had received bad reviews before, but none had been threatened with dissolution. There was neither precedent nor warning. Nor had the threatened unit a chance to present its own case before the recommendation was made. In both the professional review and quasi-legal approaches to evaluation, proper procedure and due process are the bases of fairness. The College of Communication is still there.

Confidentiality is another problem. To instill public confidence and public knowledge, there must be a public report. Yet professionals are reluctant to have their activities fully exposed to public view. Normally, as in the case of COPE, there are two reports, one an inside confidential report revealing warts and blemishes, the "real" report, and a public report which has been edited somewhat. This dual reporting seems to be necessary for professional cooperation, but of course it makes the public distrustful.

This point is dramatized by the evaluation system at a western university, which evaluated departments and published the actual reports in a form similar to a student newspaper. Predictably, this created great dissatisfaction among the faculty. The university happened to be in the process of selecting a new chancellor. The major topic of discussion during faculty interviews with the candidates for chancellor was the candidates' attitudes toward the evaluation system. The system died aborning. Generally, both professionally and personally, we can stand far less public criticism of ourselves than we think we can.

Quasi-legal

The strength of the quasi-legal approach to evaluation is that it incorporates the procedures and authority of the law. The weakness is that it also incorporates some of its liabilities. In some ways the fit between actual legal procedures and quasi-legal procedures is not a good one. For example, there is no body of case law by which to decide cases in fields such as education. Nonetheless, quasi-legal procedures have proved to be valuable in deciding controversial public issues.

Quasi-legal evaluation procedures consist of such things as blue-ribbon panels, most types of public hearing, and mock trials. A major advantage is that pressing public issues can be addressed quickly by the appointment of a commission or panel. Members of the public who are most significantly involved can be called to testify and present their views. Participation can be very broad, involving groups that might be excluded by most other approaches. A major appeal of the quasi-legal one is its potential openness to diverse viewpoints.

For example, in the panel hearings sponsored by the National Education Association to evaluate the Michigan Accountability System, more than twenty groups, ranging from the League of Women Voters to the art teachers' association, presented testimony. Previously agreed-upon procedures for hearing evidence were followed (House et al., 1974). The hearings themselves took on the trappings of a legal proceeding: The panel sat behind a table facing the witnesses, the testimony was tape-recorded, the written documents were noted and indexed, and so on. Symbolism seems to be a part of such hearings.

Another critical element is the constitution of the commission, panel, or jury. In the Michigan hearing, the panel consisted of three known evaluators. These panelists were chosen, however, by the National Education Association, which, in a sense, was a plaintiff in the case. A similar selection procedure was followed in the investigation of the Florida Competency testing assessment (Tyler et al., 1978). Credibility is always at issue. The identity of the panel and its procedures are balanced against the manner of its selection and what it may have to gain or lose, i.e., its impartiality, in such matters. The question of impartiality is not whether the panelists have expressed previous opinions about similar issues. If they are experts, they will have. The question is whether their own interests are at stake somehow and how the total panel is constituted. In mock trials the juries have so far consisted of professionals who are in some way involved with the public.

Mock trials themselves, or adversary proceedings as they are sometimes called, have been strongly criticized by some evaluators (Popham and Carlson, 1977). The adversary evaluation is based on the idea of two advocates presenting opposing sides of the issue. Critics charge that the two proponents are seldom equal in ability, and hence the case may be won by the abler debaters regardless of the merit of the issues.

Another criticism is that law judges are extremely fallible. Yet in education and other social areas, there is no appeal court by which procedural mistakes can be corrected. A third criticism is that the adversary model is not effective in arriving at the truth of a matter. While it may resolve conflicts, its potential for enlightenment is limited. Ramsey Clark, the former attorney general, puts it most strongly: "If there is a worse procedure for arriving at the truth, I don't know what it is."

A fourth criticism is that social issues do not lend themselves to "go/no-go" formulations required by the legal model. The issues are too complex and involve finer gradations of judgment. Also, unscrupulous decision-makers may use the approach to reconfirm and justify what they have already decided. They can allow themselves to be persuaded by the weaker arguments in a mock trial. Finally, critics contend that adversary proceedings are extremely expensive, often requiring the expenses of both data collection and a trial.

In defending the adversary proceeding (remembering that not all quasi-legal approaches are adversarial in nature), Thurston (1978) argued that the jury trial has three main advantages: Publicity about the trial communicates what it is about; at least two sides of an issue can be argued; and any type of evidence can be presented and must be presented in a way that is understandable. Thurston argued that the disparity of ability among adversaries and the fallibility of the judges are overstated. In any case, any evaluator using any approach is fallible. Other approaches may also be misused and cost too much. In addition, statistical evaluation methods are not likely to produce "truth" any more than are adversary approaches.

More serious problems for the adversary procedures, Thurston contended, are issue definition and the use of the jury. In social fields like education, there are no traditions or precedents for framing issues, nor is there agreement on standards, as there is on legal standards. In a particular legal case, attorneys know what the legal standards are. Yet in law courts all issues are not black or white. They can be more complex than that.

A second major dilemma is the nature and role of the jury, according to Thurston. Educational juries might be better served by members with expertise and by allowing them to deliberate on evidence external to the trial, both practices not permitted in law. All in all, from his position as both a lawyer and an education researcher, Thurston recognized certain difficulties with adversary proceedings but suggested that these can be alleviated by taking appellate court hearings or administrative hearings as models rather than the better-known jury trial.

In summary, one might say that quasi-legal proceedings, such as hearings and panels, are useful ways of conducting evaluations, depending on the nature of the problem. Controversial public issues that must be addressed quickly and which require a great deal of judgment call for panels of professionals or members of the public to hear all sides of the issue before resolving the matter (insofar as such a controversy is ever resolved). These panels are speedy and produce a sense of focus and resolution. Of course, since the members of the panels are ordinarily drawn from the ranks of the prominent, the conclusions usually represent establishment positions.

For example, the panel evaluating the Michigan Accountability System generated considerable interest and brought public attention to the characteristics of that system. As a result of the hearings and the panel's widely publicized report, several features of the Michigan system were changed. Also, many other states that were considering similar programs revised their own plans as a result. The results of the panel's evaluation had to be defended to the professional evaluation community itself. So there were both widespread public and professional repercussions of the hearings. Probably no other approach could have generated so much publicity and interest.

On the other hand, the efficacy of jury trials seems more questionable. There does seem to be some serious problems with them, though perhaps not as many as critics contend. Full-scale trials are likely to be relatively expensive and long in preparation, although so are many other evaluations. The trials (and other quasi-legal procedures) offer open participation by all members of the public. Yet there is no guarantee that people will actually participate even when given a chance. Many such hearings play to small audiences. Perhaps large-scale jury trials should still be limited to deliberately experimental cases. For the time being, other quasi-legal procedures would seem more efficient.

Case Study

The case study approach is becoming increasingly popular, although like the other subjective approaches, there is some difficulty in establishing its credibility in a predominantly scientific community. Some theorists would contend that it is indeed scientific, but most serious case study workers would deny that two different studies would discover the same thing.

For example, in a case study of a computer-based education system, Gjerde and I emphasized the technological and political features (House, 1974). Those features were definitely there, yet other evaluators might well have selected equally relevant features to emphasize, giving the case study quite a different slant. Most of the problems with case studies involve matters of emphasis rather than matters of truth or falsity. Different observers report different events. Although these issues have been discussed often, methodological consistency and interpretation remain primary problems in case study credibility.

On the positive side, case studies provide rich and persuasive information that is not available from other approaches. Everything from the personalities of the participants to the views of persons far removed from the program can be portrayed. This leads to power and utility of the information. Our case study was passed avidly from hand to hand among the administrators in the central office making decisions about the computer-based education systems.

Portraying events so personally also results in problems of confidentiality, fairness, and justice. It is difficult to disguise people and personalities so that they cannot be identified. Since one never has a total picture of the participants, it is also difficult to portray them accurately. Every case study has such problems, problems that are not nearly so severe in more impersonal forms of evaluation.

A strength of the case study approach is that it allows the representation of diverse points of view and different interests. In this sense, it can be one of the most democratic approaches. Depending upon the skill and effort of the evaluator, the evaluation can be extremely democratic in representing the interests of the parties involved, as contrasted to the systems analysis approach which tends to exclude diverse viewpoints and interests. If one does a reasonably decent job of locating and interviewing the diverse groups involved with a program, most interests will be represented. As I have indicated elsewhere in this book, those most frequently excluded in such a pluralistic approach will be the least advantaged and least powerful. Of course, the evaluator *can* exclude diverse interests. The systems analysis approach requires a deliberate effort not to do so.

The representation of diversity of interests leads to another formidable problem: How shall the evaluator balance and resolve the various interests? Case study theorists differ on this point. Some believe that they should balance the interests according to their own sense of justice. Anthropologists, in particular, have a long-established tradition of "going native," of siding with the underdogs. This throws the impartiality of the evaluation into question, however. Generally, evaluators do not appeal to principles but rely on their intuitive judgments.

Another position is that the evaluator should remain disinterested. He should not favor any particular interests in the evaluation, but should treat all the same. In this view, the evaluator neutrally represents and portrays, leaving the weighing and balancing of the various interests to the judgment of the reader. The evaluator makes none. A sophisticated proponent of this position might say that the information contained in the case study should be of equal utility to all interests. Equal access to knowledge will provide the audiences with equal opportunity to influence educational practice. Hence, the evaluator should be procedurally neutral with respect to different audiences (Elliott, 1979).

This presumes, however, that people are actually able to make use of the information. An argument might be made that the powerful are far more likely to do so than the powerless. In other words, such a position neutralizes the evaluator but does not neutralize the power relationships that already exist. Disinterestedness actually works to help the powerful.

A related issue is whether the evaluator should draw explicit recommendations from the study or whether this should be reserved for the reader, i.e., the evaluator should draw no conclusions of his own. It seems to me that either position is permissible, and that which is preferable should depend on the audience. It is true, as proponents argue, that the evaluator may not know enough about the circumstances of the program to draw good conclusions. Only in the case where the alternatives evaluated are identical to the recommendations would the evaluator understand the particular circumstances enough. On the other hand, it seems unlikely to me that the readers will be intimidated by the evaluator's recommendations if they are not good ones.

There are many instances in modern life where one would rather read and accept the recommendations than read the entire evaluation and extract one's own recommendations. For example, I am willing to accept Consumers' Union recommendations on many consumer products without having to read every evaluation on electric blenders or short-wave radios. To have to read every evaluation for every recommendation one acts on in modern life would be far too time-consuming, even if I could understand the evaluation and extract my own recommendations. Forcing each reader to draw his own conclusions and recommendations in every area where she must take action is an interesting, democratic idea, but utterly impractical if widely applied to all the specialized areas of modern society. In modern society, some specialization in decision-making seems inevitable. What the case study must do, it seems to me, is present the reader with information by which she can judge the soundness of the conclusions and recommendations if she so desires.

Connected to this issue is the claim that most proponents make for case studies. They claim that case studies are more useful than other types of evaluation. And there is some truth to this, I think, in the kind of information that a case study provides, information that allows one to come to grips better with the inner workings of a program. But the claim that case studies are more useful in all situations is considerably overstated. Case studies are always long and involved. One does not have the time to read one in preparation for every decision. There are some efficiency trade-offs, and the belief that case studies are more useful generally is more an article of faith than an empirical fact.

One more problem: Case studies are not for everyone. Writing a good case study is a difficult job, and only certain people have the talent for doing it. It looks easy, just as writing a novel looks easy, and many are tempted by it who would not be attracted to other approaches. Unfortunately, the lack of methodological guides, strictures, and procedures often leads to poor quality work. And a bad case study is bad indeed. The ability to focus on relevant issues and put these in perspective in such a way that one is not simply writing personal opinion are not universal talents. Those who do case studies need more rigorous training than they now receive. Of course, other approaches are subject to poor quality applications as well.

In spite of these caveats and reservations, the case study approach is one of the most promising and worth developing. Other things being equal, it is often my personal choice. If it is credible to its intended audience, a well-constructed case study is a most powerful evaluation. It has the potential for being persuasive, accurate, coherent, and just in its representation of diverse views in complex situations. On the other hand, it is no panacea and entails a distinctive set of problems of its own. Its theory and methodology have not yet been thoroughly thought through.

NOTE

1. This section is based on Ernest R. House and Rochelle S. Mayer, "A Critique of the Educational Imagination in Evaluation," *Journal of Aesthetic Education,* July 1980.

CONDUCTING VALID EVALUATIONS

A key concept in this book has been that of validity. In a broad sense I take validity to mean something like "worthiness of being recognized." The dictionary definition is, "the quality of being well-founded on fact, or established on sound principles, and thoroughly applicable to the case or circumstances; soundness and strength (of argument, proof, authority, etc.)" (*O.E.D.*). The concept of validity that I have applied to evaluation is considerably expanded from the traditional notion of validity as prediction, although inclusive of it.

The modern practice of evaluation is properly seen as a social decision prodecure. In the first chapter of this book, three basic evaluation situations were delineated—the personal, the interpersonal, and the public. In the personal situation, the evaluator and the audience for the evaluation are one. As a minimum validity claim, one would expect that the evaluation be true. There are different ideas and methods for arriving at the truth.

In the interpersonal situation, the evaluator works in service to the audience, but the evaluator and the audience are different private parties, as in a Consumers' Union evaluation. In this case, one would demand that the evaluation not only be true but that the evaluation be credible to the audience. The audience must trust it. There are various ways of demonstrating credibility and trustworthiness.

In the third basic situation, the evaluator evaluates a public program for an external audience. In this case it is not enough for the evaluation to be true and credible; it must also be normatively correct, for now the evaluation has been transformed from a private into a public affair. The third case is the one that confronts most evaluators. They face triple validity demands that the evaluation be true, credible, and right. Again, there are several ways in which the rightness of an evaluation can be construed. The task before the evaluator is most formidable because a failure in any one of the three areas invalidates the evaluation.

Each of the eight approaches to evaluation makes a validity claim, a claim of being "worthy of recognition." Within each validity claim is revealed, in shorthand as it were, the strengths and weaknesses of each approach. The systems analysis approach claims that it is scientific, that by following explicated procedures it produces reliable information, "hard data." By focusing so exclusively on the truth aspect of validity, these evaluations are often not credible to those evaluated and are sometimes undemocratic, unfair, or otherwise normatively incorrect.

The behavioral objectives approach claims validity in a different way based on the notion of technology. It attempts to determine the evaluation by specifying desired outcomes and then defining the means to those ends. The methods are specifications of the domain and the behavior to be observed. Face validity is derived from holding the program accountable for its prespecified goals. The approach does not include methods for judging the correctness of the goals themselves.

The decision-making approach claims validity by virtue of its utility to decision-makers. The usefulness of the data collected is the primary consideration, so the credibility of the evaluation to the audience is high. One must ask again whether service to the decision-maker is sufficient for correctness. The goal-free evaluator claims validity because of his lack of bias. Protection from improper influence makes him an objective judge of the consequences of the program. However, his credibility is often called into question since external audiences and those evaluated often question whether he really appreciates what the program is doing.

In Chapter 3 I have labeled these four approaches "objectivist" in their epistemology. All rely to a greater or lesser degree upon explicated methods for their claim to validity. Observation is the primary method of data collection. Replication is a key criterion, and this is achieved by externalizing and explicating procedures so that events can be witnessed by several observers. Reliability in measurement is highly valued.

Validity is usually assessed by replication or by inter-instrument agreement. The strength is the rigor of method, to which these approaches give great attention. Testability of hypotheses is highly valued. The weakness is that in their focus on the truth aspect of validity, they neglect the normative basis of what they are doing. If this is a weakness in the conduct of science, in evaluation it is a fatal flaw.

Generally, objectivist approaches to evaluation are derived from the empirical theory tradition in the social sciences. Evaluation is seen as an applied social science. Advocates of empirical theory hold that social science differs only in degree and not in kind from the natural sciences. There are only two models for legitimate knowledge: the natural sciences or the formal disciplines like logic and mathematics. Anything which cannot meet the standards of knowledge set by these disciplines is suspect (Bernstein, 1978).

A widespread, unsophisticated view is that the basis of all empirical knowledge is the ream of basic, uninterpreted "hard" facts. Empirical claims are legitimized by an appeal to these facts. Hence, science consists of collecting data and making generalizations from them. Presumably, the evaluator likewise investigates the effects of programs, using the methods of social science to ensure the objectivity and hence the validity of the evaluation: validity rests on the employment of the prescribed methodology.

Fundamental to this view is the categorical distinction between theory and practice. The scientist or evaluator discovers empirical relationships, and this knowledge is applied in practice. Explicated methodology leads to explicit, validated knowledge. Action is the technical application of this validated knowledge. Consequently, the proper role for the investigator, like the natural scientist, is one of "disinterest." He is value-neutral. Through his methodology he discovers the facts but does not criticize or convert them into practice. It is up to others, particularly decision-makers, to draw implications for action. In a sense, the notion of a free market of ideas and of everyone drawing her own conclusions and implications is intrinsic to the philosophy of liberalism.

There are many criticisms of such an objectivist epistemology. The relevant one here is that it focuses on the truth aspect of validity to the exclusion of the credibility and normative aspects. It presumes validity because of its methodology, and it is credible only to those who believe in such a methodology. To those who are evaluated, it is often not credible, unless they believe in "science" as a legitimating force. For example, in the Follow Through evaluation, the people evaluated felt that the evaluation did not examine relevant outcomes even though it was rigorously conducted.

The second criticism is that the objectivist approach harbors implicit values of which the investigators are themselves unaware. For example, standardized achievement tests are not value-neutral but are based on certain value premises such as maximizing individual differences. The very concepts, categories, and techniques, such as the "basic skills" categorization in the Follow Through evaluation, are value-laden. The fact that objectivist evaluators are often unaware of the biases of their techniques and presume to be value-neutral makes such evaluations potentially dangerous. In truth, the use of such techniques presupposes certain background axioms, such as an ethical system and system of justice indicating how wants and interests are to be determined. These are taken for granted. The investigator's information is assumed to feed into the presumed social decision system, such as, for example, individuals making use of the information to satisfy their own wants.

A more sophisticated notion of objectivity than the correspondence of theory to a realm of uninterpreted facts is the notion of intersubjective standards of rationality or norms of inquiry by which one attempts to eliminate various forms of bias and distortion (Bernstein, 1978). To a certain degree, Scriven's goal-free evaluation uses an expanded notion of objectivity and is an exception to the general critique of objectivist approaches. In fact, he goes much further and contends that the evaluator can determine objective "needs" that exist independent of the audiences' preferences. Hence, his position is objectivist in that not only the information derived but presumably the standards of evaluation themselves can be objectively determined by the evaluator. Values are facts, and the evaluator is justified in making strong value judgments about the program. This is not a common view among either evaluators or philosophers.

The other four approaches—the art criticism, professional review, quasi-legal, and case study approaches—are "subjectivist" in that they base their validity claims on an appeal to experience rather than to scientific method. Knowledge is conceived as being largely tacit rather than explicit. In the art criticism approach, one relies on the experience of the connoisseur. His training and credentials are important. The validity of evaluation depends on his perceptions. Teaching, or the social activity itself, is viewed as an art in which the ends are realized in the means and not separated from the means as in a technology (Elliott,

1979). Holistic perception is the critic's method. He relates the parts to the whole in an integrated fashion, thus making his judgments. The key to validity is his ability to do this. The weakness is that different critics may arrive at different criticisms of the program.

In the professional review approach, one relies upon the collective, traditional experience of the profession. Professional judgment based on professional standards is why the evaluation deserves attention. The model of the profession is that of craft rather than art or technology. There are internalized rules, knowledges, and exemplars by which the performance may be judged. Hence, validity depends on subscription to these intersubjectively held, if tacit, rules of competence. Only a professional who has participated in the professional culture can have acquired this knowledge and be a competent judge. It should be noted that the art criticism and the professional review approaches have high credibility among audiences of professionals but low credibility among positivist scientists, who see the rules of practice as "unvalidated" by scientific method, and among members of the public, who fear that strong professional interests exclude the public interest.

In the quasi-legal approach, one relies upon the experience of the legal profession, adopting "due process" procedures that have been developed in the English common law. The degree to which the evaluation follows the proper procedures is a measure of its validity. Procedural fairness is at issue. It is the experience of the law as embodied in the legal tradition that serves as the basis for validity. If the procedures are fair, whatever the results, the evaluation is valid.

Finally, in the case study approach, one relies upon the experience of the participants and the audience. Audience comprehension is a primary consideration. The evaluator records the participant's experience in such a way that the audience will understand. Validity depends on the match between the evaluation and the experiences of the participants and the audience.

The subjectivists, of course, also claim that their evaluations are true, but they attempt to achieve insights within the frame of reference of the audience and the participants themselves. Meaningfulness is important. The evaluation must be capable of being understood. The subjectivists assume that each investigator and each reader is capable of arriving at conclusions individually. A strength of these approaches is that they often communicate important insights. A weakness is that the conclusions may vary considerably, even be contradictory, and that there is no clear way to reconcile them. What is valid for one person may not be valid for another.

The subjectivist epistemology, and particularly the case study approach, is closely linked to a phenomenological view of man. Contrasted to the view that science alone is the measure of reality and the standard for legitimate knowledge, phenomenologists maintain that one's everyday view of the world, focusing on persons and their behavior, is more fundamental. Particularly if one thinks of human action, one must think in terms of intentions and of people who guide their behavior by principles and standards based on community values. This is the domain of practical rather than theoretical reason (Bernstein, 1978).

Similarly, subjectivist approaches to evaluation appeal to experience with the actual situation as the basis for validity. The experience may be manifested in a connoisseur, in a profession, in the tradition that deals with conflicting points of view, or in the actual participants and audiences for the evaluation. Accuracy in reflecting the situation and utility for the audience are key concepts. This, to be "adequate" the evaluation must be understandable to the actor and reflect the social reality in which he lives.

Critics of the phenomenologist epistemology note that there is often confusion over whose common sense perceptions are to be taken as the basis for understanding. Furthermore, if one takes everyday understanding as the foundation of inquiry, does one not merely reconstruct whatever ideologies, biases, and false beliefs already exist? How can one distinguish causal determinants and regularities, the strength of the positivist epistemology, from perceived beliefs? How can one evaluate conflicting interpretations? Phenomenology provides no way of doing so. Phenomenology has something of a conundrum in that what one takes to be causal determinants of social action is dependent on one's substantive theories. Yet interpretation itself is at least partially dependent on one's causal analysis (Bernstein, 1978).

Finally, both phenomenologists and positivists take as their ideal the role of the investigator as "disinterested" and aloof from the interests of the everyday world. The positivists substantiate their empirical regularities, and the phenomenologists elucidate fundamental subjective structures, arriving at pure description. If the positivists can be accused of covertly reflecting establishment biases, the phenomenologists can be accused of reflecting the biases of those portrayed. In either case, for evaluation at least, the role of the "disinterested" evaluator removed from all practical concerns is morally deficient.

The evaluator must be impartial. This is not the same as being indifferent to which interests are represented or being removed from the real world. The evaluator is engaged with the world. His work directly affects who gets what. He is engaged by essence of his social function. The evaluation should be impartial in that all relevant interests are represented. This should be an active concern of the evaluator, and insulation from external interests is not attainment of this moral obligation. There is a tradition in liberal science which contends that isolation of the theorist and the theory from worldly influences insures truth and fairness. But this is certainly wrong. Being indifferent to whose interests are advanced is not the same as advancing the interests of all.

In summary, then, the validity of an evaluation depends upon whether the evaluation is true, credible, and normatively correct. Each approach to evaluation claims validity in its own way, but employing a particular approach does not guarantee validity. The closer the evaluation situation matches the assumptions of a particular approach, the more likely the evaluation will be valid. Most commonly, validity is taken as identical to truth, but this is insufficient for the evaluation of a social program. As indicated by the contrast among the personal, interpersonal, and public situations, the evaluator incurs additional obligations.

Certainly, an evaluation would be invalid if it were untrue, and truth is established in many ways. The positivist temper sees truth as equivalent to replication and prediction. If one knows the cause of something, one can observe and predict accurately. Truth, however, is far broader than the positivist conception would allow. Criteria for truth depend upon the intersubjective agreement of the involved community and change from time to time. In the personal, individual situation, one can imagine the search for truth as an individual effort, even if it is not so.

In the interpersonal situation, discovery of the facts is insufficient. They must be communicated to an external audience. The evaluation must be credible so that the audience finds it trustworthy. Credibility is a function of the evaluator as well as the evaluation. The evaluator's credibility is enhanced if his own interests are not at issue. For example, one would doubt an evaluation of automobiles if the evaluator were paid by General Motors, whatever the quality of work. The evaluation must be authentic in the sense that it is entitled to acceptance or belief because of agreement with known facts or experience. The objectivists stress agreement with facts and the subjectivists agreement with experience. In both cases the evaluation must be trust-worthy.

Generally, the evaluator's trustworthiness will be strengthened if people understand and believe the evaluator's intentions. Expression of intentions is taken as a sign of truthfulness. Sincerity is often judged by the evaluator's consistency of actions. Within the evaluation report itself, credibility and authenticity are influenced by the coherence, voice, and other aesthetic elements as analyzed in Chapter 5. Overall, the evaluator must prove trustworthy.

Still, in the evaluation of public programs, this is not enough. One might accurately and sincerely enhance the welfare of a particular group while seriously damaging the public welfare. Service or utility to a particular group cannot be the ultimate criterion. A public evaluation must be normatively correct. Along with truth and beauty must come justice although, again, this is conceived in different ways. In Part III I have tried to indicate what these normative considerations should be. Public evaluation should be democratic, fair, and ultimately based upon the moral values of equality, autonomy, impartiality, and reciprocity. Admittedly, this is only a initial fromulation of such considerations.

No evaluation approach, no method, will guarantee validity in advance. One must step back and examine a particular evaluation in its situation to see whether it is valid. In most cases, several evaluation approaches will be appropriate, and the evaluator can choose an approach on the basis of his and his client's preferences. Many evalua-tions will be mixes of different approaches. Ideally, the evaluator should be trained in several approaches and should not mechanically apply whatever he has learned. He should know the weaknesses of his favorite approaches so that he might guard against threats to their validity.

The device of a fair evaluation agreement is one way in which the client's interests and those of affected parties may be included. It guards against the autocratic behavior of either evaluator or client. One can arrive at an evaluation approach or a combination of approaches in a morally acceptable way. Unfortunately, the contractual notion impli-cit in the fair agreement does not always sufficiently protect the interests of those not a party to the agreement.

The most frequent defect in an evaluation is a moral one. A liberal society sees itself as composed of independent, autonomous units who cooperate only when it furthers the ends of the parties. In such a society evaluation is likely conceived as a private or interpersonal matter, as an agreement between two parties for their mutual benefit, without regard for others. Obligations to the larger society are frequently overlooked. The evaluation of public programs is clearly a situation in which such obligations do exist, and the concept of validity must be extended to apply to such a significant social practice.

Appendices

APPENDIX A
An Analysis of the Logic of an Evaluation

Modes of Reasoning

In this section an evaluation report is analyzed for its argumentative structure. The report is Glass's "Educational Product Evaluation" (Glass, 1972), an evaluation of some audio tapes developed by Michael Scriven. After an analysis of the report, Scriven's (1972) response to the evaluation is also analyzed for its logical structure. First, however, it is necessary to delineate the categories of analysis, the modes of reasoning that both evaluators employ.

No doubt there are circumstances in evaluation where formal logic is applicable. For example, deductive logic is certainly appropriate in determining the internal consistency of mathematical models, and inductive logic is indicated in problems of statistical inference. Where appropriate, this reasoning should be applied. For the most part, however, evaluators must rely on extraformal modes of reasoning. I will enumerate some of these techniques of argument based on Perelman and Olbrechts-Tyteca's treatise (1969) on argumentation. The list is by no means exhaustive of man's informal reasoning powers. In the next section I shall illustrate the use of these arguments by an analysis of a well-accepted evaluation study.

The techniques of argument presented here are divided into three types: quasi-logical arguments, arguments based on the structure of reality, and arguments establishing the structure of reality. The first of these types, quasi-logical arguments, derive their credibility from their similarity to formal logic or mathematical reasoning. However, it is only by a reduction that the quasi-logical argument appears to be formal. The argument is essentially nonformal rather than formal and must ultimately be defended by resort to other forms of argument.

The first type of arguments depends on its similarities to logical relationships. They include contradiction and incompatibility, identity and definition, transitivity, and reciprocity. The other group of quasi-logical arguments depends on its similarities to mathematical reasoning. These are inclusion of the part into the whole, division of whole into parts, comparison, and arguments of probability.

Incompatibility. In a logical system two theses that contradict one another show that the system is logically inconsistent. The quasi-logical analog is incompatibility in which one is forced to choose between two theses that are not logically but are practically incompatible because of circumstances. In extreme cases, holding incompatible theses may invite ridicule, the argumentative equivalent of logical absurdity. For example, in an evaluation the director of the project may present one view of the project while a teacher working in it may present quite a different view. The two viewpoints are not logically contradictory since both may be true as viewed from different circumstances. Nonetheless, the incompatibility may be an important point in the total evaluation. In fact, the director whose view is incompatible with the views of others in the project does begin to look ridiculous.

Total identity and definition. Insofar as definitions can be stated unambiguously and unequivocally, they belong to systems of formal logic. As soon as they are applied to real world problems, definitions become quasi-logical. One must choose among many possible meanings. Only purely conventional systems can escape these identity problems. For example, validity is defined in at least five different ways, ranging from a general justification to the ability to predict one event from another. One can employ any one of the definitions, but the choice must be defended as appropriate and applicable if challenged.

Partial identity. The "rule of formal justice" requires that identical treatment be given to beings or situations of the same kind. This provides for consistency of action, the basis of formal justice. "Reciprocity" of behavior rests on defining situations as symmetrical. These arguments require partial reductions, such as in the prestige and status of the parties involved, which of course depend on argued positions. For example, "It was only fair that the teacher provide special assistance to the child since she had already given extra help to others." More arguable would be, "They deserved equal grades since they had exerted the same effort, although with far different results." These statements rest on definitions of partial identities.

Transitivity. A is greater than B, and B is greater than C, so therefore A is greater than C–but the basis of "greater than" is arguable. For example, "Program A is better than B because test scores are higher. A must be better than C because B's test scores are better than C's." Of course, the criteria for comparisons are arguable as is the transitivity of the relationship itself. Program A may not be better than C even if the first relationship holds.

The arguments based on similarity to mathematical reasoning include the following:

Inclusion of the part in the whole. The whole is greater than each part. For example, "Having a higher total test score is better than a high score on one of the parts because the total score includes the parts."

Division of the whole into the parts. Exhaustive division into parts leads to the conclusion that the part left is necessary in some way. "I will list my biases for the study and against it." "Either we have a Type I error or a Type II error."

Comparison. Direct comparison of objects is based on an idea of measure, but any standard of measurement is lacking. Criteria are often cited. Choice always implies comparison. "Argument by sacrifice" is a form of comparison: what sacrifice would one be willing to make to achieve an end? Perhaps all evaluation is basically comparative.

Probabilities. Argument by probability and variability usually entails a reduction of data to monistic and homogeneous values and to elements by which they can be compared. But it is usually powerful because it imparts an empirical character even when nonquantitative—e.g., Decision Theory, which requires that the decision situation be reduced to a particular decision model.

An entirely different class of arguments is based on the "structure of reality." Reality is sufficiently agreed upon and unquestioned, like facts and truths, so that one tries to establish a connection between accepted notions and those being promoted. These arguments can be more finely classified as realtions of succession, which relate a phenomenon to its causes or consequences; and relations of coexistence, which relate an "essence" to its manifestations, e.g., a person to his actions. Among the sequential relations in which time plays a major factor are the following:

Causality. Demonstrating causal links may be based on many different methods and obviously play an essential role in evaluative argument. The attempt to establish a causal link may involve establishing a relationship between two successive events, reasoning from a given event to a presumed cause, or projecting a causal consequence as the result of an event. In any case, the causal statement requires certain value judgments (see Ennis, 1973).

Pragmatism. An event is evaluated by its consequences. Value of the consequences is transferred to the cause. The value of the consequences must be agreed upon or one must resort to other arguments to establish their value.

Ends and means. Determination of the best means depends on exact definition and agreement on the end pursued. Only values relating to the end are likely to be discussed. In a technologically oriented society, ends-means arguments are particularly potent. Example: Behavioral objectives programs are good which achieve these ends. Separating means and ends allows maximum agreement by separating the ends and means analytically, although it is doubtful if a particular means accomplishes only one effect. Practically, ends and means are more closely entwined.

Waste. Since an effort has been exerted to this point, it would be a waste to give up now. "It would be a shame not to reanalyze these data since they have been so costly to collect." "Develop the child's talent to the fullest."

Direction. If we give in this time, where will it lead? The domino theory. "Knowledge can be indefinitely increased. There is no limit to learning."

Unlimited development. More is better and can be obtained. Whereas sequential relations are on the same phenomenological level, relations of coexistence connect two objects or events in which one is more basic and explanatory of the other. The order of events is of secondary importance. These include the following:

The person and his acts. Our conception of a person is usually influenced by his actions, though ordinarily the two are not equated as they are in behaviorism. Interpreting an event by ascribing it to the personality is common practice in evaluation studies. How the "intention" of the person is handled is particularly critical. The intent is often inferred by correspondence among actions. But there is always ambiguity. Most attributions of motivation are examples of this type of argument.

Authority. Although rightfully excluded from demonstrations in logic, since the logic must stand on its own, the prestige of the person making an assertion is important in argument. It is essential in legal reasoning. Only if the assertion is agreed upon by the universal audience and hence considered a "fact" is it beyond the reach of authority.

"Objectivity" is often achieved by separating the person from his act, e.g., taking the author's name off proposals before judging them. However, the person may be the best predictor of the success of the project. Impartiality may be sought by bias reduction techniques rather than through complete severance of the agent from his act (Scriven, 1975). In argumentation and evaluation the relation between a person and his assertion is important.

Person and group. "He did that because he's a behaviorist." This category includes arguments expressing concern about maintaining or establishing relations with others. Characterizing a person through his group membership is far more common in evaluation than is realized. Not only are quantitative studies set up to reveal differences among groups, qualitative evaluations often interpret the social system under study as a set of interacting groups. In addition, the evaluator is often at pains to demonstrate his concern and/or impartiality by showing what groups he himself does or does not belong to.

Act and essence. What is a good director? A good director is one who conforms to the ideal of a director. In the absence of such conformity there is a "deficiency." The essence of an object under evaluation is often defined by a set of intuitive criteria one would expect to apply. For example, a "good project director" would be expected to be and to do certain things. The evaluator may elicit this normally implicit set of criteria in order to judge the director. The same thing can be done with a good program, a good textbook, etc. The list of criteria is never inclusive and is always arguable. Nonetheless, the list is often effective in persuading the audience as to quality. Example: Consumers' Union reports on manufactured products.

Symbolic relation. Only members of a particular group believe in the magical relationship between the symbol and the thing, such as a national flag. Symbolic relationships are important in describing certain aspects of social systems and statuses. These relations are somewhat different in that they cannot be justified to others. Educators often attach such special meanings to particular facets of their program and to particular charismatic leaders within it. People and things become the objects of faith in and of themselves. This is a common puzzle to the evaluator who may look in vain for more material relationships underlying the faith.

The third class of arguments assumes the fewest premises in advance. These arguments neither rely upon similarity to formal logic nor argue from the already agreed upon structure of reality. Rather they try to *establish* reality. Example and illustrations do so by resorting to the particular case. Analogies and metaphors do so by showing new conceptual relationships to the audiences. This mode of argument is relied upon heavily in "naturalistic" evaluation.

Example. Resort to example implies lack of agreement on a particular rule but a prior agreement that one might eventually come to an understanding. A series of examples induces one to generalize. Sometimes the reasoning is from the particular to the particular with no rule being stated. The examples operate implicitly. The technique of the "closed case" and the legal "precedent" is built on such a technique. This argument values the actual and the habitual. To be effective the example itself must be accepted as factual.

Illustration. Whereas example is used to establish a rule, illustration is used to clarify one and strengthen adherence to it. It promotes understanding. Illustrations of forms of arguments in this section attempt to clarify the categories, but the categories are not dependent on the illustrations.

Analogy. Analogy strikes a relation between two previously unrelated spheres and is hence essential in invention and imagination. It develops and extends thought.

Metaphor. Metaphorical assertion opens new realms of thought by moving from the known to the unknown and by helping indicate things unspecifiable in ordinary language. Metaphoric assertion is most used in conjunction with examples and illustrations. How it works to extend the audience's ideas will be discussed as part of naturalistic evaluation.

These techniques of argument are not exhaustive and are not intended as a list of techniques from which to construct evaluations. Rather they are meant to illustrate the kind of reasoning that is actually employed in evaluations.

Analysis of Glass's "Educational Product Evaluation"

I have chosen Glass's "Educational Product Evaluation: A Prototype Format Applied" (Glass, 1972) to analyze in terms of the arguments enumerated in the last section. I selected this evaluation because it is highly accessible, it is succinct, the authority of the author is unassailable, it exhibits a variety and complexity of evaluative arguments, and I find it personally quite persuasive.

My technique will be to paraphrase Glass's work and to identify the arguments in parentheses as they occur. I would not contend that I have found all the arguments in Glass's work, that the ones I have emphasized could not be categorized otherwise, or that the types of argument I have enumerated in the last section are exhaustive. It would be impossible to list all arguments or types or to classify them unambiguously. My purpose is to illustrate from a very good piece of work that those arguments play a critical role in evaluative reasoning. The overall logic of the Glass piece is somewhat more complex than the arguments I have discussed, and I will save it until after a discussion of particulars.

Glass begins with a brief introduction stating the tentative nature of evaluation techniques and describing what he intends to do. The body of the paper is divided into ten parts.

Part I is a description of the AERA cassette recording he intends to evaluate, which is itself a discussion of evaluation by Michael Scriven.

Part II lists the three goals of the product and evaluates them. Training evaluators is good since there is a need for evaluation skills because of legislation mandating evaluation (cause and effect). Producing a casette that can be used while commuting to work may or may not be desirable because it may infringe upon a person's private time in unanticipated ways (pragmatic argument—valuing an event from consequences). Experimenting with new media is commendable if it is not "mere technological tinkering" (person and his actions—intention of the actor). The evidence will be whether the cassette is properly evaluated (intention constructed from consistency of actions—person and his actions).

Part III describes where things stood as the evaluator entered. The director, the topics of the tape, the lecturer, the subject matter, and the initial copies have already been agreed upon. The vending of the cassettes, the choice of materials, and marketing plans are not settled. This signals where it is reasonable for Glass to focus attention. Implicit is the argument that it would be a waste of the evaluator's and audiences' time and effort to address issues already decided (argument of waste).

Part IV is entitled "trade offs" and is a brilliant turn in the overall argument. Glass enumerates what could be purchased with the resources used to produce the cassette—one day of training session for 100 researchers, printing of 20,000 copies of prose materials, a half-year stipend for a research trainee, or four scholarships to AERA training sessions for minority researchers. This is the trade-off for the sponsor, the USOE. Trade-offs for the other major audiences—the director, AERA, and the consumer—are also listed.

The reasoning begins by asking what would be given up by the cassette approach (argument by sacrifice). It establishes the equivalence of the trade-offs in terms of their being purchasable with the resources devoted to the cassette approach (argument by identity). The trade-offs are also equivalent in that they are all consistent with the producer's intent. Without making explicit the reasons, Glass chooses the typescript alternative as the trade-off "with the greatest leverage" (argument by comparison). Why choose the strongest alternative with which to make further comparisons? Implicit in the reasoning is the idea that one should choose the technique which will *best* further the end of the producer (argument by ends and means).

Having chosen the strongest competitor, Glass, in Part V of the study, expands the cost comparison between the cassette and typeset approaches to the fullest (arguments by comparison and sacrifice). In exploring cost considerations, he argues that the cost would be worthwhile for groups of ten-fifteen; that the tape is too expensive and could be cheaper—for this he cites the Colorado audio-visual instruction department as authority (argument by authority); that typescripts could be better stored; and that the typescript's cost could be further reduced. All these arguments are variations based on comparisons between the two approaches and what each might cost under various contingencies.

Part VI is the "intrinsic" evaluation, labeled secondary by the evaluator. It is an evaluation of the technical quality, content, and "utilization of uniqueness" of the medium. This series of arguments deals with issues that are secondary to the entire cassette versus typescript comparison but which might be important to a potential consumer who wishes to purchase the cassettes.

The evaluation of the technical quality and content are based on an ideal of what the technical quality and content should be—deviations from these ideals are deficiencies (argument by act and essence). The evaluator lists criteria which he considers to be relevant and commonly agreed upon, since he does not attempt to justify them. Technical quality contains tape quality, recording fidelity, aesthetic quality, editing, and packaging. Each criterion is accompanied by a judgment and a few remarks enumerating observations on which the judgment is based. Similar "a posteriori" criteria are applied to the content.

The second part of the intrinsic evaluation is of the "utilization of uniqueness" of the cassette medium. This is again basically an argument based on the "essence" of the cassette (act and essence). Two producer claims are explored. The fact that one can stop the tape advantageously is refuted by the evaluator by counting the number of stops. The second claim that a significant number of people have cassette players and time in which to listen to the cassettes is confirmed by a mail survey to 100 AERA members (argument by probability). Knowing he is addressing an audience of educational researchers, Glass reports the confidence intervals in a footnote. Throughout the second part the dormant comparison with typescript is utilized by refuting producer claims that reading typescript cannot do the same things. Glass argues against the producer's "unique features" claim for the cassette approach (argument by act and essence).

Part VII is the "outcome" evaluation and is labeled as primary by the evaluator. The comparison between cassette and typescript is head-on in terms of outcomes. He argues that even if the aural medium is as effective in transmitting information, it is slower. This is a comparison implying measurement. It is a comparison based on pragmatic consequences (argument by comparison; pragmatic argument). Access is also much slower on the cassette (argument by sacrifice).

Glass cites a review of experimental studies comparing the aural versus visual mode as being inconclusive because relative efficiency depends on several contingencies. This is noncontributory to his argument, other than increasing the evaluator's credibility, but it allows Glass to describe a particular study in detail which shows the superiority of visual learning (argument by illustration).

Part VIII is a summary of conclusions and a separate set of recommendations for each separate major audience. The recommendations are quite direct, explicit, and specific in their direction. In fact, the recommendations establish a hierarchy of actions each audience might take, depending on contingencies. Part IX lists the special audiences who might benefit from the cassette approach. The arguments are that cassettes may be beneficial to sightless learners, large groups, "Reverse Luddites." All these arguments in Parts VIII and IX are variations of costs and benefits (arguments of ends and means; pragmatic arguments).

Part X is unusual in its reflexiveness. It is entitled "Evaluating the Evaluator" and explores the evaluator's own biases. Of course, simply undertaking such a consideration enhances the evaluator's credibility. Glass points out that evaluations themselves involve costs, especially in destroying a sense of community (arguments of person and group). In this case, he undertook the study because he was asked by the product developer (person and act). He establishes his credibility by showing that he took actions which are inimical to his own interests, thus giving evidence of his impartiality.

Glass divides his motives into the exclusive categories of motives for a favorable evaluation and motives for an unfavorable evaluation (argument by division of whole into parts). Biases for a favorable review derive from the fact that Glass is a member of the AERA Executive Board, the benefactors; and the fact that the producers are his close colleagues (argument of the person and his group).

Motives for the unfavorable review are that he himself declined to participate on the grounds the cassette approach is not cost effective and the fact that he was once beaten in table tennis by the project director. These arguments depend on the construct of the person behind the acts (argument from person and acts). He concludes the evaluation by pointing out that he has collected no data on attitudes toward the product or on its effectiveness. He leaves the audiences to draw their own conclusions on the balance of biases and overall credibility.

The *overall* structure of the study is well worth examining. It consists of a complex form of argument called the "double-hierarchy" argument (Perelman and Olbrechts-Tyteca, 1969). The double-hierarchy argument consists of two hierarchies of values or objects which are usually connected by relations from the structure of reality. For example, Leibniz's statement that "since [God] cares for the sparrows, he will not neglect reasonable creatures who are far dearer to him" is based on implicit hierarchies of creatures and God's caring and connected by implied cause and effect. Double-hierarchy arguments often take the forms of "if . . . then" conditional statements and are usually implicit.

The overall logical structure of Glass's evaluation seems to consist of a double-hierarchy argument. One hierarchy is a hierarchy of costs. The other hierarchy is one of benefits. The two hierarchies are connected by a means-ends relationship. In fact, the entire study is based on establishing this logical structure and orchestrating the subarguments within the grand overall design.

For example, after the context of the study is defined by the product description, the producer's goals, and the entry point of the evaluator, Glass builds a hierarchy of trade-offs in Part IV. In part V he selects the strongest competitor and builds the cost comparison hierarchy between the two approaches in Part V. In Part VII he builds the benefits hierarchy, again based on comparisons between the two approaches. The means-ends relation connects the two hierarchies. It demands that the best means be chosen to accomplish given ends. The contingencies in Parts VIII and IX are explorations of what would happen if one moved up or down the cost hierarchy or the benefits hierarchy.

Thus Glass has conducted a cost-benefit analysis without precise measurement of the costs or the benefits. And it is persuasive. It is so compelling, I think, because of the integration of the arguments. All the arguments work economically within the overall structure. There is very little extraneous movement. Only the introduction and the final section on the credibility of the evaluator do not contribute directly to the overall argumentative line. Aesthetically these two sections are appropriately placed at the beginning and end. One is inclined to agree with Polanyi that the ultimate test of truth is the coherence and beauty of the structure.

The most difficult part to handle in the overall design is Part VI, dealing with the quality of the cassette. Glass was actually asked to evaluate the cassette itself. I would surmise that the basic problem of intellectual incompatibility from which the evaluation grew was that the cassette itself was good but Glass did not see the investment as being worthwhile. He redefined the problem such that he was evaluating the cassette approach rather than just the cassette itself. Yet he could hardly evaluate the product without direct evaluation of the tape. Also, one of his audiences had to be potential consumers who might buy the tape and not just AERA board members who wanted to know if the entire activity was worthwhile. He labeled the cassette evaluation secondary as opposed to the primary outcome evaluation. Aesthetically he also deemphasized it by tucking the intrinsic evaluation into the middle of the overall presentation.

In addition to the logical coherence of the evaluation, it is also persuasive because the premises of agreement are well chosen for the audiences. Costs/benefits are powerful values for the audiences and means-ends relations are nearly unquestioned by people versed in utilitarian ethics. Glass takes the audiences from values they agree with to conclusions they may not have accepted initially. He is keenly aware of who his audiences are, even addressing each directly and giving each different recommendations. One may suspect, however, that his arguments are not equally persuasive to all. Some groups are likely to harbor values and conditions untouched by the evaluation. Yet he has solved the problem of composite audiences with differing demands beautifully, both logically and aesthetically.

How would one deny such an evaluation? One could attack the basic argumentative structure by denying the equivalence of the trade-offs and by questioning the selection of the strongest competitor, thus denying the means-end relationship. One could attack the costs and deny the comparative benefits that result from the typescript approach. Attacking the secondary evaluation of the tape quality itself does little good since it is not integral to the overall logic of the study. Glass can concede points there and still arrive at negative conclusions. One can also claim the evaluator is unduly biased and attack the credibility of the study in that way, although Glass's discussion of his own biases make this difficult to do. Any evaluation is assailable, even one that is highly persuasive.

It is noteworthy that in this masterful evaluation, Glass has used most of the types of argument previously enumerated. He relies heavily on arguments from the structure of reality, especially sequential relationships linking phenomena to consequences such as ends and means arguments, and on quasi-logical arguments such as comparisons. He has very few arguments which attempt to establish the structure of reality such as examples and metaphors.

Formal data collection procedures are used only moderately, and where employed do not contribute critically to the import of the evaluation. Most data consist of already accepted "facts." Formal data collection procedures are not essential to evaluation; argumentation is.

Analysis of Scriven's Response to Glass's Evaluation

This section was written five months after the rest of the paper because I did not know of Scriven's response to Glass's evaluation until informed of it by Glass. The timing is important because Scriven attacked Glass's evaluation in precisely the way it was suggested in the previous section one would have to do. One must deny the equivalence of the trade-offs and question the selection of the strongest competitor, thus denying the means-end relationship, as well as attack the costs and deny the comparative benefits of the typescript alternative. This is what Scriven does, and comparing his reasoning to Glass's is interesting.

Scriven (1972) begins by saying he has been invited to respond to the Glass evaluation of his cassette (intentions of the actor—argument relating a person and his acts). He sketches the background conditions surrounding his decision to redo the entire second cycle rather than revise the first product. The argument is laid out rationally as a choice among three alternatives (pragmatic argument). However, Scriven devotes so much space to developing the context of his action that he clearly wants his audiences to understand his motivations (argument relating a person to his acts).

Scriven also has a much larger problem with bias than does Glass because Scriven is responding to an evaluation of his own product and is immediately suspect. Interestingly, he argues that the direction of bias is so obvious that it can do no harm (pragmatic argument). This argument attempts to *sever* the relation between the act of counterargument and the motivation (bias) of the actor (argument relating a person and his acts). It is an attempt to reduce perceived bias on the part of the actor. Scriven buttresses his impartiality by showing his ability to distinguish between "excuses" and "criticisms" (in itself an argument by division of whole into parts). While there are several kinds of arguments in the first two sections of his response, Scriven organizes them toward disassociating himself from bias.

In the third section Scriven turns to a consideration of the conclusions about the hardware. He accepts most of Glass's criticisms (enhancing his credibility) but dismisses the desirability of cheap tapes because they will wear badly (pragmatic argument) due to heating and friction effects (cause and effect). He also dismisses distortion in the cassettes if they are played on the proper equipment. The mention of Advent and MacIntosh equipment immediately captures the audiophiles in the audience and shows that Scriven knows what he is talking about (argument by authority). Now it is clear why he started with an analysis of the relatively unimportant area of hardware; Scriven has better information in this area than does Glass. It is also an attack on Glass's cost analysis in terms of the size of the audience reachable and the cost of the tapes.

There is little to argue about in software since Glass's evaluation of Scriven's tape is a string of "excellences." Scriven dismisses the criticism that lack of citations is a handicap, based on the feedback he has received from the field (argument by probability).

Then comes Scriven's basic attack on the logic of Glass's evaluation. Scriven concedes that "the general procedure of really working to get estimates of comparative cost-effectiveness seems to me absolutely correct and indeed the method of choice in all educational evaluation." But he is not in agreement with Glass's assessments of the costs and benefits and particularly the way Glass has them linked together. Scriven's basic thrust is that Glass has chosen the wrong competitor (the typescript) for comparison.

Scriven contends the cassette serves different ends than does the typescript; it is more useful than listening to a car radio and it can be a cheap surrogate for a visiting lecturer in a course. (These two exclusive purposes are established by definition.) These arguments deny the equivalence of outcomes that Glass has established (the argument by identity). The cassettes accomplish different ends, and therefore the trade-offs are not equivalent. The cassette is a motivator in places where written material is not (pragmatic argument). Also, the costs are the same as for commercial tapes (comparison with the norm).

Scriven admits cost, speed, and replay advantages for the typescript, but again the cassette introduces a new element the written material does not. Scriven gives several reasons for using the cassette in class: hearing the authority himself; several speakers are better than one; and the tape provides variety (arguments of pragmatism, the whole greater than its parts, and unlimited development). While not generally superior, it is "repertoire-enlarging." Notice that, overall, Scriven is arguing for the *uniqueness* of the cassette while Glass is arguing that the typescript accomplishes more of the common goals (loci of quality versus loci of quantity).

The cost trade-offs Scriven treats as problematic. Perhaps the funds for producing the cassettes were not available for anything else under the circumstances (argument of waste?). Even if they were, AERA should be doing experimental things (act and essence—"being experimental" an implicit criterion for AERA); and this is a reasonable experiment, given other attempts (argument by comparison with the norm). Also, it is better to try it in education if it is to be used in education (partial identity?).

But Scriven's main objection to Glass's evaluation is the object of comparison: "So my principal criticism of the Glass evaluation concerns the choice of the main crucial comparison. It should not have been the typescript but just the better content—cheaper package cassette." The disagreement is not merely one of comparison. The disagreement is whether to connect the costs and benefits by a means-ends argument, which suggests the *best* competitor—the typescript—or by a pragmatic argument, which suggests a *lesser* competitor.

Scriven insists on the uniqueness of the medium. Although Glass has refuted the uniqueness argument by counting the number of times Scriven stopped the tape, Scriven argues he is not persuaded because Glass did not offer what would be a unique utilization. Scriven switches to "comprehensibility" as the uniqueness factor, admitting that the number of stops on the cassette is a poor indicator of that criterion (argument by act and essence).

In the last section of his response, Scriven suggests that Glass's "Reverse Luddites" category of potential audiences is too narrowly conceived and that there are many normal people who would benefit from a cassette because there are people who prefer listening to reading (arguments by frequency). In fact, everyone does so at some time of the day (cause and effect). These arguments are supported by Scriven asking his wife (argument by illustration) just as Glass used a study by one of his graduate students. Finally, Scriven says one must also consider the additional benefits of what has been learned by the intermediary population—himself and the producer (pragmatic argument). All these arguments increase the benefits, thus making the cost-benefit ratio more acceptable.

The overall logic of Glass's original evaluation is a double hierarchy argument of costs and benefits linked by a means-ends relationship. Scriven sees this structure clearly and accepts the basic comparison of costs and benefits as the method of choice for all evaluations. He tries to show how the costs are not extravagant and unreasonable and that the benefits of the cassette are significantly underrated by Glass. But the main criticism is to challenge Glass's means-ends argument by substituting a pragmatic argument as the link. The means-ends argument requires that the cassette be compared to the *best* alternative available. Scriven's pragmatic argument requires only that the cassette be better than what now exists among other cassettes. Scriven's strategy is to claim unique features for the cassette so it does not have to compete totally head-to-head with the typescript approach on each dimension. Scriven is arguing for a qualitatively different field of comparison.

The pragmatic argument in its elemental form consists of evaluating an event in terms of its consequences. The means-ends argument, on the other hand, depends on agreement on the ends. Determining the *best* means to the ends depends on *exact* definition of the ends pursued. Values not related to the ends are eliminated from consideration. If the ends are exactly defined and agreed upon, the determination of the best means becomes a technical problem. Such reasoning, appropriate for the technical disciplines, is quite different from everyday reasoning.

Generally speaking, Glass's work as a whole has tended to be more means-ends and more technically oriented while Scriven's has tended to rely more on pragmatic argument. In fact, Scriven's goal-free evaluation might be regarded as an ultimate expression of pragmatic argument. One does not care about the expressed ends at all but only about the consequences of the object under evaluation. Generally, conceiving an evaluative problem in "means-ends" logic tends to devalue the means in relation to the ends, while conceiving the same problem in "event-consequences" logic tends to make the event relatively more important. Scriven's challenge to Glass culminates eventually in a discussion over the ends of the cassette approach.

On a more abstract level the dispute is between two principles of rational choice: the principle of effective means and the principle of inclusiveness (Rawls, 1971). The principle of effective means stipulates that, given the objective, one is to achieve it with the least expenditure of means or, given the means, one is to fulfill the objective to the fullest possible extent. In other words, one is to adopt the best alternatives.

The principle of inclusiveness stipulates that one alternative plan is to be preferred to the other if it would accomplish all the aims of the other plan plus some additional aims. In arguing for the cassette approach as "repertoire" expanding but not as a total substitute for the typescript, Scriven is so arguing.

The few differences between Glass and Scriven should not obscure the many similarities of their evaluative argument. Both accept comparison of costs and benefits as the method of choice. Both rely heavily on "structure of reality" arguments, Glass relying a little more on relations of coexistence, e.g., the relations between a person and his acts and between a person and his group. Scriven relies slightly more on sequential relations arguments, especially pragmatic argument. In spite of structure of reality arguments there is little surveying of others for information. Both rely on their own personal observations for primary data.

Secondarily, both use quasi-logical arguments, though only about half as often as the above arguments. Both use arguments attempting to establish the structure of reality, e.g., examples, analogies, etc., only once. An entirely different type of evaluation would have been to put the cassettes into use in the field and to collect anecdotes about how they are used.

Both Glass and Scriven use more than twenty-five arguments in their articles, although Scriven's article is half as long as Glass's. Scriven's high argument density reflects his general style: He is apt to spin out a number of reasons for a given judgment one after the other in a profuse and linear fashion. Here and elsewhere, Glass offers fewer reasons but they are more carefully articulated with one another, some arguments carefully nested within others.

Partly because of this, Glass's piece is more coherent and aesthetically pleasing than is Scriven's. Scriven is at the disadvantage of having to respond to Glass's paper rather than creating a full-fledged argument form of his own, as he did, for example, in his goal-free evaluation paper (Scriven, 1973). The somewhat rambling flow of Scriven's response as he answers various points in Glass's paper detracts from the overall persuasiveness of his arguments. It is a serious disadvantage that every respondent to a document must face.

Finally, it should be noted that this exchange between two of the foremost evaluation theorists is not primarily over data. Rather the dispute is over the proper comparison for the object under evaluation, which is eventually traceable to the argument form preferred and the audiences addressed. Some people think that all disputes can be resolved by data but such is not the case. It is often the logic of the evaluation that is in dispute.

APPENDIX B
Naturalistic Evaluation

When one reads a novel or poem, something is learned. If someone were to ask what has been learned, it would be difficult to say. Often the knowledge gained from such reading is not in propositional form. Yet in the reading of such works, experience from the novel or poem is mapped onto the mind of the reader. The kinds of generalizations the reader acquires have been called "naturalistic" (Stake, 1976) or "spontaneous" (Perelman and Olbrechts-Tyteca, 1969). Naturalistic generalization employs a special kind of qualitative argument.

Arguments that try to establish a structure of reality and assume the least agreement in advance between the author and audience are those most used in "naturalistic" evaluation. They include example, illustration, analogy, and metaphor. I would label as "naturalistic" an evaluation which attempts to arrive at naturalistic generalizations on the part of the audience; which is aimed at nontechnical audiences like teachers or the public at large; which uses ordinary language; which is based on informal everyday reasoning; and which makes extensive use of arguments attempting to establish the structure of reality. In this category I would include most case study evaluation and also those employing legal procedures.

Denzin (1971) described the naturalistic approach in sociology. It attempts to blend the "covert, private features of the social act with its public, behaviorally observable counterparts. It thus works back and forth between word and deed, definition and act." The observer is a part of the research act, and reflections on the self may be important data. The research begins with troubling issues and admits any and all relevant ethical data.

The focus is on the complexity of everyday life, and naturalism tries to understand the everyday world in the experience of those who live it. The naturalist shows profound respect for the empirical world. Participants serve as constant sources of ideas and as checks on the developing ideas of the naturalist. Multiple perspectives are essential to portray the whole picture. The naturalist carries on and perhaps records covert dialogues with himself as he tries to explain events.

Since the focus is on understanding various interactions, the naturalist must follow events over time. He searches for explanations, rather than predictions; and explanations must usually be grounded in the retrospective reasons people give for their own and others' behavior. This necessitates considerable submersion in the participants' culture and language. Joint actions are major points of attention, and they have to be seen in some historical perspective.

Validity is provided by cross-checking different data sources and by testing perceptions against those of participants. Issues and questions arise from the people and situations being studied rather than from the investigator's preconceptions. Concepts and indicators "derive from the subject's world of meaning and action." In constructing explanations, the naturalist looks for convergence of his data sources and develops sequential, phase-like explanations that assume no event has single causes. Working backwards from an important event is a common procedure. Introspection is a common source of data.

Of course, the sociologist is interested in constructing a generalizable theory. The naturalistic evaluator is interested only in the case he is evaluating. The sociologist will try to justify his conclusions to a universal audience. The naturalistic evaluator must adjust his work to a particular audience, who may be the participants of the program he is evaluating. In presenting their studies both will rely heavily on examples and illustrations drawn from the field. The evaluator may or may not draw specific conclusions from the examples. If the examples are collected and presented systematically, their logic will resemble that of inductive reasoning. However, in naturalistic evaluation the audience always has the choice of how to interpret the findings and of how much credibility to assign them.

Evaluations using examples and illustrations extensively, even evaluations which consist entirely of one extended example, are becoming commonplace. They are particularly important when appealing to non-technical audiences who are not familiar with more arcane forms of quantitative argument and to audiences for whom the evaluator can make few assumptions about the premises of agreement. School practitioners fall into both these categories. It is dangerous to presume that practitioners start from the same values and see reality the same way as evaluators or government officials.

Analogies and metaphors are seldom used in evaluation, because they are often perceived as mere figures of speech and thus unreliable data. They are, however, important ways of arriving at naturalistic generalizations. Petrie (1976) suggested that Kuhn's exemplars convey cognitive categories essential for an initiate to understand scientific theories. Ortony (1975a, 1975b) discussed the ways in which metaphors work to extend thought.

Ortony contends that words do not precisely convey the flow of experience as it is presented to the human mind. Experience is continuous and nondiscrete; and even though words do not have distinct meanings like logical symbol systems, nor do they accurately represent all forms of experience. By "particularization" metaphors help bridge the gap between language and experience. Particularization conveys mental images to the mind of the reader. A term like "fearless warrior" evokes meaning more succinctly and compactly than does a longer description. In addition, metaphors can capture distinctions that are otherwise inexpressible.

According to Ortony, another characteristic of metaphors is their vividness. They are closer to experience and convey emotional as well as cognitive and sensory meanings. This imagibility is associated with learnability. Metaphors facilitate insight and personal understanding by moving from the known to the less known. They facilitate naturalistic generalization on the part of the audiences. It is critical, however, that the author understand his audiences in order to know whether a metaphoric assertion will expand understanding or simply pass the audiences by.

Ortony also extends this conception of language into the teaching-learning situation. Drawing upon Polanyi's idea of tacit knowledge, he contends that the teacher must always know much more than he can express in propositional form. It is this tacit knowledge, partially a knowledge of contextual application, that is the deep understanding of a field or discipline. In order to communicate knowledge to a student, the teacher must select from his tacit knowledge and try to represent it in propositional terms. The propositional form is always somewhat removed from the full tacit understanding.

The student initially sees only the propositions. It is like learning to ride a bicycle by reading a set of instructions. The beginner's behavior is controlled by the explicit propositional knowledge which is inadequate. It is here that the teacher can aid the student by examples, metaphors, and nonliteral language.

Scientists trying to learn their discipline have similar problems. According to prominent critics, it would be impossible to learn a scientific discipline solely by following a set of rules (Polanyi, 1958; Kuhn, 1970). According to Kuhn, a scientist learns his discipline through a set of exemplars—concrete problems permitting solutions that enable the novice to make comparisons with other disparate problems. The shared meaning is transferred through these experiences and not only through rules.

The similarity between naturalistic generalizations in evaluation through the use of examples and metaphors and other arguments which attempt to establish a structure of reality is clear. Understanding and insight on the part of the audience are facilitated even though there may be no scientifically verified propositions in the sense of formal logic. Even though its epistemological and psychological assumptions are somewhat different from other types of evaluation, naturalistic evaluation is still a form of argumentation.

APPENDIX C
An Evaluation Agreement

(Memorandum of Agreement Between
"Blue Ribbon" Panel and MEA/NEA)

1. Charge

The external evaluation panel consisting of Dr. Wendell Rivers, Dr. Ernest House, and Dr. Daniel Stufflebeam has been engaged by the Michigan Education Association and the National Education Association to evaluate the educational soundness and utility for Michigan of the Michigan Accountability Model with a particular focus on the assessment component.

2. Audiences (in priority order)

NEA/MEA
Decision makers in Michigan's educational system (State Board of Education and State Department of Education).
The media (the public).
Consumers (Parents, PTA, the public, etc.).
Technical persons (especially in the area of Educational Measurement).

3. Report/editing

The panel will be solely in charge of developing and editing its final report. NEA/MEA may write and disseminate any separate statement (such as an endorsement, a rebuttal, a commentary, or a descriptive piece). It is understood that the panel's report is to be as short and direct as possible and to be designed to communicate with the audiences designated for the report.

4. Dissemination

The external panel has the right to release its report to any members of the target audiences or other persons following the completion of the report. The panel's release of the report will imply no MEA/NEA endorsement. Further MEA/NEA may choose to endorse or not endorse the report depending on their judgment of the quality and appropriateness of the report. Should MEA/NEA decide to disseminate their own document describing the report their document will be identified as their own and not that of the committee. Only the committee's final report as edited by the committee will be distributed with the names of the committee on it.

5. Format of the Report

The following items were identified as desirable ingredients for the panel's final report:

   a. citation of the agreements between the review panel and NEA/MEA
   b. presentation of the major findings
   c. presentation of minority opinions, if any.

6. Questions to Be Addressed in the Report

Specific questions to be addressed will include:

   a. validity and reliability of criterion-referenced tests
   b. use of tests to evaluate staff
   c. merit of the objectives on which Michigan assessment is based
   d. involvement of teachers in developing both objectives and tests
   e. the panel's recommendations for change and further study
   f. comments about the balance of the state effort and appropriateness of expanding the scope of assessment especially given cost factors associated with the projections for improving or expanding Michigan assessment
   g. quality of planning in the Michigan Accountability Program
   h. cost benefit projections for the program
   i. value of Michigan assessment outcomes and reports for different levels of audiences in Michigan.
   j. problems of bias in the Michigan Accountability Program.

7. Resources (budget) to Support the Program

Sufficient resources will be made available by MEA/NEA to the external review panel to support eight days of work per panelist to work on the program, whatever secretarial support is needed in conducting the program and whatever materials and equipment requirements, for example, tape recorders, taping, etc., in the Lansing hearings. It is understood that if any of the panelists need to make long distance telephone calls to collect opinions about the program from people in Michigan that the panelists will be reimbursed for such expenses provided that an accurate and complete report is made of the purpose of the phone call and who was contacted.

8. Delivery Schedule

The panel is to deliver its final report on March 1 or as soon thereafter as is practicable.

9. Access to Data

It is understood that the Michigan Department of Education will make available to the panel any and all data and reports required by the panel to do the job. This, of course, is restricted to those data and reports that are now available to the Michigan Department of Education regarding Michigan accountability.

10. Procedures

Pursuant to the above conditions the external three-man panel will have control over the evaluation process that it must implement to responsibly respond to the charge to which it has agreed. In accordance with this position the panel has agreed to implement the following general process.

Private interviews and hearings will be conducted solely by the panel with representatives of the Michigan Department of Education, representatives of NEA/MEA, representatives of selected groups (teachers, administrators, board members, and educational action groups). The panel will also review documents made available to it by NEA/MEA and the Michigan Department of Education. Finally the panel will conduct a hearing to obtain additional information concerning issues identified by the panel in the course of interviewing various client groups and studying various documents.

REFERENCES

ALKIN, M. C., R. DAILLAK, and P. WHITE (1979) Using Evaluations. Beverly Hills: Sage Publications.

ALKIN, M. C. and F. S. ELLETT (1979) "The importance of category systems in evaluation theory: a personal viewpoint." CEDR Quarterly 12 (Fall): 3-5.

AMAREL, M., E. R. HOUSE, D. LANGMEYER, D. LORTIE, R. MAYER, L. McLEAN, and L. SEALEY (1979) Reform, Response, and Renegotiation-- Transitions in a School Change Project. New York: Ford Foundation.

APPLE, M. (1979) Ideology and Curriculum. London: Routledge & Kegan Paul.

ATKIN, J. M. (1968) "Behavioral objectives in curriculum design: a cautionary note." Science Teacher 35 (May): 27-30.

BAKER, E. L. and E. S. QUELLMALZ [eds.] (1980) Educational Testing and Evaluation: Design, Analysis, and Policy. Beverly Hills: Sage Publications.

BARNES, R. E. and A. L. GINSBURG (1979) "Relevance of the RMC models for Title I policy concerns." Educational Evaluation and Policy Analysis 1 (March-April): 7-14.

BARRY, B. (1973) The Liberal Theory of Justice. London: Oxford Univ. Press.

——— (1965) Political Argument. London: Routledge & Kegan Paul.

BEARDSLEY, M. (1958) Aesthetics. New York: Harcourt Brace Jovanovich.

BERGER, P. L. (1974) "Policy and the calculus of meaning," in Pyramids of Sacrifice. New York: Basic Books.

BERNSTEIN, R. J. (1978) The Restructuring of Social and Political Theory. Philadelphia: Univ. of Pennsylvania Press.

BEYER, L. E. (1977) "Schools, aesthetic meanings, and social change." Educational Theory 27 (Fall): 274-282.

——— (1974) "Objectivity, autonomy, and aesthetic evaluation." Journal of Aesthetic Education 8 (July): 107-118.

BLOOM, B. S. (1956) Taxonomy of Educational Objectives. New York: McKay.

———, J. T. HASTINGS, and G. MADAUS (1971) Handbook on Formative and Summative Evaluation of Student Learning. New York: McGraw-Hill.

BOULDING, K. (1956) The Image. Ann Arbor: Univ. of Michigan Press.

BOWLES, S. and H. GINTIS (1972-1973) "I.Q. in the U.S. class structure." Social Policy 3 (November-December, January-February): 65-96.

BRONOWSKI, J. (1956) Science and Human Values. New York: Harper & Row.

BROUDY, H. (1972) Enlightened Cherishing. Urbana: Univ. of Illinois Press.

BURKE, K. (1945) A Grammar of Motives. New York: Random House.

CALLAHAN, R. E. (1962) Education and the Cult of Efficiency. Chicago: Univ. of Chicago Press.

CAMPBELL, D. T. (1975a) "Assessing the impact of planned social change," in
    G. M. Lyons (ed.) Social Research and Public Policies. Dartmouth College,
    NH: Public Affairs Center.
——— (1975b) 'Degrees of freedom and the case study." Comparative Political
    Studies 8, 2.
——— (1974) "Qualitative knowing in action research." Presented at the American
    Psychological Association, New Orleans.
——— (1966) "Pattern matching as an essential in distal knowing," in K. R.
    Hammond (ed.) The Psychology of Egon Brunswick. New York: Holt, Rine-
    hart & Winston.
——— and J. STANELY (1966) Experimental and Quasi-Experimental Design for
    Research. Chicago: Rand McNally.
CARE, N. S. (1978) "Participation and policy." Ethics 88 (July): 316-337.
COLEMAN, J. S. (1975) "Racial segregation in the schools: new research with
    new policy implementations." Phi Delta Kappan 57 (October): 75-78.
——— et al. (1966) Equality of Educational Opportunity. Washington, DC: U.S.
    Government Printing Office.
COOLEY, W. W. and P. R. LOHNES (1976) Evaluation Research in Education.
    New York: Irvington.
CRONBACH, L. J. (1979) Design of Evaluations. Stanford: Stanford Evaluation
    Consortium.
——— (1974) "Beyond the two disciplines of scientific psychology." Presented at
    the American Psychological Association, New Orleans.
——— (1971) "Test validation," in R. L. Thorndike (ed.) Educational Measure-
    ment. Washington, DC: American Council on Education.
DATTA, L.-E. (1976) "The impact of the Westinghouse/Ohio evaluation on the
    development of Project Head Start: an examination of the immediate and
    longer-term effects and how they came about," in C. C. Abt (ed.) The
    Evaluation of Social Programs. Beverly Hills: Sage Publications.
DENZIN, N. K. (1971) "The logic of naturalistic inquiry." Social Forces 50, 2.
DICKIE, G. (1971) Aesthetics. Indianapolis: Bobbs-Merrill.
DIGGS, B. J. (1974) The State, Justice, and the Common Good. Glenview, IL:
    Scott, Foresman.
EGBERT, R. (1977) Interview conducted at the Center for Instructional Research
    and Curriculum Evaluation, University of Illinois, Urbana, IL, April 28.
EISNER, E. (1979) The Educational Imagination. New York: Macmillan.
ELLIOTT, J. (1977) "Democratic evaluation as social criticism: or putting the
    judgment back into evaluation," in N. Norris (ed.) Theory in Practice. Univer-
    sity of East Anglia. Centre for Applied Research in Education, Norwich,
    England.
——— (1979) "Educational accountability and the evaluation of teaching," in A.
    Lewy (ed.) Evaluation Roles.
ELMORE, R. F. (1976) "Follow Through: decision making in a large-scale social
    experiment." Unpublished Ph.D. dissertation, School of Education, Harvard
    University.
ENNIS, R. H. (1975) "Equality of educational opportunity." Urbana: College of
    Education, University of Illinois. (mimeo)
——— (1973) "On causality." Educational Researcher 2, 6.
EPPS, E. G. (n.d.) Memorandum to Debbie K. Walker—Re.: Test battery for
    national Follow Through evaluation.

FRANKE-WIKBERG, S. (1979) "The LONG project: an example of educational evaluation given from Sweden." Umea University. (mimeo)

GARDNER, J. (1978) On Moral Fiction. New York: Basic Books.

GARDNER, M. (1976) "Mathematical games." Scientific American 234, 3.

GLASS, G. V. (1972) "Educational product evaluation: a prototype format applied." Educational Researcher 9, 1.

GOTTSHALK, D. W. (1962) Art and the Social Order. New York: Dover.

GUBA, E. G. (1978) Toward a Methodology of Naturalistic Inquiry in Educational Evaluation. Los Angeles: Center for the Study of Evaluation, UCLA.

GUSFIELD, J. (1976) "The literary rhetoric of science." American Sociological Review 41 (February): 11-33.

GUTTENTAG, M. (1973) "Subjectivity and its use in evaluation research." Evaluation 1, 2: 60-65.

——— and K. SNAPPER (1974) "Plans, evaluations, and decisions." Evaluation 1, 2: 58-74.

HABERMAS, J. (1973) Theory and Practice. Boston: Beacon.

HAMILTON, D. (1977) "Making sense of curriculum evaluation," in L. Shulman (ed.) Review of Research in Education, Vol. 5. Itasca, IL: F. E. Peacock.

——— (1976) "A science of the singular?" University of Illinois. (mimeo)

HANEY, W. (1977) The Follow Through Evaluation: A Technical History. Cambridge, MA: Huron Institute.

HARRINGTON, P. and J. R. SANDERS (1979) "Guidelines for goal-free evaluation." Evaluation Center, Western Michigan University. (mimeo)

HERBERT, M. (1975) Extended Pilot Trials of the Comprehensive School Mathematics Program. St. Louis: CEMREL, Inc.

HOGBEN, D. and K. SIMPSON (1978) "Evaluator authority and responsibility: a delimitation." Flinders University of South Australia. (mimeo)

HOUSE, E. R. (1979) "The role of theories of justice in evaluation—justice on strike." Educational Theory 29, 4.

——— (1978a) "Assumptions underlying evaluation models." Educational Researcher 7 (March): 4-12.

——— (1978b) "Evaluation as scientific management in United States school reform." Comparative Education Review 22, 3: 388-401.

——— (1977) The Logic of Evaluative Argument. Los Angeles; Center for the Study of Evaluation, UCLA.

——— (1976) "Justice in evaluation," in G. V Glass (ed.) Evaluation Studies Annual Review, Vol. 1. Beverly Hills; Sage Publications.

——— (1974) The Politics of Educational Innovation. Berkeley: McCutchan.

——— (1973) "The conscience of educational evaluation," in E. R. House (ed.) School Evaluation. Berkeley: McCutchan.

——— and N. S. CARE (1979) "Fair evaluation agreement." Educational Theory 29, 3.

HOUSE, E. R., G. V GLASS, L. D. McLEAN, and D. WALKER (1978) "No simple answer: critique of the Follow Through evaluation." Harvard Educational Review 48 (May): 128-160.

HOUSE, E. R. and D. HOGBEN (1974) "A goal-free evaluation for 'Me and My Environment'." Formative Evaluation Report No. 3, Biological Sciences Curriculum Study: 14-16.

HOUSE, E. R. and R. S. MAYER (1980) "A critique of the educational imagination in evaluation." Journal of Aesthetic Education (July).

HOUSE, E. R., J. STEELE, and C. T. KERINS (1971) The Gifted Classroom. Center for Instructional Research and Curriculum Evaluation, University of Illinois, Urbana.

HOUSE, E. R., W. RIVERS, and D. STUFFLEBEAM (1974) "An assessment of the Michigan accountability system." Phi Delta Kappan 55 (June): 663-669.

ITTELSON, W. and H. CANTRIL (1954) Perception: A Transactional Approach. Garden City, NY: Doubleday.

JENKINS, D. and B. O'TOOLE (1978) "Curriculum evaluation, literary criticism, and the paracurriculum," in G. Willis (ed.) Qualitative Evaluation. Berkeley: McCutchan.

KALLOS, D. (1978) "Notes on schooling, curriculum, and teaching," in G. Willis (ed.) Qualitative Evaluation. Berkeley: McCutchan.

KARIER, C. J. (1973) "Testing for control and order in the corporate state," in C. J. Karier, P. Violas, and J. Spring (eds.) Roots of Crisis: American Education in the Twentieth Century. Chicago: Rand McNally.

KEARNEY, C. P., D. L. DONOVAN, and T. H. FISHER (1974) "In defense of Michigan's accountability program." Phi Delta Kappan 51 (September).

KELLY, E. F. (1978) "Curriculum criticism and literary criticism: comments on the anthology," in G. Willis (ed.) Qualitative Evaluation. Berkeley: McCutchan.

KELLY, E. G. (1980) "Evaluation as persuasion." Educational Evaluation and Policy Analysis 2, 5.

KEMMIS, S. (1976) "Evaluation and evolution in knowledge about educational programs." Unpublished Ph.D. dissertation, University of Illinois.

KOGAN, M. and T. PACKWOOD (1974) Advisory Councils and Committees in Education. London: Routledge & Kegan Paul.

KOHLBERG, L. and R. S. MAYER (1972) "Development as the aim of education." Harvard Educational Review 42: 449-496.

KRULEE, G. K. (1973) An Organizational Analysis of Project Follow Through Evanston, IL: Northwestern University.

KUHN, T. (1970) The Structure of Scientific Revolutions. Chicago: Univ. of Chicago Press.

LANGER, S. K. (1942) Philosophy in a New Key. New York: Mentor.

LEVIN, H. M. (1972) "The social science objectivity gap." Saturday Review (November 11): 44-51.

LUKES, S. (1974) Power. London: Macmillan.

LUNDGREN, U. P. (1977) Model Analysis of Pedagogical Processes. Stockholm: Stockholm Institute of Education.

MacDONALD, B. (1977) "A political classification of evaluation studies," in D. Hamilton, D. Jenkins, C. King, B. MacDonald, and M. Parlett (eds.) Beyond the Numbers Game. London: Macmillan.

——— (1974) Evaluation and the Control of Education. Norwich, England: Centre for Applied Research in Education.

——— and R. WALKER (1974) "Case-study and the social philosophy of educational research." University of East Anglia, Norwich, England.

MACPHERSON, C. B. (1966) The Real World of Democracy. Oxford, England: Oxford Univ. Press.

MAGER, R. F. (1972) Goal Analysis. Belmont, CA: Fearon.

——— (1962) Preparing Objectives for Programmed Instruction. San Francisco: Fearon.

MARCUSE, H. (1978) The Aesthetic Dimension. Boston: Beacon.

McCUTCHEON, G. (1978) "Of solar systems, responsibility and basics: an educational criticism of Mr. Clement's fourth grade," in G. Willis (ed.) Qualitative Evaluation. Berkeley: McCutchan.

McLAUGHLIN, M. W. (1975) Evaluation and Reform. Cambridge, MA: Ballinger.

MILL, J. S. (1893) A System of Logic. New York: Harper.

——— (1861) Utilitarianism. Indianapolis: Bobbs-Merrill.

MORGAN, T. (1976) "The good life (along the San Andreas Fault)." New York Times Magazine (July 4).

MORRIS, L., C. FITZ-GIBBON, and M. HENERSON (1978) Program Evaluation Kit. Beverly Hills: Sage Publications.

National Study of Secondary School Evaluation (1969) Evaluative Criteria Washington, DC: Author.

National Study of School Evaluation (1978) Evaluative Criteria. Arlington, VA: Author.

NOVAK, M. (1971) Ascent of the Mountain, Flight of the Dove. New York: Harper & Row.

O'CONNOR, J. J. (1976) "Wiseman's latest film is another reality fiction." New York Times (November 7).

ORTONY, A. (1975a) "Knowledge, language and teaching." University of Illinois. (mimeo)

——— (1975b) "Why metaphors are necessary and not just nice." Educational Theory (Winter).

OWENS, T. R. (1973) "Educational evaluation by adversary proceeding," in E. R. House (ed.) School Evaluation. Berkeley: McCutchan.

PARKER, J. H. (1960) "The problem of esthetic form," in M. Rader (ed.) A Modern Book of Esthetics. New York: Holt, Rhinehart & Winston.

PARLETT, M. and D. HAMILTON (1977) "Evaluation as illumination: a new approach to the study of innovatory programmes," in D. Hamilton et al. (eds.) Beyond the Numbers Game. London: Macmillan.

PATTON, M. Q. (1978) Utilization-Focused Evaluation. Beverly Hills: Sage Publications.

PAULSTON, R. G. (forthcoming) "Paradigm conflict in the assessment of educational reform: evaluation as social critique." Educational Evaluation and Policy Analysis.

PERELMAN, C. and L. OLBRECHTS-TYTECA. (1969) The New Rhetoric: A Treatise on Argumentation. Notre Dame, IN: Univ. Dame Press.

PETRIE, H. G. (1979) "COPE begins second evaluation cycle." Illini Week 1 (October 12): 5.

——— (1976) "Metaphorical models of mastery: or, how to learn to do the problems at the end of the chapter of the physics textbook." University of Illinois. (mimeo)

POLANYI, M. (1958) Personal Knowledge. Chicago: Univ. of Chicago Press.
——— and H. PROSCH (1975) Meaning. Chicago: Univ. of Chicago Press.
POPHAM, W. J. (1975) Educational Evaluation. Englewood Cliffs, NJ: Prentice-Hall.
——— and D. CARLSON (1977) "Deep dark deficits of the adversary evaluation model." Educational Researcher 6 (June): 3-6.
POPHAM, W. J. and R. L. EBEL (1978) "Annual meeting presidential debate." Educational Researcher 7, 11: 3.
RAWLS, J. (1971) A Theory of Justice. Cambridge, MA: Harvard Univ. Press.
Report of the Fourth Annual Follow Through Working Conference (1974). High Scope Educational Research Foundation.
Education Daily (1977) "Results of Follow Through evaluation disappointing but useful, OE says." August 10.
RIVLIN, A. M. (1971) Systematic Thinking for Social Action. Washington, DC: Brookings Institution.
ROSSI, P. H., H. E. FREEMAN, and S. R. WRIGHT (1979) Evaluation: A Systematic Approach. Beverly Hills: Sage Publications.
SCHON, D. (1979) "Generative metaphor: a perspective of problem-setting in social policy," in A. Ortony (ed.) Metaphor and Thought. New York: Cambridge Univ. Press.
SCRIVEN, M. (1976) "Bias control systems in evaluation." Presented at the annual meeting of the American Educational Research Association, San Francisco.
——— (1976a) "Evaluation bias and its control," in G. V Glass (ed.) Evaluation Studies Review Annual, Vol. 1. Beverly Hills: Sage Publications.
——— (1976b) "Maximizing the process of causal investigations: the modus operandi method," in G. V Glass (ed.) Evaluation Studies Review Annual, Vol. 1. Beverly Hills: Sage Publications.
——— (1973) "Goal free evaluation," in E. R. House (ed.) School Evaluation. Berkeley: McCutchan.
——— (1972a) "Educational product re-evaluation." Educational Researcher 1, 5.
——— (1972b) "Objectivity and subjectivity in educational research," in L. G. Thomas (ed.) Philosophical Redirection of Educational Research. National Society for the Study of Education.
SHAPLEY, D. (1976) "Earthquakes: Los Angeles prediction suggests faults in federal policy." Science 192 (May).
SIMONS, H. (1977) "Building a social contract: negotiation and participation in condensed field research," in N. Norris (ed.) Theory in Practice. University of East Anglia. Centre for Applied Research in Education, Norwich, England.
SMITH, L. M. and P. A. POHLAND (1974) "Education, technology, and the rural highlands," in D. Sjogren (ed.) Four Evaluation Examples: Anthropological, Economic, Narrative, and Portrayal. AERA Monograph Series in Curriculum Evaluation, No. 7. Chicago: Rand McNally.
SMITH, M. L., R. GABRIEL, J. SCHOTT, and W. L. PODIA (1976) "Evaluation of the effects of outward bound," in G. V Glass (ed.) Evaluation Studies Review Annual, Vol. 1. Beverly Hills: Sage Publications.
SNYDER, W. P. (1967) Case Studies in Military Systems Analysis. Washington, DC: Industrial College of the armed Forces.

SOAR, R. S. (1973) Final Report: Follow Through Classroom Process Measurement and Pupil Growth (1970-71). Gainesville, FL: Institute for Development of Human Resources.

SONTAG, S. (1977) On Photography. New York: Farrer, Straus & Giroux.

STAKE, R. E. (1978) "The case study method in social inquiry." Educational Researcher 7 (February): 5-8.

––– (1976) Evaluating Educational Programmes: The Need and the Response. Washington, DC: OECD Publications Center.

––– (1975a) Evaluating the Arts in Education: A Responsive Approach. Columbus, OH: Merrill.

––– (1975b) "Some alternative presumptions." Center for Instructional Research and Curriculum Evaluation, University of Illinois. (mimeo)

––– (1973) "Measuring what learners learn," in E. R. House (ed.) School Evaluation. Berkeley: McCutchan.

––– and J. EASLEY (1978) "Case studies in science education." Center for Instructional Research and Curriculum Evaluation, University of Illinois.

STALLINGS, J. A. (1973) "Follow Through classroom observation evaluation 1971-72." Menlo Park, CA: Stanford Research Institute.

Stanford Research Institute (1972) "Summary of plans for longitudinal evaluation of the national Follow Through program, 1969-1970." (mimeo)

Steering Committee for a National Follow Through Parent Advisory Council (1972) Parent Resolution. Denver Conference, November 1. (mimeo)

STENZEL, N. (1979) "Committee Hearings as an evaluation format." Portland, OR: Northwest Regional Educational Laboratory.

STRAUCH, R. E. (1976) "A critical look at quantitative methodology." Policy Analysis 2, 1.

STRIKE, K. (1979) "The role of theories of justice in evaluation–why a house is not a home." Educational Theory 29, 3.

STUFFLEBEAM, D. L. (1973) "An introduction to the PDK book," in B. Worthen and J. R. Sanders (eds.) Educational Evaluation: Theory and Practice. Worthington, OH: Charles A. Jones.

––– (1969) "Evaluation as enlightenment for decision-making," in Beatty (ed.) Improving Educational Assessment and an Inventory of Affective Behaviors. Washington, DC: Association for Supervision and Curriculum Development, NEA.

SUCHMAN, E. A. (1967) Evaluative Reserearch. New York: Russell Sage Foundation.

SULLIVAN, E. V. (1977) Kohlberg's Structuralism. Ontario: Ontario Institute for Studies in Education.

TAYLOR, P. W. (1961) Normative Discourse. Englewood Cliffs, NJ: Prentice-Hall.

TEMPLIN, P. S. (1978) "Photography: can it provide program portrayal?" Presented at the American Education Research Association, Toronto, March.

THURSTON, P. (1978) "Revitalizing adversary evaluation: deep dark deficits or muddled mistaken musings." Educational Researcher 7 (July-August): 3-8.

TOLSTOY (1960) "The communication of Emotion," in M. Rader (ed.) A modern Book of Esthetics. New York: Holt, Rinehart & Winston.

TURNER, T. (1973) "Piaget's structuralism." American Anthropologist 75: 351-373.

TYLER, R. W. (1950) Basic Principles of Curriculum and Instruction. Chicago: Univ of Chicago Press.

TYLER, R., S. LAPAN, J. MOORE, C. W. RIVERS, and D. SKIBO (1978) "Impact of minimum competence testing in Florida." Today's Education 67 (September-October): 30-38.

U.S. Office of Education (1969) Follow Through Program Manual. Washington, DC: Department of Health, Education and Welfare.

VALLANCE, E. (1978) "Scanning horizons and looking at weeks: a critical description of "The Great Plains Experience'," in G. Willis (ed.) Qualitative Evaluation. Berkeley: McCutchan.

WAKS, L. J. (1975) "Educational objectives and existential heros," in R. A. Smith (ed.) Regaining Educational Leadership. New York: John Wiley.

WALKER, D. R. and J. SCHAFFARZICK (1974) "Comparing curricula." Review of Educational Research 44 (Winter).

WALLER, J. J. (1967) "Identification of problem drinkers among drunken drivers." Journal of the American Medical Association: 124-130.

WEIKART, D. P. and B. A. BANET (1975) "Model design problems in Follow Through," in A. M. Rivlin and P. M. Timpane (eds.) Planned Variation in Education. Washington, DC: Brookings Institution.

WEIZENBAUM, J. (1976) Computer Power and Human Reason. San Francisco: W. H. Freeman.

WELCH, W. (1978) Goal-free formative evaluation—an example." Presented at the American Education Research Association, Toronto, March.

WILLIS, G. [ed.] (1978) Qualitative Evaluation. Berkeley: McCutchan.

WIRTZ, W. (1977) On Further Examination. New York: College Entrance Examination Board.

WOLCOTT, H. F. (1977) Teachers vs. Technocrats. Eugene, OR: Center for Educational Policy and Management, University of Oregon.

WOLF, R. L. (1974)) "The use of judicial evaluation methods in the formulation of educational policy." Educational Evaluation and Policy Analysis 1 (May-June): 19-28.

——— (1975) "Trial by jury: the process." Phi Delta Kappan 57 (November): 185-187.

WOLFF, R. P. (1968) The Poverty of Liberalism. Boston: Beacon.

WOODWARD, B. and C. BERNSTEIN (1976) The Final Days. New York: Simon & Schuster.

WORTHEN, B. R. and J. R. SANDERS (1973) Educational Evaluation: Theory and Practice. Worthington, OH: Charles A. Jones.

ABOUT THE AUTHOR

Ernest R. House is Professor of Administration, Higher, and Continuing Education in the Center for Instructional Research and Curriculum Evaluation (CIRCE) at the University of Illinois in Urbana. He received a bachelor's degree from Washington University in 1959 (graduating Phi Beta Kappa), taught high school, received a master's degree from Southern Illinois University in 1964, and a doctor's degree from the University of Illinois in 1968.

His first project was a large-scale evaluation of the Illinois Gifted Program. Since that time he has been evaluating educational and other social programs. In recent years he has been evaluating evaluations. Previous books include *School Evaluation: The Politics and Process* (1973), *The Politics of Educational Innovation* (1974), and *Survival in the Classroom* (with S. Lapan, 1978). He has served as consultant to many organizations in the United States and other countries. In 1976 he was chairperson of the annual meeting of the American Educational Research Association, and he is currently on the editorial board of *Educational Evaluation and Policy Analysis.*